'A howling success, which plugs a big and obvious gap'
Professor Ronald Hutton

There have been fascinating developments in the study of folklore in the last twenty-or-so years, but few books about British folklore and folk customs reflect these exciting new approaches. As a result there is a huge gap between scholarly approaches to folklore studies and 'popular beliefs' about the character and history of British folklore. *Explore Folklore* is the first book to bridge that gap, and to show how much 'folklore' there is in modern day Britain.

Explore Folklore shows there is much more to folklore than morris dancing and fifty-something folksingers! The rituals of 'what we do on our holidays', funerals, stag nights and 'lingerie parties' are all full of 'unselfconsious' folk customs. Indeed, folklore is something that is integral to all our lives – it is so intrinsic we do not think of it as being 'folklore'.

Explore Folklore provides a lively introduction to the study of most genres of British folklore, presenting the more contentious and profound ideas in a readily accessible manner.

Bob Trubshaw has been researching and writing about British folklore for over fifteen years.

Explore Folklore is the first in a series of books that will provide accessible introductions to folklore and mythology. Some books will provide 'overviews' of quite broad topics, drawing together current academic research with popular beliefs. Other books in the series will deal with more specific topics, but still with the aim of providing a wide-ranging introduction to the topic.

Titles planned for 2003 include:

Explore Mythology
Bob Trubshaw

Explore Fairies
Jeremy Harte

Explore Green Men
Mercia Macdonald

Explore Holy Wells and Springs
Ian Thompson

EXPLORE FOLKLORE

Bob Trubshaw

Heart of Albion Press

Explore Folklore
Bob Trubshaw

Cover design and photograph by R.N. Trubshaw

ISBN 1 872883 60 5

Explore Books

An imprint of Heart of Albion Press
2 Cross Hill Close, Wymeswold
Loughborough, LE12 6UJ

albion@indigogroup.co.uk

Visit our Web site: www.hoap.co.uk

Printed in the UK by Booksprint

For Elizabeth

CONTENTS

ACKNOWLEDGEMENTS

My debt to Ronald Hutton is a deep one. His generous help has been invaluable over many years. His books prove that the most arcane aspects of British folklore can be unravelled academically yet, through lucid writing, shared with 'popular readers'. And, not least, a passing comment from Ronald fired me up sufficiently to write this book, even though the scope is sufficiently broad that all the 'angels' of British folklore would understandably fear to tread. (To add to my hubris I also set out to do it in far fewer pages than is reasonable.)

Along with so many other people involved in the study of British folklore, my debt to Hilda Davidson is also deep-rooted and extensive. Jeremy Harte has repeatedly inspired me and lifted my spirits through his writing and company. Research for a number of sections of this book has benefited greatly from his bibliographies (Harte 1998d and 1999). Alby Stone's assistance and friendship over many years has also been too extensive to itemise.

My grateful thanks to all the people have helped with specific topics. Gillian Bennett kindly commented on sections of an earlier draft and made important suggestions for improvements. Kathryn Denning provided a copy of her thesis which shed light on a number of theoretic issues, and drew my attention to the work of Bernard McGrane; her friendship has also provide considerable insight and inspiration in many other ways. Frank E. Earp suggested the possibility of multiple levels of meaning in plough plays. Terri Enyon introduced me to recent cognitive linguistics publications; my world has never been the same since. Brant Gardner made helpful improvements to my summary of his work on the Maya glyphs. My knowledge of holy wells and 'Celtic' saints has been greatly enlarged by Tristan Hulse. Robert Layton kindly provided a copy of his notes for the discussion he chaired during the archaeology and folklore session at the 1996 TAG Conference. David Lazell shared his perceptive thoughts on fairies. Alison Skinner drew my attention to *Flora Britannica*. Ivor Perry noted how contentious Shakespeare's ghosts would have been. Wade Tarzia provided stimulating email discussions regarding folklore theory (and the lack of) and a helpful summary of Mary Hufford's article on 'Context'.

Tom Dillingham, Kim Hoag, Alejandro Gonzalez, Philip Hiscock, Paul Nasrat, Dave Postles, Michael Preston, Natalie Marie Underberg and Ralf Wolz all provided helpful responses to postings to the Folklore Discussion List and H-Net List for British and Irish History.

A number of people kindly commented, in some cases extensively, on an earlier draft of this work. They know who they are and I am especially grateful for their time and effort, although perforce they remain anonymous as I wish to take full responsibility for any remaining errors.

Given the extensive reading necessary during the preparation of this book it is entirely true to say that it would not have happened without the efficient assistance by staff of Leicestershire Libraries, for which I am most appreciative.

Inevitably book writing proceeds only at the expense of a semblance to normal life and, in addition to all other reasons for being deeply grateful, special thanks to Elizabeth Fairhurst for her forbearance.

Inevitably in a book that tries to cover a large number of topics in an overly-concise manner there may be occasions where my opinions and summaries are contentious. My sincere apologies to anyone cited in this book who feels that I have oversimplified or misrepresented their ideas. I hope there will be a future edition of this work where I can respond to suggestions for improvements. Please write or email such suggestions to the publisher's address.

Abbots Bromley Horn Dance, 1989.

Ladies and jelly beans, hobos and tramps,
Cross-eyed mosquitoes and bow-legged ants.
I come before you to stand behind ye
To tell you something I know nothing about...

1: INTRODUCTION

What is folklore?

What do you think folklore is? If you walked down any High Street in Britain and asked this question the answers might include morris dancing, Abbots Bromley Horn Dance, Padstow Mayday celebrations, Castleton Garland Ceremony, folk singers, Robin Hood and King Arthur. In some ways 'folklore' is seen as a survival of an idyllic rural lifestyle, lost sometime about a hundred years ago.

If you asked an academic folklorist you will get an answer such as Gillian Bennett's succinct definition:

> Academic folklorists today define their subject matter in a way which runs counter to popular conceptions... They see the "lore" as a body of beliefs, activities, ways of making, saying and doing things and interacting with others that are acquired through informal, unofficial channels by the processes of socialising in family, occupational, or activity-related groups. The "folk" in the old sense of a group of people distinguishable by class, education or location therefore disappears from the modern equation, for it follows that we are all folk... It follows that 'folklore' can be found anywhere and among any group of people, urban as well as rural, professional as well as "peasant".
> (Bennett 1993)

However academic folklorists can be further subdivided according to the type of folklore they are dealing with. American folklorists are diverse in their interests but most are concerned with *contemporary* folklore and rarely take too much interest in the historical background.

In contrast, British folklore studies are typically (although certainly not always) linked to the problems of 'continuity' of customs and lore – the historical 'depth', with all the problems this entails, is a key aspect of both the activities and their study. The Marxist social historian E.P. Thompson bluntly observes:

> Folklore, in England, is largely a literary record of eighteenth and nineteenth century survivals, recorded by parsons and by genteel antiquarians regarding them across a gulf of class condescension. (Thompson 1979: 6)

This remark was part of a fascinating but little-known lecture on folklore, anthropology and social history delivered in India in 1976. Thompson contrasted the 'dead, inert and corrupt' materials of British folklore with the living lore of India. In the intervening years since Thompson made these remarks British folklore studies have begun to look at the extensive 'living lore' of this country too. So, Thompson's outline of the situation in the mid-twentieth century needs to be tempered with the subsequent greater interest in contemporary lore. However the problems associated with historical folklore and looking past the 'class condescension' of the earlier folklorists have certainly not diminished.

Thompson was also well-aware that the class gulf led to nineteenth century folklore studies being 'divorced from their total situation or context.' Folk customs were seen as relics of a remote and lost past, akin to the crumbled ruins of prehistoric monuments. They were perceived as the early phases of a cultural evolution.

Sadly, as we will explore in the next chapter, throughout the first half of the twentieth century folklorists failed to address the various weaknesses inherent in earlier studies. This has led to a popular understanding of folklore that is thoroughly muddled and muddied. Since about 1960 British folklore studies have been 'painfully redefined' but 'failed to carry public opinion along with it.' (Bennett 1993) The main aim of this book is to provide an overview of folklore studies over the last two decades or so, with the emphasis on how the underlying approaches differ from popular ideas about folklore.

Social historians also study folk customs and the like but rarely look at the 'continuity' (real or imagined) of these customs. In ways that we will explore throughout this book, folklorists make more efforts to 'interpret' their material whereas social historians tend more to record when and where it happens.

In contrast, other scholars explore European folklore in the medieval period, when the evidence is most tenuous. These people usually have a good grasp of historical method and the difficulties of working with incomplete data. Some aspects of their approach have been of benefit to folklorists studying later historical periods. However, there has been little overlap of subject matter between the topics that interest medieval folklorists and the topics that usually interest British folklorists.

Some folklore, especially the study of people outside Europe and America, is done by people who call themselves 'ethnographers' or 'ethnologists'. They see themselves as a part of anthropology (in a way that British folklorists seldom do). In reality the definition of an ethnologist hardly differs from Gillian Bennett's definition of a folklorist. There may be more than a hint of reality in the cynical remark that 'ethnology' sounds more academic and is more likely to attract funding ...

The inescapable reality is that academic folklore studies in Britain have been 'marginalised' and underfunded. Many of the folklorists working in higher education are doing their folklore studies as a 'part-time' activity that is quite secondary to their academic post. At the time of writing there are no folklore undergraduates in Britain, although an increasing number of MA and PhD candidates are researching aspects of folklore.

Until the 1990s British folklore lacked a Mortimer Wheeler, a David Attenborough or a David Bellamy. Then in 1991 a charismatic historian, Ronald Hutton, published the first of an impressive series of studies of British folk customs. These lucidly written books, together with frequent lectures to non-academic audiences and television appearances, popularised his extensive research on seventeenth century customs, and also his assessment of the work of other folklorists studying nineteenth and early twentieth century customs. Sadly the work of other excellent folklorists, studying areas of British folklore other than folk customs, has so far mostly failed to reach a wider audience.

Three 'levels' of folklore

In a number of chapters of this book I have drawn attention to Gerald Warshaver's helpful distinction between three 'levels' of folklore (Warshaver 1991).

Level 1 may be termed 'customary practice', that is customs where the participants do not consider themselves to be 'doing' folklore. Examples include funerals, weddings, stag nights, hen nights, Tupperware / lingerie / Ann Summers parties and a wide variety of practices adopted within occupational or leisure-interest groups. In other words it is not 'self-conscious' folklore.

Level 2 is what most people would think of as folklore – whether it is morris dancing, mummers' plays, folk singing, fairy stories or folk crafts. This level includes the collecting, analysis and revival of folklore.

Level 3 is where folklore is self-consciously incorporated into entirely modern activities. Examples abound, including various video games, *Dungeons and Dragons*, Terry Pratchett novels, films as disparate as *The Wicker Man* or *Shrek,* and a host of 'invented' folk customs from Penzance Mayday celebrations to numerous National Trust 'activity days'. In some cases there is an intentional irony in the incorporation of 'archaic' folklore.

I do not regard these three 'levels' as any kind of 'magic spell' that makes it easy to understand folklore studies. However, these distinctions are helpful and succinct, if far from mutually exclusive.

Folk-somethings are processes

Throughout this book there will be references to folk *custom*, folk *lore*, folk *tale*, folk *narrative*, folk *song*, folk *dance*, folk *drama*, folk *crafts*, and the like. At one level this denotes customs, lore, tales, songs, etc as shared by a specific folk 'group', however the group is defined or identified. At another level, and the one predominately implied in this book, it is a 'meta category' that contains all the tales, songs, dances, etc of all the different folk groups.

But these suffixes remain problematic. What is being defined is not simply a collection of 'objects' (be they songs, tales, dances, craft items, or whatever). Part of the interest of folklore studies is how these 'objects' are passed on, and to what extent they adapt and mutate over time. These suffixes to the prefix 'folk' denote not so much *objects* as *processes* – processes of transmission. American folklorists' 'form, function, transmission' approach will be discussed in more detail in Chapter 3.

The scope of this book

The 'folk groups' of Bennett's definition who share – transmit – one or more genres of 'folklore' (whichever of Warshaver's 'levels' these may operate at) share *values, activities,* and possibly *artefacts*. In the final analysis, these are symbolic expressions. So folklore takes its place alongside most aspects of culture, in being amenable to 'semiotic' analysis.

In this book we will explore various specific genres; occasionally specific folk groups; the processes of transmission; and the symbolism 'embedded' in specific aspects of folklore. There is more than one way of approaching each of these, and the overall aim is to demonstrating how an interwoven range of approaches are appropriate to the study of folklore.

These explorations mostly concern British folklore (in the broadest sense of that term) and attempts to illuminate how the 'painful redefining' of the last 40 years has changed our understanding. I have aimed to summarise the work of the key people in different fields. However, the brevity of this book and breadth of the scope, has meant that my own interests and enthusiasms have influenced what has been included and – perhaps more importantly – what has been omitted.

I consider that folklore studies are now far more exciting than at any time in the past but, with the possible exception of the study of folk customs, too little of this 'excitement' has got beyond the pages of academic journals and monographs. Therefore, the full, if impossibly idiosyncratic, title of this book might have been *Explore the Excitement of the Latest British Folklore Studies.*

Origins of the word 'folklore'

In a letter to *The Athenaeum* published on 22 August 1846 William Thoms added, in parentheses, the word 'folk-lore'. He gave a name to a source of data that had first been studied in the late sixteenth century and developed, as part of a widespread enthusiasm for 'antiquities' in the seventeenth and eighteenth centuries.

The hyphen in 'folk-lore' became less frequently used; in 1960 the Folk-Lore Society, founded in 1878, recognised that 'folklore' was now the common usage and changed its name accordingly to the Folklore Society, although retained the acronym 'FLS'.

The 'otherness' of the 'folk'

In the eighteenth century folklore collecting was not distinguished as a separate activity, but instead was part-and-parcel of a range of topics that interested early 'antiquarians'. But clearly what they were collecting – what we would later term folk customs and lore - were not part of what the gentry regarded as 'culture'. They were clearly activities that 'others' do. The 'others' were the rural 'peasants'. And 'peasants' were not thought to have culture; that was reserved for the élite classes of European cultures. (Bennett 1994: 35)

This perceived divide between 'peasant customs' and 'élite culture' is something that grew from mid-seventeenth century attitudes and can, in a sense, be seen as the origins of the concept of 'folk customs'. The dominance of Puritan ideologies led to all popular revelries being regarded as ungodly. The resulting prohibitions led to a break in continuity during the 1640s and 1650s. Many 'traditional customs' simply did not reappear. Those that were 'restored' were much more organised by the gentry for the populace than before the Commonwealth, when the customs had been sustained by the populace with little reliance on the gentry (Hutton 1994). This rift between gentry and populace in folk customs is just one aspect of a rift that was opening up in society at the time. It is why the seventeenth century is seen as 'early modern' rather than 'late medieval'.

By the later part of the nineteenth century folklorists saw themselves as restoring or regenerating a traditional rural culture that, they believed, had been all but obliterated by the advance of industrialisation. 'The songs and dances of the "folk" were, it was believed, in a literal sense the voice of the people, a distillation of that authentic English culture which was on the verge of extinction...' (Martin 1993: vii-viii). The reality is that anachronistic, already marginalised rural dancing from one district of England was 'revived' as the source of national culture. So white-clad, handkerchief-waving teams of men came to embody lower-class Englishness. Thriving popular dance traditions, such as those of the industrial north-west, were underrepresented in this 'revival'. (Boyes 1993: 102; see also Bennett 1993.)

However there is more to the folk song and dance revival than a gulf between the myth of 'merrie England' and historical reality. The concept 'of the "folk" and their music served as powerful ideological weapons in debates about political direction, cultural values and national identity.' (Martin 1993: viii)

But why should England be different from Scotland or Wales? As Hugh Trevor-Roper and Prys Morgan showed in their contributions to *The Invention of Tradition* (Hobsbawm and Ranger 1983) 'national traditions' such as Scottish bagpipes and tartans, and Welsh harps and 'national costume' were invented in the nineteenth century. And, in a further twist of irony, Sir Walter Scott invented Scottish 'national tradition' at the request of King George IV, and an English woman, Augusta Waddington (Lady Llanover), invented Welsh 'national costume' and imposed the harp on that country, even though Welsh bagpipe traditions are as rich as the Scottish harp playing tradition once was. This is doubly ironic given that the success of Scottish and Welsh nationalistic folklore and custom was partly because it helped to reinforce a strongly anti-English political stance.

Introduction

Defining the other defines ourselves

In Scotland, Wales and Ireland the underlying 'folk' of folklore and folk custom became more a case of other-than-English rather than other-than-gentry. But these are just different ways of defining a 'folk group' by its (perceived or actual) 'otherness' to other group(s). The way the 'otherness' of the 'folk' was defined or invented in the mid-nineteenth century is exactly paralleled by the way pioneer ethnographers of the same era emphasised the 'otherness' of non-western societies.

The construction of 'otherness' was famously explored by Edward Said in his influential book *Orientalism* (Said 1978). Europeans have a complex concept of the Orient. Indeed, the Orient is one of the West's deepest and most recurring images of the Other. 'The Orient', however poorly defined, is habitually used in contrast to 'The West'; i.e. the Europeans who created the term 'Oriental'. No one from 'The Orient' would normally refer to themselves as 'oriental'; rather they may consider themselves to be Japanese, Thai, Egyptian, etc. - and more probably would label themselves in terms of ethnic or religious subgroups. In the same way, no one (except out of irony) ever labels themselves as 'folk'.

The distinction between 'The Orient' and 'The West' has been the starting point for numerous epics, novels, elaborate theories, political narratives, and much else. Such writers implicitly 'define' the Orient in terms of dominant Western ideas. The cycle is a vicious one, as the underlying Western ideas then become reinforced by the constructed contrast with the Orient. The real significance is that the 'otherness' of the Orient implicitly helps to define the West.

Making people 'primitive'

In a similar way 'temporal otherness' was emphasised by early ethnologists. They played down the on-going changes among 'primitive' societies and regarded them as almost 'outside' of time. This was followed by a scheme in which past cultures as well as living societies were placed along an evolutionary 'time line'.

Similar ideas are conspicuous in nineteenth century British folklore studies. As will be discussed in the next section, this has led to a widespread popular belief that in some strange way folklore and customs stand 'outside' of time and are regarded as 'surviving' from a ('primitive') rural lifestyle. This belief has been rejected by anthropologists since the mid-twentieth century. Richard Dorson documented the rise and fall of this approach to British folklore in his book *Peasant Customs and Savage Myths* (Dorson 1968b). Twenty years later Adam Kuper's *The Invention of*

Primitive Society (Kuper 1988) looked at the whole anthropological fallacy.

Folklore and time

However ethnology is not just about 'primitive' societies. It also encompasses the study of our own culture and customs. And, if one is looking for different approaches to the idea of time, where better to look than folklore?

As Robert Layton has outlined (1996), folklore is an alternative way of representing space and time. Just think of the archetypal opening line 'Once upon a time ... ' and we are immediately amidst a timeless world that is not quite now but not quite past.

Folkloric representations of time may involve such dramatic contrasts as between the mundane world and the Otherworld, or it may reflect different ways of approaching space and landscape. Most certainly, folklore is radically different from modern Western thinking when it comes to representing time. Think of how prehistoric earthworks and burial monuments are given such anachronistic names as Grim's Ditch and Devil's Dyke, or Giants' Graves and Wayland's Smithy.

Once we step aside from modern preconditioning about the experience of time, we can easily grasp what Christopher Gosden meant when he wrote 'We do not pass through time, time passes through us.' (Gosden 1994: 1)

More specifically, there seem to be two time-scales operating in traditional cultures – a domestic time-scale measured in generations and a 'mythical time-scale' which is, paradoxically 'timeless'. An example is a Navaho native American craftswoman who '... instead of standing on a straight ribbon of time leading from the past to some future point, stands in the middle of a vortex of forces exerted in concentric circles upon her by her immediate family, her extended family, the clan, the tribe, and the whole living ecological system within which she lives and functions... Time surrounds her, as do the dwelling place, her family, her clan, her tribe, her habitat, her dances, her rituals.' (Toelken 1996: 277; see also Tolan-Smith 1997: 7)

However 'paradoxical' traditional ideas on time might seem, they are close to the way modern physicists see time. For them, time is not an immutable forward progression but one factor in a space-time model of relativistic causality and determinism. Both 'folkloric' ideas of time and the cosmology of modern physics show that modern 'everyday' concepts of time are, far from being 'common sense', really rather odd.

Introduction

Western causality is weird

Only relatively shallow encounters with non-western ideas reveal that western 'mental models' of such fundamental concepts as space and causality are as ethnocentric as our 'mental models' of time. While you and I would think little of arranging to meet at the junction of Oxford Street and Tottenham Court Road in London at 10.30 a.m. a week on Friday, to many non-western people such exactness of space and time would appear ludicrous, if not difficult to grasp. Conversely, the 'common sense' notions of cause-and-effect that you and I take for granted appear to be little more than medieval mythology to, say, a modern physicist who lives in a world structured by chaos theory and quantum mechanics.

If different cultures do not share a common understanding of such fundamentals as space, time and causality, how should we presume to understand the ideas, beliefs and customs of people separated from us in both space and/or time; still less to impute any cause-and-effect to specific transformations? My aim is not to contemplate the abyss of such total relativism, but rather to illustrate that modern western ideas are only one way of thinking about the world. But, of course, this risks defining 'modern western ideas' by their 'otherness' …

Let us move swiftly on to outline the way British folklore studies evolved.

2: HISTORY OF BRITISH FOLKLORE STUDIES

Comparative folklore

The history of British folklore studies has been covered in detail by Richard Dorson in his book *The British Folklorists: A History* (1968a). The way mid-nineteenth century British folklorists created and established a 'cultural evolution' interpretation that fully integrated with concurrent debates about Darwinian evolution has been described by Gillian Bennett (1994). Both these works deserve reading in their entirety so, in the next few pages, I will merely cream off some of the most pertinent issues.

Dorson's *The British Folklorists: A History* is nothing if not detailed. First there is the emergence of folklore as a distinct aspect of antiquarian studies in the eighteenth century. Then, by the middle of the nineteenth century, the study of mythology dominated folklore. This was instigated by the Grimm brothers in Germany and the work of Friedrich Max Müller (1823–1900), who 'postulated a "mythopoeic" age when the truly noble conceptions of the Aryan gods first arose.' (Dorson 1968a: 162). Nietzsche had started this ball rolling, Müller fuelled the scriptwriters, Wagner wrote the soundtrack, and the Holocaust followed.

A key aspect of Müller's mythological interpretation revolved around 'solar myths' where the sun is swallowed by the night and then disgorged at dawn. A wide range of folk narratives were 'fitted' into this grand scheme – from underworld journeys to Red Riding Hood (in the German version the girl is swallowed by the wolf and only released when the hunter rips the wolf open).

In Britain, Müller's work was taken up by Sir Edward Burnet Tylor (1832–1917). In his early work, in the 1860s, Tylor follows Müller's solar analyses and indeed broadened the scope. However Tylor's eventual claim to fame was much greater – he was 'the father of anthropology and the godfather of the anthropological school of folklorists' (Dorson 1968a: 187).

Tylor and his followers were primarily interested in folklore and customs so they could find 'evidence bearing on the early history of mankind' and how far these customs showed that the people who observed them 'are allied by blood, or have been in contact, or have been influenced indirectly one from the other, or both from a common source… ' (Tylor 1865: 273)

Tylor's comparative approach was flawed; right from the outset his ideas were contested by Andrew Lang (1844–1912). Sir James Frazer's attempt at comparative studies, *The Golden Bough* (to be explored in Chapter Four), demonstrated just how flawed this approach could get.

The county collectors

Andrew Lang, George Laurence Gomme, Edwin Sidney Hartland, Edward Clodd and Alfred Nutt dominated the FLS in its first forty years (1878 to about 1920). Dorson calls them 'The Great Team'. Georgina Boyes less charitably calls them a 'metropolitan clique' (Boyes 1993a: 14–15) . Dorson also displays a similar bias as he is dismissive of perhaps the leading folklorist of this time, Sidney Oldall Addy, conceivably because Addy was Sheffield-based (Widdowson 1973: vi).

While the 'Great Team' ran the FLS, throughout the country the fieldwork of 'collecting' from 'informants' was being done at a local, usually county-base, level. Much of the work of these 'county collectors' was based around Gomme's *Handbook of Folklore* of 1890. This provided both guidance and a substantial list of topics to be covered. There are no less than 784 questions for belief and customs alone, such as 'What is the local name for a goblin, how does he behave, who has seen him?' (Dorson 1968a: 317)

At the same time Cecil Sharp was 'collecting' folk song and dance.

> … the "folk" were always someone else – never us, rarely even real people. The elderly rural worthies from whom Sharp and his collaborators "collected" (if that is the right word) their little hoard of "folk songs and dances" were almost invariably consigned to historical oblivion, whereas the collectors received lasting recognition in the movement. (Needless to say, royalties on publications were payable to the latter rather than the former, an arrangement which suggests much about the social relationships of those involved, and emphasises the specifically ideological nature of the concept of "folk".)
> (Martin 1993: ix-x)

There was no awareness of the 'false otherness' of folklore among these collectors. Instead, their concerns were to restore or regenerate a traditional culture that, they believed, was being all but obliterated by the advance of industrialisation.

Many of these collectors laboured for a lifetime and never prepared their material for publication. Indeed the number of completed county volumes numbers less than two dozen. Ethel Rudkin's volume on Lincolnshire folklore (1936) was a late example of county-based folklore collections.

After the Second World War popular interest in British folklore was met by the seemingly-endless recycling of previously-collected material. Only in recent years has a new generation of folklorists felt inspired to take up a revised form of this approach, such as the recently-collected lore that Katy Jordan brings together in *The Haunted Landscape: Folklore, ghosts and legends of Wiltshire* (Jordan 2000).

Gentrification and bowdlerisation

The collection of folklore and customs was strongly influenced by two inter-related processes. Bawdy and sexually-explicit material in folk tales and songs was invariably suppressed and bowdlerised. Fortunately there were occasional exceptions. When Thomas Percy's pioneering collection of English ballads (published 1765 but based on a manuscript already about a hundred years old) was re-edited in the 1860s, it was supplemented by a privately-published infamous 'fourth volume', which ensured the survival of some of the bawdier ballads. The *Oxford English Dictionary* excluded sexual slang and 'dirty words', leading to John S. Farmer and William Henley's *Slang and its Analogues Past and Present* – in no less than nine volumes published between 1890 and 1904.

Feasts or wakes to celebrate the festival of the patronal saint of the parish church had their origin in the medieval era and maintained their popularity into the eighteenth century. The 'many disorders and abuses' that resulted led to 'the strongest possible official disapproval' (Hutton 1996: 352). Nevertheless at least half the parishes in the English midlands were celebrating such feasts in the 1750s and probably almost as great a number a hundred years later. Although no attempt was made to regulate such parish revels by national legislation, there was widespread concern by local magistrates and clergy, who felt that they led to 'rioting and drunkenness, lewdness, and debauchery and other immoralities' (Hutton 1996: 353, citing a Gloucestershire petition of 1710). Instead, as Hutton describes, during the second half of the nineteenth century the processes of urbanisation and the rise of evangelical 'temperance' Nonconformist denominations, such as the Baptists and Methodists, together with the increasing importance of commercial shows and rides, led to a change in the character of the annual 'parish revels' to the fairs associated with towns and cities that continue to this day.

The rowdier aspects of these annual revels sometimes included 'street football'; in reality more an opportunity for 'ritualised violence' and the settling of quarrels of the last year. The problems these caused led to their widespread suppression, although the custom has survived (despite repeated serious attempts at curtailment) at three towns – Corfe Castle, Atherstone and Ashbourne. At least two villages have maintained related customs – the Haxey Hood Game (Lincolnshire) and Hallaton Bottle Kicking (Leicestershire) – although the rough play here is to gain possession of objects other than a football.

Ironically, in Leicester the attempt by residents to clear the streets after the annual revels – by whipping anyone who still loitered – itself became a folk custom, known as the 'Whipping Toms' and, apparently, took on the character of the ritualised violence of street football and the like. In the end local magistrates prohibited the Whipping Toms but it was several more years before the local constabulary could suppress the custom, leading to 'serious clashes' in 1846 and 1847.

One aspect of this move against popular folk customs received the attentions of national legislation in the 1830s. This was the popular 'blood sports' – cock fighting and the baiting of bulls, badgers and dogs. However, as if to underline the distinction between the 'folk' and the 'gentry', while the blood sports enjoyed by the 'populace' were suppressed, the rise of the gentry's blood sport, fox hunting, continued unabated. The humanitarian sentiment that outlawed badger baiting in the 1830s was only matched by parliamentary concerns about 'fox baiting' in the 1990s, which have not been resolved at the time of writing (2002).

The 'gentrification' of popular customs during the eighteenth and nineteenth centuries was thoroughly investigated by two researchers, who published their work in the early 1980s – Hugh Cunningham's *Leisure in the Industrial Revolution c.1780-c.1880* (1980) and Bob Bushaway's *By Rite: Custom, ceremony and community in England 1700-1880* (1982). David Underdown's *Revel, Riot and Rebellion* looks at the preceding period in the seventeenth century (1985). This aspect of folk customs, from the Reformation to the twentieth century, is also explored in Hutton's *The Stations of the Sun* (1996).

What all this research reveals is the extent to which the 'bawdier' aspects of folk customs were being repeatedly contested and suppressed, where possible, by the 'gentry'. As part of this, nineteenth century folklore collectors, themselves very much part of the 'gentry', were ignoring or actively suppressing the 'less gentile' aspects of popular customs and actively promoting, through their processes of collecting and publication, the more 'genteel' aspects that they and their social peers condoned. In the case of folk dancing, this went so far as to 'revive' customs and styles that were regional and already marginal within their own social groups; a fuller discussion of this appears in Chapter 10.

Twentieth century British folklore studies

The First World War was a watershed. We can only speculate how many young men who may have gone on to become folklorists were killed in the trenches. Certainly as the generation of folklorists who Dorson dubbed the 'Great Team' died off there was no one from the new generation with the same vigour. The amount of folklore material being published dropped off sharply from 1918. With the establishment of the Irish Republic a flourishing branch of fieldwork was cut off from British folklorists (Irish folklorists instead cultivated contacts with Scandinavia, a relationship that still holds strong). Traditional storytellers – the 'informants' of collectors – were dying off and the new post-war generation was too 'modernist' to have much interest in sustaining tradition. The rural economy and lifestyle was becoming increasingly marginalised to industrial manufacture and urban life but folklorists had yet to regard urban lore as worthy of serious collecting.

As universities increasingly usurped the role played in the nineteenth century by learned societies of amateurs, so scholarship became an increasingly academic profession. Sadly, folklore never took its place as an academic discipline, even though anthropology did. The social historian E.P. Thompson has suggested that the comparative studies of Tylor and his followers dragged folklore studies into academic disrepute in British universities, in a way that it did not in many other countries. Furthermore he notes that the collection of folk songs, dances and customs had been a cause which enlisted the sympathies of the intellectual Left in the early years of the twentieth century but this sympathy had dispersed by the 1930s.

Despite the inability of British folklore studies to achieve the academic acceptability gained elsewhere, between the World Wars the English Folk Dance and Song Society gained in popularity. Revival ruled while folklore studies, including the FLS, floundered.

The prevailing mood among folklorists of the time was to develop taxonomies and hierarchical classification systems. The heroic efforts of Stith Thompson led to the first edition of his six-volume *Motif Index of Folk Literature* appearing between 1932 and 1936, although the fulfilment of this project was not reached until 1958 when the final volume of the revised edition appeared. Helpful as such a classification system can be, it is easy for 'folklore collecting' to become akin to the worst kinds of 'bug collecting' or train spotting – 'Oh golly gosh, I think I've found the earliest-known Lithuanian example of motif Q493.1.'

Stith Thompson's taxonomy fitted in well with the underpinning theory of 'cultural evolution' nourished by many nineteenth century folklorists. However by the 1920s the cultural evolution theory was sorely in need of replacement. Instead the Second World War intervened. Only in the late 1960s, with the indefatigable enthusiasm of Hilda Davidson, did the FLS begin to exhibit increasing scholarly rigour. Under the Presidency of Katherine Briggs something of a revolution took place between 1967 and 1970. Davidson's own term as President, from 1973 to 1976, consolidated many of these changes. The FLS had been raised, not without difficulty, 'to a level nearer that of its continental equivalents' (Billington 1996: xii). In 1987 Davidson herself wrote an account of this time entitled 'Changes in the Folklore Society 1949-1986' although, characteristically, her central role in these changes disappears from view; Billington (1996) augments this account from a more detached viewpoint.

In 1975, Charles Phythian-Adams attempted to inject life into British folklore studies with his booklet *Local History and Folklore: A new framework.* He approached social customs at a parish level, as recorded in the sorts of historical documents more familiar to local historians than national researchers. Sadly, although his suggestions were aimed at local historians rather than folklorists, few local historians have followed his precedent. However, his approach was followed by various social customs researchers, usually as regional studies; Hutton extended this approach to re-evaluate national customs in the seventeenth century.

Folk customs and the like began to fall under the gaze of social historians of the 70s and 80s, although usually in a way that was secondary to their main pursuits. Likewise the interdisciplinary 'cultural studies' approach that originated in 1980s has occasionally cast glances at the same territory, although rather too much of the writing about cultural studies has been about how to conduct cultural studies and how the power of 'dominant cultural practices' are to be resisted. In such broad critiques of McDisneyfication, folklorists' notions of 'folk groups' are usually too fine-grained to feature.

Popular British folklore

The 'recycling' and 'repackaging' of British folklore collected in the nineteenth century has led to a substantial quantity of books aimed at 'the general reader'. Understandably, as the scholarly counter-attacks of the last 20 to 40 years were not widely publicised, these books often retain the notions of 'cultural evolution' and the fossilisation of a lost rural idyll. As a result, popular perceptions of British folklore have little overlap with the activities of British folklore scholars in recent years.

A number of works aimed at the wider public do embody some sound approaches to their material; Jennifer Westwood's *Albion: A guide to legendary Britain* (1985) and Jacqueline Simpson and Steve Roud's, *Oxford Dictionary of English Folklore* (2000) deserve special mention. However neither of these works outline the way their approaches differ from older, less acceptable ideas.

There is no advantage in trying to speculate why leading British folklorists have not attempted to popularise the changes in approach to folklore studies – for a variety of reasons their time has been given to other priorities. Clearly I feel strongly that there is a need to popularise the recent scholarly thinking and this book is an attempt to fill this perceived gap, even though my relationship with British folklore studies is somewhat as an 'outsider' looking in.

But what is so wrong with the popular understanding of British folklore? Why am I seemingly so obsessed with this question? Well, it is easier to answer both those questions by first of all exploring the problems with the theories that have underlain British folklore studies.

3: FOLKLORE THEORY

Those accustomed to thinking of the various aspects of folklore as things that float off the ground in their own little spaces, rather like children's soap bubbles, may find this chapter alien to their assumptions. Far from floating off the ground, folklore has deep roots. Rather than independent 'bubbles', there are inter-connected branches. The 'branches', and indeed 'twigs', have taken shape as a result of very specific efforts of propagation – and pruning. Whether the various individuals who have cultivated folklore have created the most vigorous or attractive of species is another matter again.

This chapter addresses three inter-related issues:

- why do we need to think about the 'underlying theories' of folklore studies?
- what is wrong with these underlying theories?
- could the underlying theories of other fields of study be of benefit to folklore studies?

The words 'folklore' and 'theory' do not often occur together. Indeed most people interested in folklore have no concern about underlying theories. This lack of concern about underlying theories characterises British folklore studies between about 1920 and the 1980s. As a result, folklore students have been left with a muddled and confused legacy. In contrast, American folklorists have endeavoured to address issues of theory, although they have not addressed some issues of key importance to British folklore studies..

As we will explore in the course of this chapter, folklore cannot be studied effectively without giving due consideration to the underlying theories, whether they are unwittingly 'assumed' or consciously adopted. As Bruce Lincoln notes, scholars:

> ... exist within a time, a place, and a social situation, and their speech, thought and interests originate in, reflect, and engage these givens of their own experience in some measure, although this is not all that they do. Still, the books and articles which scholars write and the lectures they give are not just descriptive accounts of something that unproblematically "is". Rather, these are synthetic constructions which partake in varying degrees of the people who are speaking, that of whom they speak, and those to whom their speech is addressed. Such processes can be

> extremely accurate, revealing, and enlightening; but they can
> never be perfectly neutral and disinterested, no matter how
> much those who are involved as speakers or hearers may
> sincerely take them to be so.
> (Lincoln 1991: xvii)

Cultural evolution

> ... there is no practice without theory, however much that
> theory is suppressed, unformulated or perceived as "obvious".
> (Belsey 1980: 4)

British folklore studies have had a fairly consistent underlying theory, as
Gillian Bennett has described:

> Almost since the inception of the Folklore Society (FLS) in 1878,
> folkloristic concepts and methods have been dominated by a
> single theory of culture – "cultural evolution" (alternatively called
> "social evolution" or "sociocultural evolution")
> (Bennett 1994: 25)

'Cultural evolution' took its inspiration directly from pioneer geologists,
especially the palaeontologists who fuelled much of the debate about
Darwinian evolution.

> It was obvious how folklore fitted into this scheme. European
> folklore was to the history of human civilisation what the fossil
> record was to earth history. ... Folklorists were not slow to see
> the significance this gave to their researches. Above all, cultural
> evolution gave them the opportunity to transform their "trivial
> pursuit" into (a least a part of) the most exciting endeavour of the
> age and join the scientific community on the coat-tails of
> anthropology.
> (Bennett 1994: 29)

Bennett notes that the perceived triviality of their materials 'had always
been a sore trial to antiquarians and collectors of folklore.' These
Victorian folklorists can hardly be blamed for wanting folklore to become
an integral aspect of what, at the time, was 'cutting edge theory'.

Nevertheless, other theories were available almost from the onset, and
trenchant criticism of the 'cultural evolution' approach came from Joseph
Jacobs in the 1890s, and was increasingly voiced from the 1920s
onwards. (Bennett 1994: 25) But the 'cultural evolution' model had over-
whelming advantages in offering folklore the opportunity to develop into
an academic discipline.

But, sadly, the accolade of academic discipline went to anthropology. British folklore never became an '-ology' (ethnology cannot be regarded as an exact synonym) and became the realm of the amateur rather than the academic. With hindsight a number of reasons can be discerned. George Stocking Jr has devoted a book to the 'interactions' between folklorists and anthropologists between 1888 and 1951 (Stocking 1996; see also Bennett 1997). E.P. Thompson adopts a wider political perspective and suggested:

> In the early years of this century, the collection of folk-song, dance, and custom in England had been a cause which enlisted the sympathies of the intellectual Left, but by the 1930s this sympathy had dispersed. The rise of Fascism led to an identification of folk studies with deeply reactionary or racist ideology. And even on less sensitive historical ground, an interest in customary behaviour tended to be the prerogative of the more conservative historians. The custom is, by its nature, conservative. Historians of the Left tended to be interested in innovative, rationalising movements, whether Puritan sects or early trade unions, leaving it to Sir Arthur Bryant and his friends to celebrate "Merrie England" with its may poles, its church-ales, and its relations of paternalism and deference.
> (Thompson 1979: 6)

Theory follows fashions

Bennett (1994: 34) considers that, had folklore developed into a discipline, it would have had to have met the 'challenge' of the pioneer anthropologist Bronislaw Malinowski (1884–1942), or of leading early twentieth century anthropological theorists, Franz Boas (1858–1942) in America and Kaarle Krohn (1863–1937) in Germany (e.g. Krohn 1926). As the path of folklore studies did not 'meet these challenges' it is largely beyond the scope of this summary to explore the intense debates within anthropology over most of the last hundred years. Regna Darnell's *Readings in the History of Anthropology* (Darnell 1974) provides a useful introduction up to the 1970s. Marilyn Strathern (1987) looks specifically at how Malinowski influenced British anthropology and mythology, not least the extreme contrast between the approaches of Sir James Frazer and Malinowski.

Just as Malinowski revealed the weaknesses in Frazer's 'comparative mythology' so, in turn, Malinowski came to be regarded as too 'functionalist'. Bruce Lincoln (1999) discusses the strengths and weaknesses of Malinowski's contribution to the study of mythology from a current perspective. Mythology came to be strongly influenced by 'structuralism', inescapably associated with Claude Leví-Strauss. Structuralism found its supporters among some folklorists in Europe (and European émigrés working in America), specifically those taking a 'Lit Crit' approach to the more literary forms of folk tale such as 'fairy stories' and other 'wonder tales'. The most-cited of these works is Vladimir Propp's 1968 study *The Morphology of the Folk Tale*.

Propp made a number of distinctions and general schemas about folk tales. For instance, he considered that these tales tend to have characteristic plots. Firstly, the protagonist is confronted with an interdiction or prohibition that he or she violates in some way. Then the protagonist departs or is banished, and either given a task or assumes a task related to the interdiction or prohibition. He or she then gets into trouble by encountering either (a) a villain; (b) a mysterious individual or creature, who gives the protagonist gifts; (c) three different animals or creatures who are helped by the protagonist and promise to repay him or her; or (d) three different animals or creatures who offer gifts to help. The gifts are often magical agents, which bring about miraculous change. The protagonist goes on to battle and conquer the villain or inimical forces. However, a sudden fall in the protagonist's fortunes creates a temporary setback that will be reversed by a wonder or miracle. The protagonist makes use of the gifts, magical agents or cunning to achieve his or her goal. The result is typically (a) three battles with the villain; (b) three impossible tasks that are nevertheless made possible; (c) the breaking of a magic spell. Thereupon the villain is punished or the inimical forces are vanquished and the protagonist usually (a) marries; (b) acquires money; (c) acquires wisdom; or (d) any combination of the first three. (Zipes 1999: 3-4, based on Propp 1968)

This 'synopsis' fits well for most of the *oral* tales Propp was analysing but, seductive as it seems, sadly represents only a minority of such tales as they intermingled with the increasingly-predominant literary forms. 'And more to the point, what Propp dismisses as mere "attributes" – names, descriptions, appearance, and other details that he finds marginal – are often, in these tales, blown up to enormous proportions and become, in fact, the repositories of the most significant cultural content.' (Canepa and Ansani 1997: 17)

A number of Propp's contemporaries in the 1970s had similar interests and approaches, among them Algirdas Greimas, Claude Brémond, Max Lüthi, Petr Bogatyrëv, Roman Jakobson and Mikhail Bakhtin. Between them they came up with a number of novel approaches to interpreting folk tales, noting that 'the repetitive and predictable features of the genre offer a highly condensed model of more elaborate narrative forms' (Seifert 1996: 1). One of the distinctive traits is the predilection for sharply-contrasted dualisms: protagonists are either kings or pauper, beautiful or ugly, good or evil (Canepa and Ansani 1997: 15).

Some of these 'structuralist' distinctions now seem to be period pieces, reflecting the obsessions of scholarship in the 1970s. But not all have been rejected by subsequent scholars. For instance, folk and fairy tales generally embody elements of 'revolt' against 'reality', although by the end this revolt has been accommodated and dissolved into conformity (Seifert 1996: 12–13). Roger Renwick also took a structuralist approach in his 1980 book on what he termed 'English folk poetry' (the lyrics of folk songs), which contains chapters such as 'the semiotics of sexual liaisons'.

The merits and otherwise of specific structuralist and 1970s 'Lit Crit' suggestions have been discussed by Richard Bauman (1982). The broader issues of structuralism and semiotics in the study of folk tales has been concisely assessed by Cristina Bacchilega (1997: 11ff) and Nancy Canepa and Antonella Ansani (1997).

British insularity

The debates that resounded among anthropologists, literary critics and mythologists through much of the twentieth century did not spill over into concurrent British folklore studies. Only with Bennett's articles in the 1990s do any of these issues begin to appear, very belatedly, in the pages of the Folklore Society's journal, *Folklore*.

Even if the debates in anthropology had benefited British folklore studies, things still would not have ended up all that cosy. Bernard McGrane pulled no punches when he wrote:

> Anthropology has been an extremely subtle and spiritual kind of cognitive imperialism, a power-based monologue, a monologue *about* alien cultures rather than, and in active avoidance of, a dialogue with them... Anthropology is interested in the Other and at the same time remains altogether alien to the Other; in the best of cases anthropology speaks well *of* the Other, but with very few exceptions anthropology does not speak *to* the Other and it is as Todorov says only by speaking *to* the Other – not giving him orders but engaging in dialogue – that I can acknowledge him as subject, comparable to what I am myself. ... Anthropological 'scientific method' is the decay of dialogue,

the sustained, cultivated, and epistemologically enforced atrophy of dialogue...

Anthropology never *listened* to the voices of 'alien cultures', it never *learned* from them, rather it studied them; in fact studying them, making sense out of them, making a 'science' about them, has been the modern method of *not* listening, of avoiding listening, to them. The Other's empirical presence as the field and subject matter of anthropological discourse is grounded upon his theoretical absence as interlocutor, as dialogic colleague, as audience.
(McGrane 1989: 127–8)

To recycle a statement that had already been applied to culture theory and to archaeology: 'It is impossible to study folklore without theory. It is quite possible to study folklore without thinking about the theory being used. The dangers in this process should be obvious.' The consequences of this have been summarised cogently by Gillian Bennett:

What perhaps bedevils folkloristics in Britain is the result of the founders' [of the Folklore Society (FLS)] successes and failures put together. Their success lay in establishing a theory of culture so comprehensive, elegant and satisfying that it became assimilated not only into the culture of the FLS, but into everyday popular conceptions of culture and society. Their failure lay in their inability to establish folkloristics as an academic discipline. ... The process of challenge-reformulation-rejection-replacement therefore never took place...
(Bennett 1994: 34).

Sadly, British folklore studies (and it is important not to include European or American folklore studies in this criticism) were carried out without consideration of the theory being used for about 70 years, from the First World War until the 1980s. The legacy of this process is now obvious. But, to some extent these are problems that another autonomous anthropological discipline began to fully recognise in the 1980s. Did that discipline fare better?

Theory in archaeology

While recognising that the differences are greater than the similarities, there is some shared blood between folklore and archaeology. Both might be considered to be aspects of anthropology, although requiring a greater appreciation of 'the past' than is typical for 'main stream' anthropology.

Unless studying contemporary lore, folklorists cannot observe the behaviour of the people they are studying. Neither do folklorists have direct access to the thoughts of the people as they are recorded in written texts, unlike historians. Again, these create an affinity between folklorists and archaeologists.

In 1989 Bruce Trigger evaluated the problematical 'theory' and dubious paradigms of folklore's not-so-distant sibling in the anthropology family, in his book *A History of Archaeological Thought.* Trigger noted that archaeological theory and practice is dominated by regionalism and regional schools, often with colonialist, nationalist or imperialist 'agendas' (although noting that a few were 'world-orientated'). Clearly the same remarks could be made about folklore research too, with the proviso that there are far fewer folklorists than archaeologists, so the divergences may be more reconcilable in folklore than they have proven to be in archaeology. (Trigger 1989: 5)

Archaeology persisted with a 'seemingly complacent culture-historical orthodoxy' until the 1950s (British folklore studies generally retained such complacency until the 1980s). However, in archaeology, 'ambitious theoretical innovations' since the 1960s 'far from producing an anticipated new consensus, have led to growing disagreement about the goals of the discipline and how these goals can be achieved.' (Trigger 1989: 1)

> As archaeologists become more aware of the complexity of what they have to explain, they have also become more interested in learning how and to what extent their experience of the present influences their interpretations of the past.... It is perhaps deceptively easy to show that throughout the world the interpretation of archaeological evidence is influenced by specific social, economic, and political conditions ... [some of these] interpretations reflect the political and economic concerns of the middle classes ... [and others are] influenced directly by gender prejudices, ethnic concerns, the political control of research and publishing... financing; generational conflicts; and idiosyncratic influences of charismatic archaeologists (Trigger 1989: 379–80)

If these are the 'benefits' of acceptance as an academic discipline, perhaps folklore studies have benefited from remaining marginal to academe.

However, one of Trigger's comments is most trenchant to folklore studies: 'social conditions influence both what data are regarded as important and how they are interpreted' (Trigger 1989: 13) And what social conditions does Trigger consider most pertinent? '... the development of archaeology has corresponded temporally with the rise to power of the middle classes in Western society.' (Trigger 1989: 14). Again, one can only concur that folklore studies have indeed gravitated from eighteenth and nineteenth century 'gentry' to their successors ostensibly lower down the social scale.

Only five years after Trigger's overview of archaeological thought, a British archaeologist who can be considered to have 'ambitious theoretical innovations', John C. Barrett, published *Fragments from Antiquity* which discusses at length the way archaeologists could, and should, investigate the less tangible aspects of prehistory such as 'ritual'. (Barrett 1994: 70–81). Given that, during the era of positivism in archaeology during the 1960s and 1970s, 'ritual' was once a 'dirty word', this is indeed a major change in emphasis.

Trigger and Barrett are only two among many who have made their name in the 1980s and 1990s from provocative rethinking of the assumptions underpinning British archaeology. However the point being made here does not require us to delve too deeply into the strata of theoretical thought deposited by such archaeologists as Ian Hodder, Michael Shanks, Julian Thomas and Chris Tilley among many others. The reaction to their writing was highly charged and extensively debated. The outcome of the controversies instigated by these writers has, however, ultimately proved invigorating to archaeology. The past is now populated by people (albeit rather sketchily drawn) rather than mere 'artefacts' and 'features'. 'Ritual' has been reinstated as a primary concern of prehistorians.

Although archaeologists, understandably, have no use for the term 'folk custom' and prefer the term 'ritual', clearly these are all-but synonymous terms. If archaeologists consider it essential to question the theories underlying the investigation of prehistoric ritual, then folklorists should have no qualms about questioning the theoretical basis of researching folk customs.

However, folklorists are only beginning to overlap with archaeologists. In 1996 the annual Theoretical Archaeology Group (TAG) conference included a session on 'Folklore and archaeology'; sadly none of the speakers were folklorists. (Augmented versions of the papers were published as *Archaeology and Folklore* (Gazin-Schwartz and Holtorf 1999).) In 2002 the Folklore Society's annual conference addressed the same topic, this time with folklorists dominating the podium. Clearly it is too early to speculate on the offspring this union may engender.

Theory in American folklore studies

Given the lack of theory in British folklore for much of the twentieth century, some might think it better if 'folklore studies' had disappeared and been replaced with 'ethnology', suitably encompassed within the discipline of anthropology and bolstered by the debates about methodology and theory that have, quite appropriately, been part-and-parcel of that discipline.

Indeed, to some extent this is exactly what American folklore did become, although not to the extent that folklore studies has completely disappeared from view as an 'entity' in its own right. This, in part, results from folklore studies having healthy roots in the English literature departments of universities in the USA. The academic study of folklore is far healthier in America than in Britain – by 1986 there were sixteen North American universities offering degrees in folklore and another eighty offering folklore as a component of degrees; a further five hundred colleges and universities offered other kinds of folklore course (Oring 1986: ix). Partly this is because a number of American academics have given folklore studies a 'cuckoo' status – even though their post is in another discipline, typically English literature, they have actively promoted the study of folklore and custom.

More importantly, American folklore studies have benefited greatly from two influential teachers and theorists. We have already met Richard Dorson (1916–1981), who took a particular interest in the history of British folklore. His legacy in his home country was to inspire widespread interest in folklore through charismatic teaching. His best-known book, *Folklore and Folklife: An Introduction,* came out in 1972 and became the workhorse of folklore textbooks in America.

Alan Dundes (born 1934) shares the honours with Dorson for being the leading American folklorist of the later twentieth century. While Dorson was inspiring students in Indiana, Dundes was charming their Californian contemporaries at Berkeley. Dundes came to prominence in 1965 when he edited a stirring collection of papers with the title *The Study of Folklore.* Some of the best of Dundes' own papers were compiled in 1980 as *Interpreting Folklore.*

The opening chapter of *Interpreting Folklore* discusses 'Who are the folk?'. After considering how the term emerged in the nineteenth century to imply 'illiterate, rural, backward peasants' (Dundes 1980: 6), he offers the following definition: 'The term "folk" can refer to *any group of people whatsoever* who share at least one common factor.' (Dundes 1980: 6; emphasis in original.)

This definition has become the basis of American folklore studies. Unlike British folklore studies there is no implied 'continuity' to a poorly-defined idealised past. This is not some sort of 'failing' on the part of American folklorists – there is, after all, real interest in the way folklore is 'passed on' – but rather reflects the failure of British folklorists to address the assumed 'continuity' with a past 'rural idyll'.

As a theorist, Dundes could be reduced to three words: 'form, function, transformation'. This is a deceptive over-simplification of his ideas, but does encapsulate the way that he suggested researchers identify clearly what it is they are studying (the 'form'), the function this has within its 'folk group', and then how the 'form' might be transformed as it is passed on or reappears in somewhat different contexts.

Clearly Dundes was inspired by Malinowski and other 'functionalist' anthropologists. From the works of Dundes that I have read it appears he was little concerned that functionalism in anthropology gave way to the structuralism of Leví-Strauss. Perhaps that was entirely valid, because structuralism was in turn to prove of limited value to anthropologists. Instead, Dundes – like so many of his generation – seems to have been seduced by Freud's speculations on human thought. Dundes' *Interpreting Folklore*, published in 1980, now seems to be overly-concerned with psychoanalytical interpretations. This was not his intention. Rather, he was trying to demonstrate alternative ways of approaching folkloric material; indeed he is critical of those who restrict their interpretation to any one arbitrary analysis.

American folklore studies have moved on significantly since Dorson and Dundes wrote their major works. *Folk Groups and Folklore Genres: An introduction*, edited by Elliott Oring appeared in 1986 and opened up new ground, at least for beginners' books, with chapters on ethnic folklore and religious folklore alongside more predictable introductions to occupational folklore, children's folklore and folk songs. But the brightest light in the next generation is Barre Toelken, whose book *The Dynamics of Folklore* was revised in 1996 and provides an excellent exposition of current folklore studies in the New World; the annotated suggestions for further reading are especially helpful. And American folklore studies acquired a modern text book in 1995 with *Folkloristics: An introduction* by Robert A. Georges and Michael Owen Jones, which combines a reasonable amount of context-setting 'theory' alongside plenty of examples and short 'case studies'.

However these three works are thoroughly American in their scope. Their authors are deeply rooted in the concerns of American folklore studies and, quite understandably, make little reference to British or European folklore or its study. The subject matter of American folklore studies often seems surprisingly far removed from the interests of most British folklorists. American folklore is something that is rooted in the present day, with plenty of active collectors, and little interest in the 'historical depth'. In contrast, British folklore seems far more concerned with analysing what has been collected in the past, and stripping away the 'distortions' of earlier interpretations (although all credit to the small number of 'collectors' who go against this generalisation). The differences between American and British interests also manifest in the content of this book, which differs significantly from the contents of any of these three American examples of 'explore folklore' books.

Excessive psychology

The complex interplay of 'symbolic' protagonists and artefacts, often in 'symbolic' contexts and settings', have made fairy tales and similar genres of folk narratives highly attractive for those attempting to explore the 'inner workings' of the mind. However, psychologists have tended to use folklore less as a 'tool' than as something to be studied and analysed to provide clues about human thought processes.

A number of American folklorists have felt compelled to consider the 'psychological context' of folklore, leading Toelken to report 'Drawing especially upon the work of Freud and Jung, folklorists have sought to relate basic mental processes to the kinds of idea sets that foster traditional behaviour and expression from culture to culture.' (Toelken 1996: 5) The main instigator of this approach seems to have been Bruno Bettelheim's influential book *The Uses of Enchantment* (1976) where tales are 'deciphered' as symbols of sexual desire and conflicts. Although not necessarily following Freudian perspectives, Bettelheim notes that the plots of fairy tale often concern the 'dynamics' of family life. Equilibrium is lost through the death of a parent or from expulsion from the family, leading the protagonist on a quest for restoring equilibrium by reuniting the original family or by starting a new one e.g. the stereotypical marriage at the end of so many tales.

Bettelheim's book was criticised by numerous subsequent writers (e.g. Zipes 1979 Ch.6; Doty 2000: 427–30) but his approach has continued to be influential for both folklorists and psychotherapists. Freudian approaches to folklore were initially criticised by Dundes (1965: 107–9) although he went on to publish a number of Freudian interpretations of folk tales, albeit with a more sophisticated treatment than Bettelheim

(Dundes 1987). Elliott Oring has also taken a more-or-less Freudian approach to aspects of folklore (e.g. Oring 1992). The validity and integrity of Freud's work has been seriously criticised by, among others, Herbert Marcuse (1956), Thomas Szasz (1978) and Richard Webster (1995). But psychoanalysis has acquired such substantial momentum that merely undermining and demolishing the Freudian edifice is not sufficient to diminish its influence.

Carl Jung has also come under criticism in recent decades. His reputation is based in great part on interpretations of myths (this will be explored in Trubshaw 2003). Thankfully folklorists have generally not been drawn into the proliferation of Jungian-inspired psychobabble about mythology, even though Jungian-inspired studies of folklore have been even more prominent than Freudian-inspired ones. In the 1970s Jung's one-time assistant Marie Louise von Franz published a series of three books (1970, 1972, 1977) taking a Jungian approach to exploring fairy tales. In 1969 Carlos Drake published a paper titled 'Jungian psychology and its uses in folklore'. One of the first British folklorists to explore symbolism with a somewhat Jungian approach was Katherine Briggs in her essay 'Symbols in fairy tales' (1977) where she looked at magical artefacts made from metal, mirrors, the sun and moon. Since 1983 Marina Warner has drawn on her Jungian interests to produce a series of entertaining and informative books, mostly exploring the images of monsters and female protagonists in folk tales, culminating in *From the Beast to the Blonde* (1994) and *No Go the Bogeyman* (1999).

If *Star Wars* (1977) might be considered the greatest commercial success for Jungian-inspired mythology (the characters for *Star Wars* were developed in conjunction with the mythologist Joseph Campbell), then the greatest commercial success for Jungian-derived approaches to folk tales has been self-help books. Robert Bly's *Iron John* (1990), aimed to heal the 'wounded masculine' and his success was followed by Clarissa Pinkola Esté's *Women Who Run with the Wolves* (1992) and Gertrud Mueller Nelson's *Here All Dwell Free* (1999) who sought to soothe the wounded feminine.

Freudian and Jungian inspired approaches to folklore should be treated with a good deal of caution. Both Freud and Jung studied myths as a way of explaining the deeper aspects of human thinking. To then turn the insights they obtained this way to try to understand myths (and, by extension, folklore) is to create a hall of mirrors, a kaleidoscope of circular arguments. As both Freud and Jung created explanations of human thinking that themselves can be regarded as having the character of myths, a further source of 'regressive reflections' arises. There have been attempts to assess Jungian approaches to mythology (e.g. Segal 1998), although none, to my knowledge, that deal with the relatively minor influence that Jungians have had on folklore studies.

Context sensitivity

In the last ten years or so American folklorists have placed considerable emphasis on putting lore and customs into the *context* of their immediate surroundings. Context clearly includes the physical and social situation. 'Context' operates at two levels: 'culture' and 'situation'. For instance, folk lore revivals celebrate a context of 'otherness', that is the 'otherness' of a 'lost past' rather than the local reality. This 'lost past' contrasts with modern urban life, creating a romanticised rural past that marginalises rather than emancipates (M. Hufford 1995).

Context at the level of 'situation' includes those practices that 'frame' a performance and the shared concepts that regulate social life, produce identity and construct a social world situating people, events and places in space and time. This framing allows the narrated events to be sufficiently distanced from the present moment to allow for reflection. For instance, the incorporation of reported speech and anecdote into tales. Such framing may in some cases create a sense of boundaries and/or relate parts to wholes.

Issues of context of folk tales are also explored by Canepa and Ansani (1997 e.g. 15–16). Indeed, the wide range of studies of literary 'fairy tales' and 'wonder tales' published in recent years often deal, either as primary or secondary issues, with various aspects of 'context' and this seems likely to continue.

To some extent Dundes' 'form, function, transformation' has now mutated to 'form, context, transformation'. However, 'function' and 'context' are not interchangeable, merely intimately intertwined. Although less succinct, I suggest American folklore studies can be thought of as concerning themselves with 'form, function/context, transformation'.

Theory in history

'Form, function/context, transformation' appears to provide American folklorists with an adequate theoretical basis for their studies of 'contemporary' lore. But British folklorists are more interested in the historical 'depth' of their material than their American counterparts. This means that British folklore studies are as much at home in history departments as anthropology departments. Indeed the most influential figure in current folklore studies, Ronald Hutton, is an historian. Intentionally or not, Hutton's approach is broadly akin to the American folklorists 'form, function, transformation' foundations.

Since the 1960s the social sciences, such as sociology, have brought different working practices to bear on topics once the domain of historians. The once-dominant position of history in academe was undermined by these 'new kids' on the academic block. Historians responded by looking at new areas of study, such as beliefs and rituals, patterns of religious behaviour, and other topics 'reclaimed' from the social sciences. Historians' analyses increasingly used quantitative tools developed by economists and sociologists. (Chartier 1988: 2-3)

Some of these new areas of study brought historians into the domains of folklorists. But, however much these attempts to emulate the social sciences might led us to believe otherwise, historical sources are not necessarily reliable and none are free from problems. The literate, mostly male, élite who left written records represent poorly the wider population. Surviving material is dominated by clerical or legal administration; the background circumstances to the brief entries have long since disappeared.

In 1970 Arthur Marwick complained that British historians are distinguished from their Continental and New World colleagues by their lack of interest in historiography (the study of how historians claim to know about the past). Over twenty-five years later Beverley Southgate wrote the 'assumption of the possibility of sharply differentiating between a supposedly pristine, "objective" historical account from any philosophical or ideological accretions, still lives on.' She notes 'Any philosophical standpoint revealed in the writing of history is frequently taken as a sort of veneer... something to be assessed, praised or condemned, independently of the underlying historical research itself.' (Southgate 1996: 2).

Despite Marwick and Southgate's books being eminently readable and passionately argued, the self-awareness of historiography and post-modernist writing has only rarely found its place in British history. The American journals *Critical Inquiry* and the *American Historical Review* thrive on the debates between competing historical ideologies, but their influence on this side of the Atlantic is apparently minimal. Far too many consider that the 'facts of the matter' exist independently of the ideologies that fashioned the so-called 'facts'. Far too few have grappled fully with the implications of postmodernism. Set afloat in a sea of relativism, there is no *unique* history, no uncontested knowledge. Truth and even morality are uncovered in specific contexts, not somehow agreed in advance.

Rethinking social history

Starting in the 1960s, a new breed of British social historians made the questioning of underlying ideologies into a key part of their studies. Commencing with E.P. Thompson's masterful rethinking of English radicalism in the eighteenth and nineteenth centuries, *The Making of the English Working Class* (Thompson 1963), other historians, such as Gareth Stedman Jones (1983) and James Epstein (1994) have reconstructed the specific political contexts in which key forms of collective identity – the nation, femininity and masculinity, class, etc – were expressed. The 'underlying ideology' of Thompson and Stedman Jones is Marxist. Thompson sought to overcome perceived weaknesses in Marxist approaches; interestingly he has specifically identified such weaknesses in the context of the study of folklore, anthropology and social history (Thompson 1979: 18–19). Their views on the way the working classes attempted to subvert the intentions of their capitalist 'lords and masters' contrast significantly with the 'school text book' versions of this period. For instance, Thompson sees the *selective* destruction of machinery by the Luddites as an early form of 'trade union' activities, not as antipathy to mechanisation. For instance, the Luddites smashed the equipment of workers producing inferior goods or undercutting prices, while leaving other workers' equipment in the same workshops unscathed. While approaching his material as an historian rather than a folklorist, James Epstein specifically looks at how rituals and symbols – such as banners and ceremonial 'liberty caps' – formed part of the 'folk customs' within radical groups of this period (Epstein 1994).

Despite their emphasis on major political developments, these social historians cannot be ignored by British folklorists because (a) their work provides a 'context' for the changes to folk customs during this period, (b) their work shows how much history changes when the underlying ideology and approach of writers differs from 'established' viewpoints.

Simplistic distinctions between 'élite' and 'popular' culture were shown to be inappropriate by social historians in the 1980s. Peter Burke was the first to explore these problems (Burke 1978). Tim Harris's study of seventeenth-century London suggests that such a 'two-tiered' model does not match the reality of a multi-tiered social hierarchy, with substantial numbers of households in the 'middling' levels; Harris suggests that the divisions caused by religion were as important as 'class' divisions (Harris 1989: 43–58). Martin Ingram has taken a different approach, showing that there was a 'cultural consensus' uniting all social levels (Ingram 1984: 113; 1987: 167). Roger Chartier goes even deeper and asks if it is possible to establish exclusive relationships between specific cultural forms and particular social groups. He suggests that historians have a predilection to create cultural distinctions, and then set about describing them (Chartier 1987: 3; 1988: 30).

All this leads Tessa Watt to ask 'Should we completely abandon the concept of 'popular culture', or can we find a more constructive way of using it?' (Watt 1991: 2) She answers her question by drawing upon the work of Peter Burke and Bob Scribner. Burke compares the 'great' tradition – the closed culture of educated élites - with the 'little' (or popular) tradition – open to everyone, including the élites (Burke 1978: 28). Scribner points out that this has a tendency to reduce the 'little' tradition to a residual or marginalized category. He suggests that popular culture is a unified system of shared attitudes and values. The existence of social stratification and subcultural identities cannot be ignored, but these overlapping segments are aspects of a functional whole (Scribner 1989: 181–4). I am tempted to suggest that such an approach has become implicit to many recent British folklore studies, although there has been little or no debate about such key issues in, say, *Folklore*.

Folklorists ideas about 'folk groups', as already outlined, are entirely compatible with Scribner's notions of a unified social system and are greatly removed from the simplistic 'two-tier' notions of 'élite' and 'popular' culture that are inherent in nineteenth century concepts of folklore and, indeed to a great extent are still assumed to be valid.

Narrative voices

In so much as British historians have embraced any aspects of post-modernism, it has been from waking up to the 'excitement' of narrative. At one level historians have always 'narrativised' their historical accounts. The newly-found excitement arises partly by exploring the process through which individuals have 'narrativised' their identities in the past, following the example set by Patrick Joyce (e.g. Joyce 1991). More especially, the excitement comes from realising that different histories emerge when different narrative stances are adopted. E.H. Carr (1964) famously observed 'History is a construct consequent upon the questions asked by the historian.' These days it might be more accurate to observe 'History is a construct consequent upon the narrative approach adopted by the historian.'

'Narrative' has evolved into a number of approaches that give 'voice' to one or more points of view, especially giving fictionalised voices to real or imaginary dead people. The evolving use of narrative, in turn, has merged with other literary techniques that have come to the fore in recent years, such as irony, paradox and self-reference. Somewhere into this also comes the issue of 'closure', a topic I will turn to in Chapter 5. Many of these techniques are used to make the writing more 'reflexive', that is, being aware of itself and 'reflecting' on itself. Reflexivity may go so far as to reject the idea that observation and description are somehow detached from the processes of observing and describing. Some celebrate the self-awareness of reflexive writing, others find it difficult to evaluate the 'instabilities' this creates.

It is not the purpose of this book to predict if, say, closure and reflexivity will create any changes to historiography, or even to what extent such developments in historiography might impact on the study of folklore. However, those who want to explore these literary ideas further should read Kearney 2002 for a delightful yet profound introduction to narrative; Lawson 2001 for a more daunting but nevertheless rewarding look at the 'closure' of narratives; and Cooper 1997 for a witty yet incisive overview of reflexivity.

Cognitive Linguistics

An entirely different group of academics, mostly from the cognitive sciences and linguistics, have developed a 'metatheory' that leads to the view that our understanding of the world around us is no more than 'myth making'. As may be readily imagined, this is but a short step from folklore itself.

This theoretical approach has labelled itself 'cognitive linguistics' and evolved from initial studies published around 1980. The initial studies in the field, such as George Lakoff and Mark Johnson's *Metaphors We Live By* (1980) and Lakoff's *Women, Fire and Dangerous Things: What categories reveal about the mind* (1987) can only be described as intense and rather indigestible. However, in recent years the ideas have been developed in detail and, simultaneously, become more 'applied' rather than merely 'rarefied theories'.

The essential character of cognitive linguistics (CL) is that we think about the world entirely through 'categories of thought' that are termed 'image schemas'. Image schemas are somewhere between metaphors and the 'literal truth'. As many of the schemas relate to concepts where there is no 'literal truth', it could be said that they are categories where the metaphor has, to all intents and purposes, become 'the literal truth' (although those within CL would dispute this over-simplification). More specifically, the metaphors we use to describe 'reality' are rooted in the way we experience the world through our bodies – this has created a sophisticated concept of the 'embodied mind', that is our more abstract thinking is ultimately based on the way our bodies experience 'reality'.

These 'frozen metaphors' become embedded in the lowest levels of our thought, such that more sophisticated thinking is best considered as more complex interplay between the underlying metaphors. For instance, we have no direct way of experiencing time. We think and speak of time as something we are 'in' or as a 'flow'. These are metaphors used throughout the world by different cultures (and indeed are seemingly the only two metaphors used to describe time) so have become deeply ingrained into our sense of 'reality'.

Any attempt to summarise CL in a short section can only result in severe oversimplification. Thankfully Mark Turner has written a lucid and easily-digested introduction: *The Literary Mind: The origins of thought and language* (Turner 1996). He illustrates the ideas behind CL with examples from literature and folklore – the opening chapter is a discussion of one of the tales from *A Thousand and One Nights*. More importantly, his detailed exposition of the ideas behind CL offers an excellent approach to folk narratives (not least the 'otherness' of other cultures) and, by easy extension, to folk customs and other aspects of folk lore.

The two leading proponents of CL, George Lakoff and Mark Johnson, have recently developed an ambitiously wide-ranging 'philosophy of thought' based on the concepts of the 'embodied mind' with their 1999 book *Philosophy in the Flesh: The embodied mind and its challenge to Western thought*. While this is unduly 'heavyweight' to be directly relevant to the study of folklore, it does indicate that CL is 'well-rooted' in philosophical principles.

While the nature of this overview of theory in folklore is largely 'descriptive' of other people's achievements rather than 'prescriptive', may I venture to suggest that cognitive linguistics deserves evaluation as an especially promising way of understanding the nested levels of metaphor in folk narrative and, by extension, other genres of folklore. Thankfully Turner's *The Literary Mind* provides an accessible introduction to this potent 'metatheory'. The 'image schemas' of CL add potency to the concept of 'context' developed in the American folklorists 'form, function/context, transformation' approach. CL also adds additional 'nuances' to old-school notions of function. Indeed, there seem to be no underlying conflicts between these approaches.

Where have we got to?

This chapter is by far the most challenging part of this book to write. Partly this is because I am attempting to concisely summarise complex and often conflicting ideas. More especially, it is because I find myself looking beyond any of the prior studies of theory in folklore.

So let me summarise my summary. American folklorists have developed a theoretical basis adequate for studying more-or-less contemporary lore, but this lacks the extra sophistication required for studying the lore and customs of people and cultures separate in time and/or space. British historians study people 'separate in time' but the discipline has been characterised by a long-standing lack of interest in historiography and different 'methodologies' to folklorists. Archaeologists too were late in awakening to a lack of theory in their approaches to prehistory. So, although debates and developments in these disciplines are sometimes of interest and relevance to folklore studies too, they have yet to yield any clear guidance, beyond an awareness that the past can be viewed in many different ways, not least when different 'narrative stances' are adopted. This is the 'relativism' endemic to postmodern ways of seeing the world, in which folklore studies is itself a form of myth-making.

Future of folklore theory

Although British folklore studies are still marginalised (especially from the perspective of academe), they are stronger now than at any time since the First World War. This is not to say that there is no room for reassessment. One concern is the way British folklore is treated as more 'transparent' than lore from non-western 'traditional' peoples. Ethnologists repeatedly report that traditional people attach multiple levels of meaning to stories and rituals (and are often constrained about reporting details because of 'secrecy' and other 'initiates-only' scenarios). European lore is rarely acknowledged as being 'multi-level'. Social historians faced with 'secondary' documentary evidence are hardly in a position to explore 'hidden' or even 'ironic' levels of meaning.

One of the problems that the modern western mind has with 'traditional' material (whether western or non-western) is that our culture is far more 'literal' than any 'traditional' culture. Distinctions we expect to make – on whether something is literally true or whether it is metaphorical – often do not make sense to cultures without our overriding sense of literalism (see Harpur 2002 for examples). When looking for multiple levels of meaning, modern literalism is a serious handicap.

As an example in British folklore, surviving rituals for the initiation of new recruits to the once-widespread secret society of 'Horse Whisperers' (or 'Horseman's Word') clearly suggest multiple levels of meaning, as might be expected. The wording and imagery apparently borrows from contemporary Freemasons rituals; the prohibition against anyone joining the Horse Whisperers if they wear an apron can be taken as an injunction not only against women but also against Masons (although anyone with sufficient social status to be invited to join the Freemasons would, presumably, consider it to be 'beneath them' to join the Horse Whisperers). So, if there is ambiguity over how we should interpret the rituals of the horsemen, then can we be so sure that the texts of the plough plays (apparently also closely linked to the horsemen) are also lacking in multiple levels of meaning? And if this applies to plough plays, what about other manifestations of the 'mumming' traditions?

Whether or not this example holds up to further examination, the history (in the strict sense of 'documentary evidence') of folk customs should sit alongside 'non-documentary' studies. As John Barrett and other archaeologists have shown, the absence of written records does not preclude reasoned approaches to the investigation of social custom (or 'ritual' as the archaeologists prefer).

Hufford's considerations of 'framing' and 'boundaries', as applied to the context of folk narratives (M. Hufford 1995: 531–7), can usefully be extended to folk customs. Hufford considers only folk narratives in her paper, so her concept of 'boundary' has more to do with narrower issues of 'context' than Victor Turner's pioneering investigations in the 1960s of boundaries and 'liminality' in non-western ritual (Turner 1967, 1969, 1974), although the two approaches intertwine when expanded to folk customs.

Above all, the sophistication of cognitive linguistics, and its direct relevance to folk narrative – and, by easy extension, other genres of folklore – strikes me as an especially promising way of understanding the nested levels of metaphor in human cultures.

Clearly these relatively superficial suggestions are not the only ideas that could be explored by British folklorists. I sincerely hope that someone considering writing an introduction to British folklore studies in, say, 2020 will have a greater variety of approaches – preferably successful ones! – to assess.

4: PROBLEMS WITH 'POPULAR FOLKLORE'

'Evolved, adopted and fabricated'

The ideas and issues explored in the previous chapter might seem almost unrelated to popular perceptions of folklore. The misguided emphasis on 'cultural evolution' and over-simplistic distinctions between 'popular' and 'élite' culture that dominated British folklore studies for far too long have, understandably, developed deep roots in popular writing about folklore. A huge gulf has opened up in the last two decades or so between academic folklore research and most books about folklore aimed at the non-specialist readers.

While folklore scholars revel in following the way folk tradition evolves, adopts and is fabricated, those outside academe think in terms of unchanging continuity verging on 'fossilisation'. Popular perceptions accept without question that folk customs are a 'survival' from a lost rural idyll. Very often, there is a more or less overt belief that this tradition goes back to prechristian paganism. Nationalistic Irish, Scottish and Welsh traditions are believed to be far older than their actual known history, and to be part of shared 'Celtic' culture.

Much as academic folklorists recognise these topics as 'problematical', the reality is that such 'paganism' and 'nationalism' is now very much part-and-parcel of British folklore. The historical arguments used to support these notions may be, at best, dubious but the ideas are deeply rooted in the continuing popularity of folk customs and lore. The folklore student, while accepting that the reasoning is flawed, observes and records this as part of the processes of adaptation and evolution. It is not for nothing that folklorists sum up the folk tradition as being 'evolved, adopted and fabricated'.

Let us explore these three 'fabrications' that pervade British folklore – 'paganisation', 'continuity' and the 'Celtic conundrum'.

Paganisation of folklore

The belief that folk customs are survivals of a prechristian 'pagan' religion is as old as the study of folklore. Indeed, it predates the study of folklore. The origin of the belief is interesting in its own right and has been documented in detail by Dorson (1968a). It all starts with a clergyman and antiquarian of the early eighteenth century. Henry Bourne was the son of a tailor in Newcastle upon Tyne. He was born in 1694 and graduated from Christ's College, Cambridge in 1720, when he became curate of a Newcastle church. Five years later, in 1725, he published a tract titled *Antiquitates Vulgares*. Far from being intended as a pioneering study of folklore, this work was 'kindled with Reformation ire and zeal, berating papist and heathen ideas insinuated into Christian rituals.' (Dorson1968a: 11)

Bourne 'took pleasure in linking pagan and papist as perpetrators of a vulgar antiquity.' His sources were his own observations of 'festal orgies' and 'papist rites'. And he was a shrewd observer. 'He wrote about the populace kindling fires on Midsummer's Eve, seeing spirits exorcized in haunted houses, carousing at wakes, worshipping at wells and fountains... He saw how the interwoven strands of folk tradition formed a separate culture from the rational, sober, and pious ways of learned men.' Theologically they 'were heathen errors renewed and enlarged by the medieval church.' (All quotes from Dorson 1968a: 12)

Bourne died eight years after this tract appeared. As the eighteenth century progressed the religious mood in England changed. Anglicanism entirely eclipsed Catholicism. Such exhortations as Bourne's lay unnoticed. But antiquarians thrived. So, over fifty years later, in 1777 another Newcastle-born cleric-cum-antiquarian, John Brand, added to and reprinted Bourne's work (under his own name) as *Observations on Popular Antiquities*. Brand did not share Bourne's religious stance and expressed disdain for the manner in which Bourne added a 'spice of Divinity' into every statement. What drew Brand to Bourne's work was the record of popular customs and Brand was able to add further information from his own extensive collecting.

Brand did accept Bourne's prefatory remarks that 'Christian, or rather Papal Rome, borrowed her Rites, Notions, and Ceremonies, in the most luxurious Abundance from ancient and Heathen Rome...' And, as Hutton has detailed in less florid pose (Hutton 1991: 284ff), a subtler version of this stance is supported by the historical evidence. However, in the pages of Brand's *Observations on Popular Antiquities* we have the first suggestions of what was to become a key feature of British folklore: 'inquiry of elderly villagers into seasonal customs supposedly reflecting primitive fertility rituals.' (Dorson 1968a: 16). This is quite a different assertion and one that Hutton has discussed in detail in several books (notably Hutton 1991, 1994a, 1996) and ultimately dismissed all but a small handful of such claims.

When Brand died in 1806 he left a vast collection of antiquarian information. Thanks to the efforts of Sir Henry Ellis, Brand's original work was revised and greatly extended. In 1813 two hefty quarto volumes appeared, retaining Brand's original title *Observations on Popular Antiquities* but vastly larger than the 1777 edition. 'This mighty work laid the foundations for a science of folklore, and became a landmark in the history of English thought.' (Dorson 1968a: 17). So Bourne's once-neglected religious exhortation, increasingly augmented, entered into the mainstream of nineteenth century reasoning. And not just the reasoning of academe, but increasingly into the minds of the non-academic public. By standing on the shoulders of Brand, Ellis had single-handedly stimulated widespread interest in what would soon be dubbed 'folk-lore'. And, implicitly incorporated into that widespread interest was an acceptance that folk customs perpetrated a prechristian past. Indeed by asking appropriate questions of 'elderly villagers' this pagan past could be 'retrieved'.

The maestro of mix and match

And why stop at elderly villagers in Britain? Why not link these 'fossils' of an ill-defined pagan past to the beliefs of 'savages' in the countries incorporated into the British Empire? This was the late nineteenth century. Pioneer anthropologists and folklorists could happily refer to their sources as 'primitives' and 'peasants'. Everything was on course for the heyday of comparative anthropology. Mix-and-match was the order of the day.

In 1890 a reclusive Cambridge don published the first volume in a series that would make him the undisputed all-time maestro of mix-and-match. By the time Sir James Frazer died in 1941, *The Golden Bough* had long become a household name and inspired shelves of books derived from his ideas.

The Golden Bough is best-known in the 1922 single-volume digest. But the whole multi-volume work is vast – and Frazer revised the entire opus twice. The whole tenor of the work is anti-Christian (although this had mellowed by the third edition). He attempts to argue that the 'myth' of the crucifixion and resurrection derives from a once-universal custom of a sacred king who reigned for a set term and was then sacrificed. Sadly, apart from a dubious example from Sudan, Frazer was never able to identify a sacred king of this kind. The multi-volume 'evidence' was a smoke screen for this crucial failure.

Indeed, as Hutton notes (1991: 326) Frazer was never accepted by most of the historians and theologians of his day. But he was accepted by the public. And he inspired such leading writers as T.S. Eliot, D.H. Lawrence and Robert Graves.

Graves combined Frazer's unbounded eclecticism with his own fertile imagination and gave us *The White Goddess* in 1948. The sacred king now had a consort – a triple-aspect goddess. By then Margaret Murray, hitherto best known for her work in Egyptology, had begun to catch the attention of the reading public with *The Witch Cult in Western Europe* (1921) and *The God of the Witches* (1933). Although Frazer might be criticised for an inability to assess his evidence, Murray combined this trait with deliberate excisions of sections of quotations so they better supported her arguments that many folk customs were evidence for continuity with prechristian religion (see Oates and Wood 1998).

Murray was actively involved in the Folklore Society of the 1930s and 1940s, as was Gerald Gardner. Gardner was to draw on Graves and Murray (and much else) to give the world Wicca. Since its origins in the 1950s Wicca has in turn spawned into a whole spectrum of contemporary pagan beliefs. That story is beyond the scope of this book (and the origins of Wicca have been covered by Hutton 1999) but suffice to say that contemporary pagans, whether Wiccans or otherwise, have nurtured the idea that traditional folk customs have an unbroken continuity to a once-suppressed pagan past.

The notions of folk customs as 'pagan survivals' was being questioned from within the FLS in the 1920s, although it would be the 1980s before this became the dominant supposition within the pages of *Folklore* and the FLS's monographs. Frazer's ideas were extensively criticised by British anthropologists, notably Malinowski, from about 1920. Marilyn Strathern's delightful article 'Out of context: The persuasive fictions of anthropology' (1987) assesses in more detail than Dorson or Hutton the contribution of *The Golden Bough* to twentieth century thought, and the debates between Frazer and Malinowski.

There were a number of books published in the 1970s that 'debunked' Frazer (notably Munz 1973 and J. Smith 1978 Ch.10) but the main thrust of these attacks was not directed at the ideas of 'pagan survivals'. Only when Hutton's book *The Pagan Religions of the Ancient British Isles* (1991) gained wide readership did it become apparent to people outside the FLS and academic anthropology that there were doubts about this 'prechristian continuity'. Decades of popular books about folk customs had reiterated this perpetuity of pagan practice. Not only was it accepted as 'fact' by the public, it had become a key factor for the people who were maintaining and reviving folk customs.

One does not have to look very far to see examples of this process – many Morris dancing teams have members who continue to maintain that this custom is a prechristian 'fertility rite' – despite the evidence long since garnered that origins lay with sixteenth century courtly dances (summarised in Hutton 1996: 262–276). My favourite example of the 'paganisation' of a traditional custom is the Hallaton Hare Pie Scramble and Bottle Kicking, which takes place each Easter Monday (as discussed in detail in Chapter 9).

'Prechristian pagans' and 'popular Christianity'

The big problem with the notion of the survival of 'prechristian paganism' is the total absence of 'prechristian paganism' since about the ninth century. The dualist distinction between Christianity and paganism is a recent one. In the form we think of it, this pairing came into existence in the mid-nineteenth century. Before that, from the later part of the seventeenth century, 'pagan' was synonymous with the Classical Graeco-Roman deities. For instance, a marble sepulchral monument to Judge Leek (died 1687) in Wymeswold church, Leicestershire, was described at the time of its construction as 'a fine pagan monument' – because the symbolism incorporated into the carvings was based on Classical motifs rather than Christian ones (which, at that date, could easily be taken for 'Popery').

When Karen Jolly researched early Christianity in the Anglo-Saxon era (eighth to tenth centuries), she was surprised at the almost complete absence of any 'pagan' beliefs in the religion, even accepting that the literature was recorded by clergy. Instead, there was a clear distinction between 'magic' (such as healing charms) and 'religion'. The 'magic' owed nothing to Christian beliefs but *was being practised by people who regarded themselves as Christian.* Jolly regards this as a 'popular Christianity' that differed significantly from the 'official' formal religion but was not intended to be 'unchristian' (Jolly 1996). In this she is following a distinction that had been made by a number of European scholars, not least Keith Thomas in his pioneering study *Religion and the Decline of Magic* (Thomas 1971) and pursued by Hutton (e.g. Hutton 1996: 416–7).

Modern minds since the mid-nineteenth century generally blur the distinction between religion and magic. This leads to claims for the survival of 'prechristian religion' when the evidence being offered is for the survival, not of religion, but of magical practices. James Oblekevich (1976) provided evidence for such survival of magic, without any claims for the survival of paganism, in the South Lindsey district of Lincolnshire in the mid-nineteenth century. David Clarke and Andy Roberts (1996) also found evidence for magical practices in the Derbyshire Peak District, although their interpretation argues for 'pagan survivals'.

Going backwards in time, Aaron Gurevich's study *Medieval Popular Culture* (Gurevich 1988) makes it clear that, despite the apparent contradictions between pagan and Christian worldviews, they were inextricably combined in medieval thinking. Whatever beliefs survived from the prechristian era did so in a form thoroughly intermingled with Christianity. The popular belief of the medieval era may appear contradictory but it lacked any 'dualism' between paganism and Christianity. Such 'dualism' is a modern way of thinking and cannot be followed back in time.

If there is a dualism in religious thought of the late medieval and early modern times it is, of course, that between Catholicism and Protestantism. Protestant rejection of 'popery' was rejection of the inextricably intertwined Christian and pagan thinking that characterised the medieval worldview. So, popular traditions retaining elements of possible pagan precursors were killed off in the seventeenth century, not for their 'pagan' content, but for their unwanted Christian connotations.

While religious thinking is often thought of in terms of the doctrines of 'formal' religion, the reality is that most Christians felt comfortable with a much wider range of beliefs. This 'popular religion' sits more-or-less comfortably alongside the 'formal' religion and both readily evolve from generation to generation. Some of these 'popular beliefs' become clear in attitudes to death and the afterlife, others in folk remedies and charms. With the increasing popularity of printing the evolution of these 'folk beliefs' can be followed as they manifested in ballads and broadsides, as Tessa Watt revealed in her fascinating study (Watt 1991).

What such sources reveal is that from the sixteenth century until the early decades of the twentieth century there was an 'Old Religion' readily discernible in British popular religion. But this was not the 'Old Religion' of witches and Devil-worship, as postulated by, say, Margaret Murray. Rather it was 'a well-documented one which was brought to an end only four or five centuries ago' (Hutton 1996: 416). The Reformation brought dramatic changes to 'formal religion' but the effects on popular belief were not so much dramatic as muddled. Theo Brown summed up popular religion of the seventeenth and eighteenth centuries as 'a mixture of ancient pagan belief, half-remembered old Catholic teaching and later Puritan doctrine possibly distorted as a result of misleading sermons' (Brown 1979, cited in Hutton 1996: 417). The passage of time did little to unmuddle this state of affairs. The lack of distinction of many scholars, especially folklore researchers, between 'formal' and 'popular' religion and between 'religion' and 'magic' has only made this muddle much messier.

Continuity

Despite Hutton's books drawing attention to the various little-known academic critiques of the myth of 'prechristian continuity', a number of people active in maintaining and reviving folk customs in Britain still argue for a more-or-less revised notion of 'pagan continuity'. This is supported by some slippery shades of meaning inherent in the word 'continuity'.

Humpty Dumpty – the manifestation Lewis Carroll met on his drug-infused travels *Through the Looking Glass* rather than the nursery rhyme father of the omelette – would feel at home with these folklorists' concepts of 'continuity'. It was Carroll's Dumpty who declared 'When I use a word, it means just what I choose it to mean neither more nor less.' Indeed, in recent years 'continuity' has come to acquire a range of distinct but overlapping meanings for folklorists. Folklore researchers usually adopt meanings that differ, at least in emphasis, from the meanings 'obvious' to folk custom practitioners. This section explores some of the ways of understanding 'continuity'.

Like Humpty Dumpty, sequences of continuity can be fragile and break down. This is because continuity is, in the final analysis, a process of collective human memory. As with all memories, the key to successful recollection lies with suitable mnemonics. And, for present purposes, folk lore and customs are 'suitable mnemonics'.

Distinguishing individual from collective memory

Individual people have experiences that can clearly be labelled 'memories'. 'Societies' may be regarded as 'social bodies' resembling an extended person, and as such may have 'collective memories', but this is only one way of alluding to the nature and function of social processes. The term 'collective memory' is a convenient shorthand but should *not* be taken to be a simple extension of individual memory, but rather the metaphorical description of far more diffuse processes.

Memories shape culture

The processes of collective memory reflect on themselves. The performance of customs and the retelling of stories are not simply the 'artefacts' of a society. The customs and the stories also shape the society. The repetition of customs, the retelling of stories, and similar performances are *in themselves* a substantial part of the society.

> Actions do not simply express norms and beliefs, they simultaneously create the later; as Sahlins pithily puts it: "If friends make gifts, gifts make friends." Couched in the broadest

terms, this means that cultural practices – telling a story, performing a rite – do not passively reflect a culture, they shape it, too. Culture is not just reflective, it is also, and above all, performative.
(Maza 1996: 1501, citing Sahlins 1985: xi)

Marshall Sahlins long ago (Sahlins 1981, 1985) showed to anthropologists and historians that cultural artefacts – and that includes customs as well as physical objects – are not inert 'containers of meaning' but actively implicated in historical change. Folklore draws upon and simultaneously recreates the underlying assumptions and preconceptions of a society.

Memories must be 'worked on'

Quite crucially, memories do not survive on their own beyond an individual lifetime. The more mundane 'collective memories' are little more than routine behaviour and habits. Most socially-sustained memories need to be 'worked on', passed on and sustained. Sometimes this process apparently persists for generations. But, even if there is continuity of outward form, do the meanings and intents remain constant?

Collective memories are socially constructed. Their permanence is dependent on their emotional importance. Rumour and hearsay may be as crucial to their perpetration as 'authorised' accounts. Indeed, as any modern office 'grapevine' will confirm, non-official and dissenting 'histories' may be more prevalent than the annals presented to the outside world would ever reveal. Which leads on the question 'How much of what we remember is "true"?' If memory is socially constructed, we must accept that invention and fiction may feature more prominently than fact. And this applies as much – if not more – to the society's 'interpretation' of *why* it does certain things as to the 'content' of what is done.

Culture shapes memory

Indeed, it often seems pointless to attempt to distinguish what is 'true'. Societies seemingly adapt and distort their customs and lore according to the purposes for which they being passed on. To a large extent it is irrelevant that there is no historical evidence for morris dancing being a prechristian fertility rite, or for clan tartans dating back before Queen Victoria. English and Scottish cultures would both be poorer without these beliefs; indeed we might not have morris dancing or tartans today without these beliefs.

We have few opportunities in Britain to study oral history operating *independently* of written history. However, the recent ability to translate Maya glyphic texts

> ... provides an insight into the pre-Hispanic mind with a potential clarity not previously available. The texts were written prior to the Conquest, the meanings were encoded by natives for natives, and the carvings in stone have been altered only by the passage of time, not by significant tampering with the texts themselves. The glyphs present the most exciting chance to glimpse the Maya at a time before there was contact with, and potential influence by, the Western world.
> (Gardner 1997)

Gardner's study demonstrates that 'The impact of the Spanish upon our record of native oral literature ranges from the subtle to the blatant, the virtually imperceptible to the grossly obvious... the types of distortions the contact with the Spanish made upon the oral literature of Central Mexico... are 1) distortion by transcription error; 2) distortion by interpretation; 3) distortion by selection; and 4) distortion by accretion.'

He concludes that :

> ... *no* text can be taken at face value, even though it be written in Nahuatl (or any other indigenous language). The processes of distortion were sufficiently powerful to reach those who wrote in their own language, and could effect both the selection of the material, its presentation, or particular aspects of the lore presented.

Although the Maya might appear exotic to the study of British folklore, they illustrate clearly the way oral traditions adapt and distort, as these processes are especially obvious in Mesoamerica because of the great contrast between the powerfully-imposed categories and the newly-subservient native population. Presumably these processes of distortion were the *normal* way for oral cultures, but the evidence elsewhere will be more subtle – but no less real.

Remembering and forgetting

The memories of oral traditions apparently distorted readily. Likewise they are easily lost. A few moments' thought reveals that *most* of an oral tradition is quickly lost. In the absence of a written record the significance of artefacts and even monuments is soon dissipated. Can you remember who gave you what for Christmas last year? Can you recall how and when (and, for gifts, from whom) you acquired the ornaments around your house? For most people the answer is probably only a small proportion, and then only partial details. The 'life stories' of those artefacts you recall comparatively well are probably the ones that you most frequently recount, if only in internal monologues.

While collective memory is, as previously noted, distinct from individual memory, both processes forget far more than is remembered. The reality is that *most* of an oral culture is forgotten quickly. What is remembered from one year to another is only a small proportion of what could be remembered. That which is passed from one generation to the next is an even smaller proportion. Memory is highly selective. The memories that do persist over generations are, in some way, exceptional.

The ways in which ideas are transmitted from generation to generation in societies without writing are very different to the 'memories' of modern literate societies. Walter Ong drew attention to these fundamental differences in his book *Orality and Literature* (Ong 1982), which remains essential reading for anyone interested in understanding 'oral cultures'.

In such oral societies, those appointed with custody of the collective memories – poets and bards, usually – were held in great esteem, at least in the minds of those who hoped that the future would retain their memory. Epic poetry that has been transcribed from more or less oral traditions revels in the genealogy that is so tedious to modern minds. Yet how many modern-day people devote considerable time and effort to family history research? If today there were no record offices, parish registers, census returns and the like, how much more important might we rate those who could trace our descent and (by implication) maintain the memory of ourselves for our descendants? Yet, in the well-documented nineteenth century only a few people (usually through contemporary fame or notoriety) left more than their names, dates of birth and death, details of marriage and children. With luck and hard work we may establish who our ancestors were. But rarely have their 'life stories' been recorded, still less remembered.

Continuity in folklore

In the days before tape recordings and video cameras (more pedantically, before wax cylinders and hand-cranked cine cameras) customs and rituals lived on, between re-enactments, only in the human memory. Only from the late eighteenth century did the early 'folklorists' begin to make written records, and few substantial or systematic records were made until well into the nineteenth century.

For over a hundred years, British folklorists created and sustained the delusion that there was a continuous, somehow unbroken and unchanged tradition that went back into the mists of time and were fossils of a pagan past. As already noted, Hutton has done much to draw attention to the work of some of the more recent folklorists who have shown instead that many 'traditional' customs have clear origins within the last two to three hundred years. Even the most deeply-rooted traditions, such as those associated with May Day, changed dramatically during the Reformation and the Civil War era of the seventeenth century (Hutton 1994a; 1996).

Far from being unbroken and unchanged, the history of folk customs reveals continuity means anything but 'fixity'. Outward forms may sustain and only slowly evolve, but the original significance and meaning may have been misunderstood or forgotten.

Jeremy Harte has assessed the 'folk memory' of lore about ancient sites (Harte 1998c) and, likewise, found that claims for oral traditions spanning a millennia or more simply do not hold up. Indeed, he was unable to find any examples where oral tradition reliably spans more than two hundred years.

The reality of many of the customs now indelibly labelled in the popular mind as 'pagan customs' originated in recent centuries as 'ritualised' seasonal begging. Even morris dancing, now widely regarded as a vernal fertility rite, can be traced back to an entirely secular royal court dance 'craze' of about 1500, paganised only by the minds of Cecil Sharp and his fellow folk dance enthusiasts some 400 years later.

All is change

Can we assume that when there is no evidence for change, there has been no change? This overview of continuity has attempted to show that the reverse dictum is more likely to be true. The processes of remembering are as much about transforming and forgetting. Sequences of continuity are fragile and often break down. 'Meaning' and 'significance' can mutate even when the outward form — say, a Mayday custom — remain largely intact.

Nevertheless, continuity is to be found in folklore. But 'continuity' is never synonymous with 'fixity'. Rather it denotes a process of evolution and change — possibly quite rapid and frequent change. This makes the study of continuity fraught with difficulty because, as the Taoist maxim aptly states, 'You cannot catch a moving stream in a bucket'.

(This section is based on a previously published overview of continuity in folklore and archaeology, Trubshaw 1999.)

The Celtic conundrum

> Today, whenever Scotchmen gather together to celebrate their
> national identity, they assert it openly by certain distinctive
> national apparatus. They wear the kilt, woven in a tartan whose

colour and pattern indicates their "clan"; and if they indulge in music, the instrument is the bagpipe. This apparatus, to which they ascribe great antiquity, is in fact largely modern. It was developed after, sometimes long after, the Union with England against which it is, in a sense, a protest. Before the Union, it did indeed exist in vestigal form; but that form was regarded by the large majority of Scotchmen as a sign of barbarism: the badge of roguish, idle, predatory, blackmailing Highlanders who were more of a nuisance than a threat to civilised, historic Scotland. And even in the Highlands, even in that vestigal form, it was relatively new: it was not the original, or distinguishing badge of Highland society.
(Trevor-Roper 1983: 15)

So Hugh Trevor-Roper opens his essay detailing the invention of the Highland 'tradition'. In the same volume Prys Morgan dismantles the invention of the Welsh 'tradition'. Both make fascinating reading. For instance, Trevor-Roper discusses the invention of Scottish clan tartans by Sir Walter Scott for George IV's state visit to Edinburgh in 1822 and Morgan summarises the role of the maverick mystic, Iolo Morganwg, in restoring Welsh culture from the Methodism that had all but replaced it during the eighteenth century.

The invention of Scottish and Welsh 'tradition' has been well-known to scholars since 1983 although sadly these excellent and easily-accessible essays have had little effect on the popular understanding of these traditions. I am reluctant to further summarise these essays as they are themselves already quite concise in their treatment of the relevant information and, frankly, deserve reading in their entirety by anyone interested in British folk traditions.

Although Welsh and Scottish traditions were resurrected and fabricated to bolster national identity, their success was intermeshed with the strengthening of an anti-English political stance. This 'stance' was even more a feature of Irish identity. Steadily the anti-English stance of the Welsh, Scots and Irish brought them together and claims were made for a common 'Celtic culture' – even though throughout history the three countries had little in common, notwithstanding the close contacts between County Antrim and south-west Scotland. And, on the basis of recent DNA analysis, between 50 and 75 percent of English people alive today (at least those south of Yorkshire, where Scandinavian and Germanic genes predominate) have clear evidence of 'Celtic' genes. This is in sharp distinction to the Welsh, whose genes betray a pre-Celtic origin on the Iberian coasts and little evidence of 'Celtic' genes. Confused? It gets worse...

'Celtic' – a people, a group of languages, or a style of art?

A vast amount of popular literature has appeared over the last 15 to 20 years with the word 'Celtic' in the title and describing some amalgam of Irish, Welsh and Scottish cultures – with aspects of European Iron Age 'La Tène' and proto-historic Germanic 'Celts' thrown in for good measure.

There is undoubtedly a group of languages that have common roots, and linguists have labelled these the 'Celtic' languages. However it is important to stress that these 'common roots' grew into a tree with many branches and twigs; each of these became more-or-less distinct from each other. There is little reason to suppose that the speakers of these varied languages actually shared a common culture, least of all from the Iron Age to the modern era. And what the Irish, Welsh and Scottish did have in common was largely shared with the neighbouring, equally Celtic country – England (see Kearney 2002 Ch.8 for a delightfully fresh narrative approach to how Irish and English identity separated).

The concept of 'Celtic art', now seemingly ubiquitous in the more commercial aspects of the 'heritage industry', has been known in Ireland and Scotland since the late nineteenth century, but only achieved wider recognition after 1951, with the publication of George Bain's influential book *Celtic Art: The Methods of Construction.*

Hutton devotes the fifth chapter of *The Pagan Religions of the Ancient British Isles* (Hutton 1991) to distinguishing the Iron Age cultures popularly lumped together as 'Celtic'. The archaeologist John Collis joined the fray a year or two later, asserting that there was 'no broad based Celtic art, society or religion' (Collis 1994), although the detail of his arguments were widely criticised. Alby Stone introduced his response thus:

> Collis asserts that there was 'no broad based Celtic art, society or religion'. This is true in one sense, and false in another. On the whole it would probably be more accurate to say that there were a series of broadly similar societies and religions among Celtic-speaking populations; and that these do not necessarily coincide exactly with the distribution of certain artistic styles. It has long been a source of pain to me that otherwise sensible scholars do persist in identifying Celtic-speaking populations with artistic styles that were far more widely dispersed, and associating them with 'Celtic-style' artefacts that have no definite Celtic

provenance at all - the Gundestrup cauldron and the Book of
Kells being the two best-known examples.
(Stone 1994)

Around the same time Simon James (1993) argued strongly for Celtic
'homogeneity' in Europe and his book also generated considerable debate
(see for instance Megaw and Megaw 1996; 1998; Collis 1997; James
1998). Interestingly, in his 1999 book *The Atlantic Celts,* James is much
more ambivalent about Celtic 'homogenity' and turns his attention more
to the invention of Celtic 'ethnicity' in recent centuries. The main
protagonists in these debates are archaeologists rather than folklorists, but
the latter nevertheless need to be aware of the consensus of opinion, at
least over the fundamental issues, that has emerged in the last three years.

The main problem is that we do not know what the people in western and
central Europe called themselves around two thousand years ago. Neither
do we know what Greek and Roman authors, such as Hecataeus and
Herodotus, meant when they used the term 'Celts' – it may just have been
as much a fiction as Columbus dubbing the natives of America 'Indians'
(Wells 2001 explores these issues).

These debates have seemingly not abated the flow of popular books and
Web sites where anything that has come to be called 'Celtic' is eclectically
concatenated. Some of these are based on the visual arts – where La Tène
brooches merge with Irish Christian crosses – and some are based on
myths. These myths has inspired numerous attempts to invent a pagan
'Celtic spirituality'. The grounds for this had already been seriously
muddied in the late eighteenth and early nineteenth centuries when Iolo
Morganwg and others invented what they considered to be a 'Druidical'
religion. The reality of this 'Druidism' was thinly-disguised Protestant
theology transposed into the radical political philosophies prevalent in
Wales at that time (the same impulses for liberty and self-determination
that led to the American and French Revolutions), augmented with some
good 'theatre'.

After Morganwg's death in 1826, what has become one of the key texts of
Celtic 'mystical mythology' was created. This is known as *The
Mabinogion.* This is a translation into English of various Welsh songs,
poems and other texts, mostly dating back to the medieval era, although
the earliest-surviving copies are often more recent. The most important of
these texts were apparently brought together from diverse, confused and
incomplete sources towards the end of the eleventh century. They were
'augmented' by modern forgeries in the late eighteenth and early
nineteenth centuries. Lady Charlotte Guest, an Englishwoman as her

name indicates, paid for this miscellany to be translated into English and gave it the title of *The Mabinogion* when it was published in 1849. The image was set of an early Irish bard, Taliesin, whose poems recorded the 'mysticism' of sixth century prechristian Wales. In the next two decades scholars drew attention to the serious deficiencies of Guest's edition, not least that these 'mystical' poems are probably much later than the sixth century, but to little avail – it has been her endeavour that has been devoured avidly ever since, providing ample fuel for the 'Celtic mysteries' – not least Robert Graves' *The White Goddess*. (For a concise summary of the critiques of *The Mabinogion* see Hutton 1991: 147; 320.)

Leslie Ellen Jones has trawled through the academic and popular literature on the Druidic revival and other manifestations of 'Celtic paganism' and distilled the results in an enthralling book *Druid, Shaman, Priest* (1998). Just as Jones reveals the supposed 'Celtic paganism' to be fuelled by fantasy not facts, so the presumed similarities between Irish and Welsh religion in the early Christian era – the so-called 'Celtic church' – are far less conspicuous than the actual and significant differences between Irish and Welsh Christian practices. Again Hutton has drawn attention to the work of religious historians such as Kathleen Hughes in questioning any concept of 'Celtic Christianity' (Hutton 1991: 287–8).

However, despite all these qualms, the large quantity of dubious popular literature is counterbalanced by a smaller quantity of much higher quality studies of 'Celtic' cultures that are built on academically-acceptable foundations.

As with 'continuity' and 'paganisation', the supposed reasons for common Celtic culture are mostly spurious. But these 'spurious reasons' are significant factors in the way these folk traditions have 'evolved, adopted and fabricated'. Even if the reasons can be dismissed as spurious, the outcomes have indelibly coloured British folklore, and are likely to remain as distinguishing features.

Some might argue that I am being unfair in singling out the fabrication of folklore to further 'Celtic nationalism' when the folklore of most European countries has been deeply linked to emergent nationalism. Giuseppe Cocchiara has argued (Cocchiara 1981) that folklore has been strongly linked to emergent nationalism throughout Europe since, arguably, the Renaissance. However the scope of this book is primarily aimed at British folklore and, within that context, this 'Celtic conundrum' is a conspicuously contentious issue. The comparatively weak sense of English nationalism (often inconspicuous beneath the better-defined *British* nationalism) is reflected in the way all genres of English folklore are less readily recognised that of Wales, Scotland and Ireland. I suspect this has had indirect consequences on the way English folklorists have been less interested in 'nationalistic' aspects of folklore than their compatriots elsewhere in Britain or Europe. After all, it is no coincidence that the countries where folklore studies developed most in the nineteenth century – such as Germany, Finland, the Baltic states and Ireland – were, at the time, dominated by other nations and had most to gain by invoking the 'folk' (and their 'lore') as emblematic of national identity.

5: FOLK NARRATIVE

This chapter explores those genres of folklore usually labelled as tales, stories, legends, fables, myths, ballads, poems, anecdotes and the like. There is an overlap with folk song, although the more 'performative' aspects of song and dance are saved for Chapter 10. For the sake of convenience I use the term 'folk narratives' for this whole bundle, although 'fairy tales' and 'wonder tales' form the central part of the discussion.

There are few, if any, topics that do not occur in folk narratives. From hagiographical legends of the lives of saints, to factual accounts of mining disasters, from bawdy drinking songs to subtly nuanced lengthy narrative ballads of the lives of the gentry, it is fair to say that all aspects of human life – and most forms of non-human life, whether of this world or not – have been honoured and dishonoured in verse and prose. As is inevitable with folklore, only a small proportion of this is well-known today.

Oral/aural and written

Although most of these folk narratives started out as spoken or sung, there has been a constant interplay with written versions, especially after the advent of the printing press. Indeed one of the 'genres' is known as the 'broadsheet ballad' because of the format in which large numbers of copies were printed.

Printing assisted the dissemination of material that would have travelled more slowly and less widely by word of mouth. But it did not slow down the processes of diversification and adaptation; far from it as, in the days before copyright was enforceable, printers of broadsheets and the like plagarised and adapted at whim.

Folklorists have, nevertheless, regarded 'oral lore' as being more important than written or printed lore. Clearly, from the perspective of 'collecting' it was more important to record the tales of older people who, in all possibility, might not pass their repertoire on to the younger generation. However, once collected and published, this once-oral lore takes on its own life among the archives of printed lore.

I have not attempted to discover when the convenient homophone 'aural' began to be used as an alternative to 'oral' to describe spoken narrative and song. Although there might be a real distinction between oral sex and aural sex (e.g. telephone chat lines), the distinction between oral lore and aural lore is a more pedantic one. 'Oral' (literally 'by mouth') is paired with 'printed', i.e. the contrast in the means of 'production'. 'Aural' (literally 'by sound') includes both 'live' speech and song plus recordings, and pairs with 'written', i.e. including both handwritten and printed lore. In this book I will usually retain 'oral' except where the wider scope of 'aural' is more appropriate.

Oral folk tales containing wondrous and marvellous elements have existed for thousands of years and were told largely by adults for adults. Motifs from these tales, which were memorised and passed on by word of mouth, made their way into the Bible and the Greek classics such as *The Iliad* and *The Odyssey*. The oldest-known written epic, *Gilgamesh*, dates from c.2000 BCE yet the fragments discovered reveal variations in the recounting of the tale, showing that this work was part of a mature storytelling tradition.

Until the 1980s few people, least of all folklorists, appreciated the extent to which cultures without writing differ from modern literature cultures in the ways they preserve ideas. Walter Ong's *Orality and Literature* (Ong 1982) provides an excellent introduction to the issues, and is essential reading for anyone dealing with the 'formulaic' aspects of fairy tales, proverbs, charms, and a whole other range of other folkloric texts that betray clearly their purely oral origins.

'Wonder tales'

A few further moments of pedantry are needed. The first concerns 'fairy stories'. We think we all know what we mean by the term. But not all, in fact rather few, so-called 'fairy stories' actually feature fairies at all. So when writing about 'fairy stories' academics often adopted the wider term 'wonder tales' (at least when not using the German or French terms *Zaubermärchen* and *conte merveilleux*). Although I accept that the term 'wonder tales' has not so far gained popular currency, I am happy to use this to refer to the genre of fairy stories, whether or not they are specifically about fairies.

'Myths'

A second pedantic distinction needs to be made regarding 'myths'. This is a word that has various uses in the English language, the commonest being the pejorative sense of something that is not necessarily true. Attempts to define myth are notoriously problematical but Elliot Oring's attempt is representative of how folklorists draw a distinction from other folklore:

Three major prose narrative categories regularly distinguished by folklorists are myth, legend, and tale. These terms do not refer to the *forms* of narrative so much as to the attitudes of the community towards them. Thus, myth is a term used for a narrative generally regarded by the community in which it is told as both sacred and true. Consequently, myths tend to be core narratives in larger ideological systems. Concerned with ultimate realities, they are often set outside of historical time, before the world came to be as it is today, and frequently concern the actions of divine or semi-divine characters. Indeed, through the activities of mythological characters, the world has come to take the form that it has today. The story of Adam and Eve in the Garden of Eden might serve as an appropriate example of a myth, even though it takes a written rather than an oral form. For those who hold the story to be both sacred and true, the activities of this primordial couple, in concert with beguiling serpent and deity, explain fundamental aspects of world order: why the serpent is reviled, why woman is ruled by her husband and suffers in childbirth, why man must toil to live, – and most importantly – how sin entered the world and why man must die. It should be noted that nowhere in this definition is myth held to be untrue – rather, that the narrative is held by someone to be ultimately true enables its characterisation by the folklorist as a myth. Myths are frequently performed in a ritual or ceremonial context. There may be special personnel designated to recite the myth; the time and manner in which it is performed may also distinguish it from the other forms of narration in the society. Indeed, the language of the myth may be as sacred as its message.
(Oring 1986: 124)

Oring continues by noting that 'There are few, if any, folk narratives in our own society which could be readily categorised as myths according to our definition. Those narratives which deal with ultimate truths are generally safeguarded through a written, indeed printed, tradition.' (Oring 1986: 124)

From a historical perspective, the term mythology was created as a clear distinction from folklore. In the mid-nineteenth century, folklore was defined as survival from the stage of savagery into more advanced stages of culture. So natives of the colonies could not have folklore in the technical sense as they were considered to be still savages. 'Mythology' was utilised for these *living* systems of 'primitive' tales and beliefs and 'folklore' was reserved for the survival of these systems in civilised societies. (Oring 1986: 8) Such ethnocentric excesses also went as far as to posit that only non-western societies have mythology as 'we' have religion.

Far more could be said about how myth has been defined by different mythologists; indeed a companion work, *Explore Mythology,* is planned for publication in 2003.

'Legend'

In contrast to myths, legends are set in the modern day world and frequently include real people and places, although not necessarily making their associations explicit, as their identity and significance is often assumed to be already known. Wade Tarzia has suggested that a legend is the narrative of any strange event – usually in a local community – that seems beyond natural laws. The 'legendary event' may be either affirmed or denied by the teller, but some aspect of the legend is often taken to be true by part of the audience. That is, Joe *did* fall in a ditch and break his neck, but one person suggests that the local demon lured him there, and a sceptic says the fog was so thick that Joe just stumbled (Tarzia 1996, based on Dégh and Vazsonyi 1976: 109; 112–113). Elliot Oring is more specific and suggests that people hearing a legend are 'required to examine their world view – their sense of the normal, the boundaries of the natural, their preconceptions of fate, destiny, and coincidence.' (Oring 1986: 126)

Elliot Oring opens up some of the complexities:

> Legends are considered narratives which focus on a single episode, an episode which is presented as miraculous, uncanny, bizarre, or sometimes embarrassing. The narration of the legend is, in a sense, the negation of the truth of these episodes. This is not to say that legends are always held to be true, as some scholars acclaimed, but that the core of the legend is an evaluation of its true status. It might be that particular narrative is regarded as false, or true, or false by some untrue by others. This diversity of opinion does not negate the status of the narrative that legend recount as, whatever the opinion, the true status of the narrative is what is being negotiated. In a legend, the question of truth must be entertained even if the truth is ultimately rejected. Thus the legend often depicts the improbable within the world of the possible. The legend never

asks for the suspension of disbelief. It is concerned with creating a narrative whose truth is at least worthy of deliberation; consequently, the art of legend telling engages the listener's sense of the possible.
(Oring 1986: 124)

'Tales'

Elliot Oring completes his hat-trick of definitions thus:

A folktale is a narrative which is related and received as a fiction or fantasy. Such narratives, unlike myths, are not sacred, nor do they challenge the world views of the audience in the same manner as the legend. Folk tales often appear in a variety of forms. They are encountered only rarely in the oral traditions of our own society, although many have been adapted for children's entertainment in hundreds of illustrated books and scores of films.
(Oring 1986: 126)

He also notes that, although the folk tale plots depend upon logic, it is not always the logic of the everyday world. Furthermore, the way the plot is presented is often highly structured. For instance European and American tales tend to rely on a threefold repetition (wishes; attempts at challenges; etc) – although fourfold, fivefold, and even sevenfold repetitions are encountered in the folk tales of other cultures (Oring 1986: 130).

Origins of folk tales

Early folk tale collectors believed that folk narratives could be traced back to any original 'source' version. But such origins proved to be elusive and chimerical. Clearly there is a distinction needed between versions of a tale or song that are collected in different places at roughly the same time (specialists call these 'synchronic' manifestations) and versions that predate each other (known as 'diachronic' versions). But, even when you think you have found the earliest known version of some lore, then that is *all* you can say – that you found the earliest known version. Perhaps another earlier version exists somewhere, recorded in some strange archive or yet-to-be-disclosed by a yet-to-be-located informant. Or, more probably, the earlier versions have been lost to posterity forever except for the survival of their 'offspring'.

Eventually a folklore item might be found to change enough (back through time) so that it seems to bear little resemblance to

the most recent avatar. Then what do we do? Move to the next item up, draw a highly artificial, arbitrary line, and say we found an "original"? Yet we might also move "sideways" (i.e. to another district or country) and encounter a similar kind of variation in a similar kind of relation to the item for which we seek an original! It's very complicated, this pursuit of folklore origins, and is likely to end in an arbitrary line drawn in the sand that can be easily challenged by another scholar who approaches the subject with slightly different criteria (perhaps the criteria not of science but of his/her own cultural upbringing).
(Tarzia 1997)

There is a distinction to be made for songs and poems, where the exact wording is passed on; these usually do have a clear 'origin' (even though it may have been forgotten or lost) and, indeed, are likely to have a clear author or authors. Nevertheless, as the frequent blending of well-known themes and 'motifs' in folk song attests, even this material is closely linked to previous works.

Interaction of oral and printed literature

The adaptation and 'evolution' of folk narratives becomes especially fascinating when trying to unravel the interaction of the word-of-mouth transmission and the printed lore, such as chapbooks and broadsheets. During the sixteenth and seventeenth centuries, aural and literate modes of communication were closely intertwined and, since the 1980s, historians have taken an increasing interest in the ways print interacted with other forms of communication in post-Reformation England (see Watt 1991). By the nineteenth century oral lore was being collected and archived; these versions and printed versions of such lore are amenable to conventional historical research. Numerous studies of European folklore have pursued such approaches.

The previous chapter outlined Brant Gardner's study of the way oral history operated independently of written history among the post-Conquest Maya, and the processes of mutation and 'distortion' of the oral lore (Gardner 1997). In an example closer to home, the Old English epic *Beowulf* has survived only from copies of one written version. Although composed in a formal literary style, it incorporates traditional 'folklore' themes. At the very least these themes were familiar to contemporary audiences and, in all probability, there were numerous now-lost variants of *Beowulf* that differ from the surviving version to greater or lesser extents. We have only the one surviving version and so do not know it would have been regarded by the original audience as typical or unusual (Tarzia 1997).

The origins of fairy stories

The oral traditions from which literary forms of the wonder tales developed must have been widespread through Europe. Zipes offers a concise and convincing account of how he believes the written versions of these tales gained in popularity:

> It is not by chance that the literary fairy tale began flourishing in Italy before other European countries. During the fifteenth and sixteenth centuries, Italian cities and duchies had prospered by developing great commercial centres, and the literacy rate had grown immensely. Cultural activity at the courts in the city-states was high, and there was a great deal of foreign influence on storytelling as well as strong native oral traditions among the people. Although it cannot be fully documented, it is highly likely that the Italian literary fairy tales were gradually spreading in print and by word of mouth throughout Europe. Interestingly, England, another powerful maritime country, was the other nation that began cultivating a literary fairy tale tradition. There are fairy tale elements in Chaucer's *The Canterbury Tales* (c.1386-1400), in Spencer's *The Fairy Queen* (1590-96), and, of course, in many of Shakespeare's plays such as *King Lear, A Midsummer Night's Eve, The Taming of the Shrew,* and *The Tempest,* all written between 1590 and 1611. However, due to the Puritan hostility toward amusement during the seventeenth century, the fairy tale as a genre was not able to flourish in England. Instead, the genre had more propitious conditions in France and virtually bloomed in full force toward the end of the *ancien régime* from 1690 to 1714.
> (Zipes 1999: 11–12)

> The very name of the genre itself – fairy tale – originated during this time, for the French writers coined the term *conte de fée* during the seventeenth century, and it has stuck to the genre in Europe and North America ever since.
> (Zipes 1999: 13)

The 'propitious conditions in France' to which Zipes refers are essentially subversive ones. Having noted that many of the leading writers of fairy tales in seventeenth century France were women (quite remarkable considering how few women at that time attempted more 'serious' literary genres) he considers that they 'preferred to address themselves to a fairy and have a fairy resolve the conflicts in their fairy tales than the Church with its male-dominated hierarchy.' The success of these fairy tales made it safer to introduce supernatural powers and creatures in a symbolical code than that officially sanctioned by the Christian code. 'In short, there was something subversive about the institutionalisation of the fairy tale in France during the 1790s, for it enabled writers to create a dialogue about norms, manners, and power that evaded court censorship and freed the fantasy of the writers and readers, while at the same time paying tribute to the French code of *civilité* and the majesty of the aristocracy.' (Zipes 1999: 13–14)

The evolution of 'wonder tales' into 'nursery tales'

Wonder tales and fairy tales are not strictly 'folklore', they are the oral 'popular' tradition appropriated as a literary genre to appeal to the aristocracy and middle classes. As more and more wonder tales were written down during the fifteenth, sixteenth, and seventeenth centuries, they lost their association with the lower classes and evolved to appeal to the aristocracy and the middle classes. Recent scholarship, which is plentiful, treats wonder tales as just another literary genre.

The considerable scholarly interest in the way 'wonder tales' evolved from popular oral culture into literature is interwoven with the way in which these written forms went on to themselves influence the oral tradition. From the perspective of folklore studies, it is this incestuous borrowing and borrowing-back that makes these literary forms of 'folklore' interesting, although clearly they also have interest in their own right as literature.

One of the leading authorities on interpreting fairy stories is Jack Zipes. Since the 1970s he has produced a series of articles and books (notably Zipes 1979, 1983, 1999) that explore the tales in an 'open-ended' manner. For instance, Zipes states that most people assume 'that fairy tales were first created for children and are largely the domain of children'. However, he goes on to state: 'Nothing could be further from the truth.' Zipes notes that fairy tales were considered 'suspect' for children until the 1830s because of their 'fantasy' elements' 'In Germany, for instance, there was a debate about *Lesesucht* (obsessional reading) that could lead children to have crazy ideas and to masturbate.' More realistic, sentimental and didactic stories were favoured by educators and church leaders. (Zipes 1999: 1, 18)

However, from about 1730 'it became more acceptable to write and publish fairy tales for children just as long as they indoctrinated children according to gender-specific roles and class codes in the civilizing process. [...] Significantly it was from 1830 to 1900, during the rise of the middle classes, that the fairy tale came into its own for children.' (Zipes 1999: 15, 20)

Zipes himself offers an alternative opinion, 'In fact, the flowering of the fairytale in Europe and America during the latter half of the nineteenth century has a great deal to do with alienation. As daily life became more structured, work more rationalised, and institutions more bureaucratic, there was little space left for daydreaming and the imagination. It was the fairytale that provided room for amusement, nonsense, and recreation.' (Zipes 1999: 21)

Hans Christian Andersen became extremely popular by combining humour, Christian sentiments and fantastic plots. The Grimm brothers began to rewrite their collections of German tales and 'cleansed' the narratives of erotic, cruel or bawdy passages to make them more suited to the nursery. The popularity of these pioneers led to a surprisingly large number of nineteenth century authors who created 'wonder tales' intended as nursery tales. Of these, Lewis Carroll's *Alice's Adventures in Wonderland* (1865) and L. Frank Baum's *The Wonderful Wizard of Oz* (1900) were to prove the most influential.

Women and children to the fore

Although not addressed directly by Zipes, the modern distinctions between 'adults' and 'juveniles' did not evolve until the nineteenth century. U.C. Knoepflmacher contends that 'The notion that "adult" and "juvenile" texts should be kept apart did not become prevalent until the end of the nineteenth century.' Well into the twentieth century some of the finest children's writers, such as Edith Nesbit, Rudyard Kipling, E.B. White, Russell Hoban and Maurice Sendak, all wrote for a 'dual audience' (Knoepflmacher 1998: viii). Indeed, as modern publishers will attest, the successful marketing of a children's book lies in appealing to the adults who will pay for it.

Knoepflmacher goes on to suggest that as (a) all 'children's books are written by adults; (b) all 'adults' are former children; (c) therefore all children's books involve, in various ways, an adult reactivation of their memories of childhood (1998: ix).

A great deal of evidence points to the 'centrality' of children in the oral forms of the tales and the early written forms. As Lewis Seifert explains in his rewarding introduction to *Fairy Tales, Sexuality and Gender in France 1690–1715*, the predominant contents of fairy stories concerns the conflicts of childhood or adolescence, and their (hopeful) resolution in adulthood.

> As such, fairy stories specify with extraordinary precision and economy a culture's prototypical quest for identity; they are *par excellence* narratives of initiation, becoming, and maturity; they are themselves susceptible to becoming (and have become) powerful instruments of socialization and acculturation.
> (Seifert 1996: 2)

Through to this day, it is women who take the lead in telling stories to children and grandchildren. Even if children were not the primary audience for *literary* forms of the tales, there seems little doubt that the *oral transmission* of some genres relied heavily on women retelling stories they had heard in their childhood to the children in their care.

In 1697 Charles Perrault published his collection of wonder tales *Histoires ou Contes du Temps Passé*. The frontispiece shows an old woman, probably a servant, spinning thread with a distaff and holding the rapt attention of three children; a sign on the wall translates as 'Tales of Mother Goose' (see illustration opposite).

There is also clear quantitative evidence for the role of women in the transmission of fairy tales. Perrault, although perhaps now the most famous, indeed notorious, of the French writers who created the first heyday of fairy stories between 1690 and 1715, was only one of sixteen writers. Quite unusually for the time, when the virtues for a woman were considered to be subdued domesticity and motherhood, seven of these writers were female. However, the nine male writers mostly produced occasional tales, whereas the women generally produced collections of tales. Of the 114 tales from these writers, *two-thirds* were authored by women (Seifert 1996: 5–8). To add a further twist to this trait, Perrault was the most prolific of the male writers – and some writers (reported by Lewis 1996: 180) consider that the content of his tales suggest he had a lifelong anguish about his sexual identity.

Be that as it may, or not, the women writers demonstrate a greater attachment to the genre or, at least, seem to have 'more to say' through fairy tales than men (Seifert 1996: 9).

Feminism and fairy tales

Although 'in their day' these tales might be regarded as 'empowering' for women, recent writers have observed the extent to which representations of gender roles are one of the most ideologically-charged aspects of fairy

tales. Numerous authors since the 1970s have subverted and inverted the gender stereotyping of classic fairy tales; perhaps the best-known is Angela Carter whose 1979 tale *The Company of Wolves* was made into a film in 1984 (for further discussions of modern – and post-modern – fairy tale writers see Chapter 7).

These authors of recent decades have their counterparts among academics and literary critics who have also provided a number of stimulating 'revisionist' studies.

> In spite of their lesser prestige compared to "high" literature, fairy tales are a particularly apt means of studying the construction of sexuality and gender differences.
> (Seifert 1996: 2)

Seifert goes on to discuss the paradox that 'sex/gender systems' arise from, and are bound by, specific social contexts. So, although fundamentally unstable and susceptible to change, at the same time they are extremely resilient as they legitimise themselves as 'natural' or 'commonsensical' (Seifert 1996: 3).

Whereas Seifert's study was centred on the origins of fairy tales, Cristina Bacchilega, in her stimulating study *Postmodern Fairy Tales: Gender and narrative strategies* (1997), extends the timeframe to consider the genre right up to the time of writing. Rather than seeing fairy stories as inherently sexist narratives that offer narrow and damaging role-models for young readers, 'Feminists can view the fairy tale as a powerful discourse which produces representations of gender – a "technology of gender" ...' (Bacchilega 1997: 9–10). She cites as an example the work of Marina Warner's *From the Beast to the Blonde* (1994) who focuses on the 'images' of women from the perspective of the story's writers and tellers (who, as previously noted, are mostly women).

Although most of the best-known tales such as 'Beauty and the Beast', 'Cinderella' and 'Sleeping Beauty' have been subjected to feminist 'deconstruction' and revision, one tale has generated a shelf-full of literature all on its own: 'Little Red Riding Hood' (summarised in Bacchilega 1997: 157 fn7). Early versions of this tale have a variety of endings, mostly unhappy. Expurgated from the later nursery versions are a series of 'tests' which lead to the heroine taking her clothes off one by one and putting them on the fire, before getting into bed with her 'grandmother' then discovering she is a male wolf. If fairy tales generally have as their subtexts the transition from childhood to adolescence and adulthood, few are as disturbing as the early forms of Little Red Riding Hood (see Lewis 1996: 167ff).

Fairies ain't what they used to be

By the time J.M. Barrie wrote *Peter Pan* in 1904, Tinkerbell would be believed by the clapping children to be a delicate gossamer-winged creature capable of being dwarfed by a dandelion. But a hundred years or more before and the word 'fairy' would have brought to mind rather nasty and not at all small beings. The image of 'gracefulness, refinement and snobbery in miniature' (Harte 1998b) is a Victorian fantasy that confounds our understanding of the already-complex issue of what people meant by 'fairies' before the mid-nineteenth century.

Jeremy Harte has studied the origins of fairies in folklore and written a number of articles exploring this issue; these form the basis of a forthcoming book (Harte, in press). He introduces the complexities of understanding fairies as follows:

> The origin of fairies is amongst the most discussed questions of folklore. They have been variously traced to nature spirits, the dead, elementals, pagan deities and so on. In support of their arguments, researchers have turned to a handful of mediaeval texts, and occasionally to the evidence of place names. But there is room for doubt whether these sources should be regarded as describing fairies at all.
>
> The fairy tradition in literature begins in the 1380s, with Chaucer and Gower. In their eyes, the fairies are already a vanishing race, partly frightening and partly comic. The implication (particularly in the preamble to *The Wife of Bath's Tale*) is that people used to believe in fairies, but don't do so any more. However, the fairy mythology as a consistent set of beliefs (dancing in rings, living in hills, the rule of a queen, and so on) is itself created by the writers who claim to be recording its final echoes. Earlier evidence does not describe these fairies. Instead it details encounters with various supernatural beings who were, in retrospect, treated as if they had been citizens of fairyland.
>
> …there is no systematic mythology of fairies before 1380. There are many unrelated motifs - barrow-dwellers, tricksters, small people, household guardians - which we know in hindsight will come together to define the fairy kingdom. But this identity is simply not there in the original references.
> (Harte 1998a)

In Harte's opinion, the origins of the fairy mythology can be found in the court of Richard II, where the creative synthesis of English and French traditions was developed. In the Tudor period this synthesis sucked in

65

tricksters of the Robin Goodfellow type, the familiar spirits of cunning men, and domestic spirits like the brownie. Although this was an English-language tradition, it assimilated the *sidhe* beliefs of Ireland and the Highlands, introducing alien notions such as small size into their narrative. By 1850 William Allingham conceived of *The Fairies* thus:

> Up the airy mountain
> Down the rushy glen
> We daren't go a-hunting
> For fear of little men

Harte brings this diffuse process of evolution into sharper focus:

> By the nineteenth century, it was possible for Anglo-Saxon spirits like the *grima*, *scucca* and *thyrs* – who had lived out a quiet rural existence as Church Grims, Black Shucks and Hobthrusts – to find themselves reinterpreted by folklorists (not the folk!) as minor figures in the fairy mythology. This means that we can no longer make out what they were like originally. The fairy glamour of the fully developed tradition has tended to obscure our understanding of the very disparate narratives of supernatural encounters which have been patched into it.
> (Harte 1998a)

Especially influential in the early decades of the nineteenth century were Crofton Coker's *Fairy legends and Traditions of the South of Ireland* (1826), Thomas Keightley's *Fairy Mythology* (1828). Although stories about fairies were mostly supplanted by tales based on contemporary children's lives and adventures during the mid-nineteenth century, later in century Andrew Lang's books, beginning with the *Blue Fairy Book* (1889), re-established the popularity of fairy stories. A number of writers, including Juliana H. Ewing, Mrs Molesworth and Rose Fyleman, created a heyday of fairy lore that lasted into the 1930s. Then, with Tolkien's *The Hobbit* (1937), fairies atavistically take up sinister elvish forms. (Information in this paragraph is mostly based on Sivier 2000.)

Harte's work shows that the modern concepts of fairies are radically different from pre-Victorian notions – although these earlier concepts in turn were invented by bringing together various aspects of previous oral traditions. If nothing else this shows again how folklore 'evolved, adopted and fabricated'. To add further complexity to the fairy issues, there are also the reports of people who claim to have seen fairies; I will discuss the 'phenomenology' of encounters with fairies in Chapter 8 (see also Trubshaw 1998).

Once upon a time...

As I have already noted in Chapter 1, folklore is radically different from modern Western thinking when it comes to representing time. Wonder tales not only begin with such ambiguous phrases as 'Once upon a time...' but they conventionally end with '... and they lived happily ever after'.

... and they lived happily ever after

Zipes contended, 'Rarely do wonder tales end unhappily. They triumph over death.' (Zipes 1999: 3). The exceptions mostly come from German tales, particularly those of the first half of the nineteenth century, which was when the Grimm brothers were collecting. In these tales the protagonists typically go insane or die. Zipes suggests that this reflects the mood of the era, dominated by the selfish interests of petty tyrants and the Napoleonic Wars (Zipes 1999: 17–18).

Despite Zipes opinion that wonder tales usually end happily, this is an evolution of the genre. The earliest written wonder tales from the late seventeenth century *rarely* end happily. Not all those tales are known today but those that are, such as 'Sleeping Beauty', tend to have 'survived' incomplete so that the ending is now happy (Lewis 1996 Ch.4).

'Closure'

> The tale begins with "once upon a time" or "once there was" and never really ends when it ends. The ending is actually the true beginning. The once upon a time is not a past destination but futuristic: a timelessness of the tale and lack of geographical specificity endow it with utopian connotations – utopian in its original meaning designated "no place", a place that no one had ever envisaged. We form and keep the utopian kernel of the tale safe in our imaginations with hope.
> (Zipes 1999: 3–4)

In some literary genres the 'Once upon a time... ' is truly futuristic, although there seems to have been little study of the interplay between sci-fi fantasy genres and folkloric genres.

Storytelling subtly creates and utilises a complex concept of time quite distinct from modern 'rational' notions of chronology. In this 'other world' of 'other time' disbelief is easily suspended. This enables subtle – yet often complex – ideas to bypass much of our 'rational' thinking. For suitably trained and experienced counsellors and psychotherapists this can be a powerful technique (e.g. O'Connor and Seymour 1990: 128).

I have previously noted (Chapter 3) that wonder tales have always been rife with paradoxes. One of these is the ambivalence in the way fairy tales accommodate 'revolt' against 'reality'. Yet, in the end, everything conforms again, so even the revolt is passed off as conformity. Or does it? François Flahault has proposed a more ambiguous model for under-standing the 'closure' of such tales. Rather than an aspirational closing message of 'things must get better', folk tales adopt an acceptance – 'we have to live with the way things are'. Flahault considers that the dynamic tension between contradictory or opposing tendencies – such as between desire and satisfaction – are rarely resolved in folk tales. 'Flahault's model openly defies finality and closure.' (Seifert 1996: 13).

Building on Flahault's recognition of the ambivalent closure of folk narratives, and drawing on the analysis of 'longing' or nostalgia by Susan Stewart (1984), Siefert looks in more detail at the idea that such tales form a 'utopian kernel' as Zipes suggested. Rather than utopia, Siefert states that 'fairy tales reveal a central ambivalence or tension between nostalgia on the one hand and utopia on the other.' Nostalgia can manifest in different ways, such as the denial of the present as decadent and inauthentic, or as a wish for a location that is neither transcendent nor earthly.

Although, strictly, nostalgia is quite distinct from utopia in that the former looks to the past whereas the latter looks to the future, Seifert sees considerable ambiguity. At the end of a carefully nuanced discussion, he quotes from the philosopher Ernst Bloch who wrote that utopia '… draws images from the still valid past insofar as they ambiguously fit for the future… '. Seifert concludes that the tension between nostalgia and utopia in fairy tales creates a sense of 'nostalgic utopias' that embodies but does not resolve this tension. This 'non-closure', he suggests, reflects the crisis and transition of the period he was studying (French fairy tales between 1690 and 1715) and to all critical moments of cultural change (Seifert 1996: 13–18).

The ambiguous closure of fairy tales explored by Flahault and Seifert perhaps is symptomatic of the nature of what is meant by closure. Hilary Lawson's in-depth study, *Closure: A story of everything* (2001) is seemingly unaware of Flahault or Seifert's work but nevertheless his prefatory remarks are pertinent:

> This account of closure is a response to the chaos and confusion that surrounds us. For we are lost. Lost in a world that has no

map, not because it has been mislaid or forgotten, but because we can no longer imagine how such a map could be constructed. In our post-modern relativistic age we find ourselves adrift in a sea of stories that cannot be fathomed nor anchor found. We find ourselves in a world without certainties; without a fixed framework of belief; without truth; without decidable meaning. We have no unique history, but a multitude of competing histories. We have no right or moral action but a series of explanations for behaviour. We have no body of knowledge, but a range of alternative cultural descriptions.

(Lawson 2001: ix)

Framing

'Once upon and time... ' and '... they lived happily ever after' are framing devices, that is they create a boundary between the tale and whatever else may be going on at the time the tale is being told. But 'framing' exists at multiple levels within the tales too. Once such ploy is a tale-within-a-tale. The ultimate exponent of this, where it becomes many-tales-within-a-tale, is the 'framing story' for Antoine Galland's well-known version of *A Thousand and One Nights* (1704–17), where Shahrazad marries King Shahriyar then uses her skills as a storyteller to cure his habit of each morning ordering the beheading of the wife he had married and deflowered the afternoon before.

Many stories and storytellers adopt more-or-less complicated 'framing stories'. Those old enough to remember the TV programmes by such comics as Dave Allen or Ronnie Corbett will recall the extended 'tales' that invariably nested framing stories one inside another like so many Russian dolls. Or the framing story may itself be humorous, as with Ciaran Carson's *Fishing for Amber: A long story*:

> It was a stormy night in the Bay of Biscay and his sailors were seated around the fire. Suddenly the Captain said, Tell us a story, Captain. And the Captain began, It was a stormy night in the Bay of Biscay...
> (Carson 1999)

There is a 'framing story' pun set in the context of 1970s computers, and often quoted by American folklorists:

> A super computer is built and all the world's knowledge is programmed into it. A gathering of top scientists punch in the question: "Will the computer ever replace man?" Clickity, click,

whir, whir, and the computer lights flash on and off. Finally a small printout emerges saying, "That reminds me of a story."

(Dundes 1980: 19)

In some tales, especially ones originating in the nineteenth century, a different type of framing is used to 'wrap' a serious moral lesson within the tale. A classic example is the heavily moralistic ending to Charles Perrault's 'Little Red Riding Hood' of 1697:

> This story teaches that the very young,
> And little girls more surely than the rest,
> – sweet, dainty things, clothed in their Sunday best –
> should never trust a stranger's artful tongue.
> Small wonder if these guileless young beginners
> Provide the wolf with some of his best dinners.
> I say the wolf, for every wolf that roams
> Is not the same.
> Some, in appearance tame,
> Gentle, well-mannered, affable and gay,
>
> Trotting beside them in the friendliest way,
> Follow young ladies right into their homes.
> Alas, how many to their cost do find
> These plausible wolves are the most dangerous kind.
>
> (Translated Geoffrey Brereton, *The Fairy Tales of Charles Perrault*, Penguin 1957.)

Clearly 'framing' is not restricted to folk narratives. Indeed, post-modern writing takes great delight in nested levels of framing, emphasising reflexivity, paradox or irony. In folk tales 'framing' or tales-within-tales is usually a simple conceit of the storyteller (as with *A One Thousand and One Nights*) although there more complex instances that may serve to overload the mind's judgmental processes so alternative belief systems can be pursued within this 'suspension of disbelief'.

Riddles and proverbs

American folklorists, to a far greater extent that their British and European counterparts, have taken an interest in teases, insults, retorts, curses, oaths, toasts, greeting and leave-taking remarks, riddles, taunts, tongue-twisters, limericks, rhymes for ball-bouncing, skipping and 'counting out', lullabies, dandling rhymes and other nursery songs. These are excellent examples of how common 'lore' helps define and 'bond' a 'folk group'.

Little Red Riding Hood (from Gustave Dore's
Les Contes de Charles Perrault, *1862)*

As many of these genres are rather 'fun' their neglect in British folklore studies for many decades is even more surprising. Examples of most of these genres, although excellent examples of the formulaic nature of orally-transmitted lore, end up written down in various more-or-less likely contexts. Nearly one hundred examples from Old English that have come down to us from the tenth century or earlier, such as:

> Soundless my robe when I step on earth
> or rest at home or ruffle the waters.
> My clothes and this lofty air
> at times lift me over human dwellings,
> and then clouds' power bears me
> far above folk; my dress
> rustles loud and whistles,
> sings clearly when I am far
> from flood and field, a flying spirit.

Translation by John Porter (Porter 1995).

(Answer on next page.)

Today's riddles are usually less literary and more punning, such as:

> What does one flea say to another as they go strolling?
>
> Shall we walk or take a dog?
>
> (Georges and Jones 1995: 248)

Although we now think of riddles as 'merely' jokes, and rather childish ones at that, in many European wonder tales, riddles often have to solved by the protagonists, to save themselves from death, or to win a partner in marriage; J.R.R. Tolkien could be drawing on either eighteenth and nineteenth century wonder tales or Old English precedents when he pits Bilbo against Gollum in a potentially deadly exchange of riddles.

F.A. de Caro has looked at the way riddles form much deeper cultural connections in places as far apart as Turkey, Borneo and the West Indies. He also looks at the way some riddles require knowledge of proverbs and other clichés, which is an overlapping genre of lore (De Caro 1986).

I have included these genres under the heading 'folk narratives'. Purists may argue that these genres are too 'fragmentary' to be considered as narratives. However, if the folklorist studies these in context then such remarks usually arise in the course of an exchange, quite probably an extended exchange, which may have its own 'framing stories', and almost invariably is a good example of the folk group defining itself through the 'narrative exchanges' taking place. It is another example of the 'context' of the folklore being as important as the 'item' of folklore itself. Clearly, the folklorist is interested too in the adaptation and mutations that may arise during the transmission of the lore.

(The accepted answer to the Old English riddle on the previous page is a swan.)

6: CONTEMPORARY FOLKLORE

While on the one hand the phrase 'contemporary folklore' might seem almost tautological to American folklorists, whose studies of folklore almost entirely look at contemporary lore, the same phrase strikes many British ears as decidedly odd because, as I have discussed, the British idea of 'folklore' is popularly linked to an imagined lost rural idyll. Tales of people who had one of their kidneys stolen while on holiday indeed seem at odds with, say, eighteenth century ballad texts about maids in the heather who met gallant gentlemen on fine white steeds.

This chapter is restricted to considering contemporary 'lore', both written and aural; later chapters will look at contemporary folk song, dance and customs. The 'folk' of contemporary folklore are:

> ... *any group of people whatsoever* who share at least one common factor. It does not matter what the linking factor is – it could be a common occupation, language or religion – but what is important is that a group formed for whatever reason will have some traditions which it calls its own.
> (Dundes 1980: 6–7; emphasis in original)

Groups can be as few as two people or as large as a nation. Not everyone in a group need know all the other members, but they will know the common core traditions belonging to the group. This 'common core tradition' is often a major component of the group identity. 'Large scale' examples of common traditions creating group identity include national identity – although all too often the highly emotionally-charged 'traditions' have little historical depth or accuracy (as with the 'Celtic' countries of Britain discussed in Chapter 4).

Families build up considerable shared lore – usually framed by such opening words as 'Remember the time at Alan's wedding when... ' or derogatory references to absent members of the group with unfortunate habits, such as 'Don't do an Aunt Beth!'. Religious and ethnic groups are bound together by their common core traditions. But the most dynamic area of such group identity lore is that of occupational and leisure-interest groups. I think we can find it fairly easy to accept that the members of such traditional trades as deep-sea fishermen or coal miners shared common lore. But common lore bonds such modern-day occupations as diverse as computer programming, ambulance and fire crews, or professional footballers. Indeed *every* place of work has its own traditions and lore. In the same way, every leisure-time pursuit acquires its customs, traditions and other traits that bond members of that group together, whether they are anglers, surfers, golfers, bridge players, mountain bikers, members of an evening class, or just 'regulars' at a local pub.

We are all folk

So, from this perspective, we are all 'folk'. Indeed, unless we are exceptionally reclusive, we are all 'lots of folk', as we shift from one group to another in the course of a day. Think again about Gerald Warshaver's three 'levels' of folklore, introduced in Chapter 1. His first level is 'customary practice', that is activities where the participants do not consider themselves to be 'doing' folklore (Warshaver 1991). The examples he gives are of customs such as funerals, weddings and stag nights. For the purposes of this chapter the emphasis will be on the customary telling of 'tales' and jokes – although nicknames (both ones known to their 'owner' and scurrilous ones used only behind their back) are also a significant feature of many folk groups.

Indeed, jokes are often a key defining aspect of a group. The type of joke shared between 'the lads' after watching a football match would probably not be appropriate for a social evening to raise funds for a religious group. Context is often critical. Catholics may tell anticlerical jokes among themselves, but not to non-Catholics. Likewise, the best anti-Semitic jokes are said to be told by Jews themselves, but Gentiles normally only hear these from other non-Jews. Barre Toelken has suggested that up to 80 percent of the oral lore that bonds groups might be considered 'crude' or 'obscene' if heard out of context (Toelken 1996: 8). Tolerating or condoning humour that would be taboo in other contexts helps to define the folk group.

Although orally-transmitted jokes and tales are still paramount for bonding groups, as any office-based worker is well aware, when there is easy access to photocopiers or email then various forms of jokes are readily circulated. 'Photocopy lore' has been a genre of folklore studies for a number of years; those researching this genre now study how such tales are transmitted and adapted by email instead. Much of this humour follows the same lines as 'Top twenty reasons why chocolate is better than sex' (see next page) – risqué but likely to be tolerated in most offices, perhaps because written from a female perspective. Clearly these jokes usually originate from outside the group but the people who 'introduce' them to their groups make some deliberate decisions, not necessarily consciously, about who would be suitable recipients. These are typically people considered to share similar 'status' in the group or are considered to have a 'good sense

Top twenty reasons why chocolate is better than sex

1. You can get chocolate.
2. "If you love me you'll swallow that" has real meaning with chocolate.
3. Chocolate satisfies even when it has gone soft.
4. You can safely eat chocolate when you are driving.
5. You can make chocolate last as long as you want it to.
6. You can have chocolate even in front of your mother.
7. If you bite the nuts too hard the chocolate won't mind.
8. Two people of the same sex can have chocolate without being called nasty names.
9. The word "commitment" doesn't scare off chocolate.
10. You can have chocolate on top of your desk during working hours without upsetting workmates.
11. You can ask a stranger for chocolate without getting your face slapped.
12. You don't get hairs in your mouth with chocolate.
13. With chocolate there's no need to fake it.
14. Chocolate doesn't make you pregnant.
15. You can have chocolate at any time of the month.
16. Good chocolate is easy to find.
17. You can have as many kinds of chocolate as you can handle.
18. You never too young or too old for chocolate.
19. When you have chocolate it does not keep their neighbours awake.
20. The chocolate, size doesn't matter, it's always good.

of fun' – unwittingly the circulation list for such lore defines a group or subgroup.

There is a long tradition of 'chain letters', which have now mutated into various email counterparts. Variants of these, very much creatures of our time, are the ever-mutating 'hoax' virus alerts, passed on in good faith by misguided computer 'newbies' (there are numerous Web sites devoted to publicising false virus warnings, although the organisers are rarely doing this for 'folkloristic' reasons). Email has become the 'natural home' of another 'tradition', that of spurious charity collection schemes. The best known of these in Britain started in 1989 when Craig Shergold, a nine year old suffering from a brain tumour, wanted to break the *Guinness Book of Records* for the number of get well cards received, then standing at about one million. Along the way the request mutated to include business cards. At the last count 350 million such cards had been received and they are still arriving at the rate of several thousand every day; Guinness have long-since closed the category. At least Craig Shergold was responsible for starting this saga, even he could never have predicted the unstoppable consequences. More typically such charity collections have no purpose at all. They date back to at least 1971, when a restauranteur in Kansas recruited Boy Scouts and Girl Scouts to collect about eight million cigarette packages to help a dying girl obtain an iron lung; he later learned that there was no little girl, and no market for the empty packages (Lindahl 1996b: 79–80).

Oral narrative as performance

Orally-transmitted tales and jokes are still paramount for bonding groups, who form the 'folk' of contemporary folk lore studies. Such oral narratives are 'performed' for their listeners. To a large extent orally-transmitted folklore is entirely a subset of the performance of folklore. Vocal emphasis and numerous 'framing techniques' in the narrative style are employed (more-or-less self-consciously) by the teller to enliven the narrative. The storyteller is not only reporting an experience, but makes the telling of it into an experience for those listening.

Narrative techniques might be expected to make the events being described as comprehensible as possible. But in many cases the object of the telling is either to 'tell a tall one', where things are not as they seem to be and the concluding remarks 'reframe' previous assumptions, or there are other reasons for 'obscuring, hedging, confusing, exploring, or questioning what went on, that is, for keeping coherence or comprehensibility of narrated events open to question.' (Bauman 1986: 5).

Richard Bauman's study of personal experience narratives in a small Texan town (Bauman 1996) revealed complex and shifting contextual issues.

Telling tall tales and other forms of what Bauman calls 'expressive lying' are combined with comic accounts of personal experiences and other ways of 'managing the point of view'. Bauman concludes that the cornerstones of these activities are 'story, performance and event' (1996: 112), and these are 'one of the most fundamental and potent foundations of our existence as social beings' (1996: 114).

FOAFs

There is much more to contemporary folklore than tales passed on within 'folk groups'. One genre is best-known to folklorists by its acronym 'FOAF', that is 'friend of a friend' tales. These are relatively short, usually plausible but rather improbable, stories that have the 'framing story' that starts 'A friend of a friend of mine ... '. The 'friend of mine' might be named, if known to the listeners, but the 'friend of' invariably remains anonymous. Often the doubly-anonymous FOAF opening alone adds sufficient 'veracity' to the tale.

The first FOAF tale to be studied by folklorists is known as the 'Vanishing Hitchhiker', although there are a number of variants. The four most common American versions are:

1: An attractive young female hitchhiker is given a lift and gives the driver details of an address where she wants to go. At some point the driver suddenly discovers she has inexplicably vanished. The driver goes to the address given and is told that his passenger has been dead for some time.

2: A lift is given to an old woman who issues a prophecy or warning before disappearing. Later the driver and/or other passengers discover that the old woman is dead.

3: A young man meets a girl at a dance and gives her a lift home. She asks to be dropped off at a cemetery. Later he finds she is dead; however a personal item of his that he had given to the girl has been left on her grave.

4: An old lady carrying a basket is offered a ride and sooner-or-later disappears. Later the traveller(s) discover they have given a ride to the Hawaiian Goddess Pelee.

(Summaries based on Bennett 1998: 2)

The first folklorists to study this FOAF tale, Richard Beardsley and Rosalie Hankey published details of 79 versions of the story they had discovered in America, mostly in the 1930s (Beardsley and Hankey 1943, cited in Bennett 1998: 1). The earliest known version of similar events dates to 1824, well before modern notions of hitchhikers. 'Token leaving phantoms' have even older roots.

Since the 1940s, versions of the story have been printed in a variety of newspapers and magazines worldwide, and the tale has mutated into a greater number of variants. However the ghostly protagonist is predominantly either an attractive young woman or a little old lady. Commonly the young woman is said to have died violently, often in a car accident at the place where she was picked up. A further twist may be that the event took place on the anniversary of her death.

Organ thieves

Whatever the tellers' and their listeners' beliefs are about the 'reality' of ghosts (a topic to which I will return in Chapter 8), the ubiquity of the 'Vanishing Hitchhiker' tales makes it easy for this to be recognised as 'just a story'. However FOAF tales also permutate into stories that initially appear plausible. So plausible that they appear in newspapers with 'actual' names to the protagonists – although follow up research reveals that they are fictional people. One such tale first appeared in the German tabloid *Bild der Frau* in September 1990. It recounted how a married man on holiday with his wife in Istanbul was 'kidnapped' by a seductive woman. He was drugged and woke the next day to discover that one of his kidneys had been surgically removed, presumably for an organ transplant.

Although hotly denied by the Turkish authorities, the story spread rapidly through Germany and official warnings were issued to tourists and business travellers. At the same time the Australian press was reporting that Australians visiting Los Angeles, California, were falling victim to 'kidneynappers'. Within months examples of the tale were being collected from around the world. Variants of the tale started to appear, such as a young English woman travelling in India who was stricken with acute appendicitis. She consented to emergency surgery but, when back in Britain, the symptoms reappeared. She underwent further surgery when it was discovered that her appendix had not been removed in India, but one of her kidneys had (this appeared in *The Observer* 4 Dec 1994). Yet another variant reports the victim was an attractive woman shopping for clothes who is persuaded to go to the cellar of the shop or to a van out the back, where she is drugged and a kidney removed.

The tale has immediate precursors in accounts from the 1980s of the theft of body parts – typically kidneys or eyes – from babies and children in Latin America. Some versions of these tales report that the kidnappers are dressed as clowns. Such allegations led to official enquiries in Mexico in 1990 and 1992.

The tales are xenophobic in that they are situated in a Third World country. They incorporate common folkloric motifs as an attractive young woman (as seducer or victim) or adding a sinister element to an 'innocuous' figure such as a clown (in this the tales may be imitating examples of sinister gun-totting hijackers dressed as clowns in films).

Although organ transplants from living donors as well as from cadavers take place throughout the world, and in some parts of the world donors may be paid for their organs (although in India legislation was passed to outlaw such 'rewarded gifting'), organ conservation needs sophisticated equipment that is improbable in the scenarios described. None of the official investigations or detailed follow-up research has found any truth in these tales. Nevertheless these rumours continue to spread, not least because tabloid journalists happily rework them in ignorance of the folkloristic aspects of the tales.

(All the above information on organ theft tales is taken from Campion-Vincent 1997 and Howe 2000.)

Contemporary legends

As these newspaper accounts of the organ theft 'FOAF tale' clearly show, such tales are not restricted to aural transmission. Variants of FOAF tales frequently appear in popular newspapers and magazines. FOAF tales are best considered part of a more general category of 'contemporary legends'. More or less the same scope of legends has also been referred to as 'belief legends', 'modern legends' and 'urban legends'. However, as Gillian Bennett and Paul Smith note, 'how does one measure the belief in a belief legend, establish beyond contradiction the modernness of a modern legend, or guarantee the urbanness of an urban legend?' (Bennett and Smith 1996: xxxix)

The way contemporary legends are told – both orally and in print – relies greatly on *what is not said*. Their interest is partly the way they are told, which forces recipients to assume the role of interpreters. This makes contemporary legends distinct – and distinctly modern. These 'elliptical plot structures', rather than the content itself, may even be their key defining feature. As an example of such 'elliptical' story telling, here is the summary of the so-called 'killer in the back seat' legend; the last line 'redefines' the preceding narrative:

> … a woman shopping late at night has forgotten to lock her car door. After reentering the car and driving off, she finds herself pursued by a fearsome stranger in a truck: after several minutes of horrifying chase, the stranger reveals himself as a saviour in disguise. The real threat, indeed, much closer to her than the woman ever imagined. Concealed in the familiar confines of her

car was a maniac; the truck driver had pursued a woman in order to protect her.
(Lindahl 1996b: 82)

Contemporary legend studies

There has been a substantial number of articles and specific studies about aspects of contemporary legends. Despite this vitality there has been no recent overview of the research, with the exception of Bennett and Smith's introduction to *Contemporary Legend: A reader* (Bennett and Smith 1996) and Smith's chapter in that work.

The relative lack of interest in contemporary legend may be because

> ... as a genre, contemporary legends have been defined solely by folklorists and, unlike other types of traditional narratives, no "folk generic" category exists for the lay person. I would argue that this has come about simply because of the diversity of content, presentational forms, and functions which contemporary legends exhibit. Thus, while the lay person can, rightly or wrongly, deal with such concepts as "myth", "folk tale" and "legend", contemporary legends are often "just ordinary" forms of communication.
> (Smith 1989: 111)

Those who are active in the genre have plenty to keep them occupied. There are lots of variants of specific legends to collect. When told orally there are 'performative' aspects to be studied. As they differ significantly from more literary stories, some scholars regard the 'narrative style' as the key area of study. The more philosophically-inclined can explore the ambiguity as to whether the teller believes the tale or not.

Contemporary legends are a comparatively recent addition to the recognised genres of folklore, although this does not mean the tales did not exist for some considerable time previously. The study of contemporary legends can be traced back to A.S.E. Ackerman's *Popular Fallacies Explained and Corrected* (1st edn 1907; 4th edn 1950), although Alexander Woollcot was probably one of the earliest to identify the contemporary legend genre, in the early 1930s. Harold Brunvand's compilation *The Vanishing Hitchhiker: American Urban Legends and Their Meanings*, published in 1981 was immensely influential in both helping to define and arouse interest in contemporary legends.

Paul Smith notes specifically that contemporary legend studies have not acquired the same academic 'status' as interest as fairy tales. This has led to few attempts at overview and synthesis of contemporary legend research, and such attempts as have been made seem too narrow in their approaches compared to comparable overviews of fairy tales and myths (Smith 1989). The key approaches to contemporary legend studies have their roots in contributions to a symposium in 1959 (the papers were published in Hand 1971). Different contributors questioned the definitions then current, drew upon psychological studies of rumour, and introduced novel approaches based on sociology and psychology. In the subsequent years the proponents of these different approaches clashed and competed with each other. Three of the key speakers at the symposium, Linda Dégh, Robert Georges and Alan Dundes, became closely associated with contemporary legend research in the 70s and 80s. (Bennett and Smith 1996: xxii–xxxix provide a detailed historical overview of this formative phase of contemporary legend study.)

Ironically, academic interest in fairy tales has grown at a time when fairy tales have become less important to popular culture than contemporary legends. '… contemporary legends abound in magazines and daily papers, comedy and horror films, and, as always, in the words of everyday people, where they are retold as jokes, ornate tales, or plain news.' (Lindahl 1996a: xi) At the same time, legends have been incorporated into all kinds of artistic expressions. 'The "pedestrian" realism of legendary – the "this-could-happen-to-you" quality of the genre – has exerted great appeal on such authors as Margaret Atwood, Anthony Burgess, Ernest Hemingway, and Carson McCullers, to name a few… ' (Barnes 1991)

Contemporary legends have been popularised in their own right. Paul Smith has edited the *Book of Nasty Legends* (1983) and *Book of Nastier Legends* (1986). Three popular paperbacks by Phil Healey and Rick Glanvill (*Urban Myths,* 1992; *The Return of Urban Myths,* 1993; and *Urban Myths Unplugged,* 1994), based on their column in the weekend edition of *The Guardian,* are significant research aids for contemporary legend researchers. However such compiling of ever-increasing examples has not been matched by much-needed 'overviews' of the genre.

Contamination and contemporaneity

One theme dominates the contemporary legend canon – contamination. The scope ranges from reptiles, spiders or insects invading someone's body; through snakes or tarantulas lurking unseen in clothes, plants or household goods; to the most abiding of all these themes – the contamination of foodstuffs. Within recent decades a new variant has arisen, of which the commonest version tells of a man who picks up a woman in a local bar, sleeps with her, and awakens to find the message 'Welcome to the world of AIDS' scrawled in lipstick on the nearest mirror.

There are clear parallels here with the fears of 'invasion' and 'contamination' underlying the widespread popular interest in UFOs and close encounters with aliens, itself only an extraterrestrial extension of the xenophobia and racism lurking rather too close to the surface of Western societies. One does not need an in-depth training in psychology to spot the insecurities about our physical and social 'boundaries' on which these scenarios feed.

Recovered childhood memories

The ideas and 'folkloric motifs' of contemporary legends can also step out of folklore and become worryingly manifest in the real world. In recent years there have been a number of 'therapists' who use exceedingly dodgy hypnotherapy attempts to 'recover' memories of abuse – usually sexual – during childhood. Needless to say the person concerned has no previous recollection of such abuse (which is not to say that there may not have been some greater or lesser 'dysfunctionality' in their family life as a child). The alleged abuser finds the accusations difficult to refute, leading to bitter tensions between various members of the family. The American Medical Association's Council on Scientific Affairs has responded to this by stating: 'Contrary to what is generally believed by the public, recollections obtained during hypnosis not only fail to be more accurate but actually appear to be generally less reliable than non-hypnotic recall.' (Cited in Watters and Ofshe 1994).

This procedure for 'recovered memories' has also led to attempts to question children about alleged 'Satanic abuse'. The origins of such allegations can be clearly traced to a small group of right-wing Christians who have widely promoted their beliefs to police authorities, social workers and child welfare charities. This phenomenon came to the UK in 1990, although the same people had promoted their ideas in the USA and Canada in previous years.

As a result of this witch hunt fuelled by Christian fundamentalism a number of families, notably in Rochdale, Nottingham and the Orkneys, were suspected of such 'Satanic abuse' in the 1990s, with tragic consequences. The anthropologist Phillips Stevens, in a number of articles published in America in 1989 and 1990, drew the parallels with historical persecution of Jews and heretics, and with 1950s American political paranoia about communism. He recognised that these were 'a particularly insidious and dangerous' form of folklore. The late twentieth century Satanic abuse allegations was mostly derived from the demonology of the late Middle Ages, as modified by the interest in 'esoteric magic' during the late nineteenth century. (Stevens 1989 (1996: 342))

The British 'Satanic abuse' controversies led to a major study of Satanic abuse by the folklorist Jean la Fontaine (1998) – 'What might be the first report on witchcraft and Satanism commissioned by a British Government for 400 years... ' claims the review in *Magonia* (Rimmer 1998). Some seven years previously *Magonia* had brought together three quite heavyweight articles mainly devoted to analysing stories of alleged Satanic child abuse and their links with so-called 'UFO abduction' reports (*Magonia* No.38 Jan 1991). La Fontaine found no evidence for such practices but did see close parallels with the witchhunts of late medieval Europe and eighteenth century America (famously the Salem community in 1692). While it would be rational to expect that, compared to the eighteenth century, witch hunts would be on the decline in the twentieth century, sadly this was not the case.

In recent years a number of studies have been made of the way children 'confabulate' their memories of real experiences with memories of 'events' they have only been told about. In contrast, people who have been undisputed victims of abuse in childhood have no need to 'recover' these memories; on the contrary they do not succeed in suppressing or forgetting the events. These studies shed considerable light on the way children and adults alike create and adapt stories; indeed, on the whole nature of how we create 'narratives' of our entire lives. The wider implications of this extend well beyond folklore studies into the realms of philosophy and psychology.

More recently Ethan Watters and Richard Ofshe's demolition of 'recovered memory syndrome' in their milestone study *Making Monsters* (1994) and Gareth Medway's *Lure of the Sinister: The Unnatural History of Satanism* (2001) have both thoroughly undermined the procedures and beliefs of the proponents of supposed Satanic abuse.

Which just leaves the 'parallel issue' of UFO abductions. The notion of people being abducted by aliens then subjected to 'examinations' (rather reminiscent of sexual abuse scenarios; see Sivier 2001) in UFOs has generated a contentious, indeed litigious, volume of literature since the 1980s. Although this notion has seemingly been accepted as 'gospel' by a rather large number of Americans, suffice to say that the proponents of this idea rely on the same recovered memory hypnosis techniques. As Peter Rogerson, Roger Sandell and Michael Goss all noted in their articles in *Magonia* 38 (1991), there are clear parallels between 'Satanic ritual abuse' and 'UFO abductions' - and with other folklore 'motifs'. But academic researchers were slow to take an interest. Perhaps their logic was that, because neither Satan nor UFOs exist, there was little or no significance to beliefs that they do exist. But the strong emotions and damage to a substantial number of people's lives most certainly exist. Significantly it was folklorists such as Rogerson, Sandell, Goss and La Fontaine who recognised that the 'motifs' here were essentially folkloric and the whole phenomena could best be approached by incorporating ideas that had arisen within folklore research.

It's all around us

Contemporary folklore is all around us in a variety of forms and genres. The remaining chapters include various other manifestations of contemporary 'lore'. Those interested in pursuing contemporary legends and folklore will find that several books by American folklorists provide adequate introductions, such as Oring (1986), Georges and Jones (1995), and Toelken (1996). Brunvand (1981) and Bennett and Smith (1995) are also essential reading.

7: MODERN FOLK NARRATIVES

As the previous chapter started with examples of folk tales that fall with the first level of Warshaver's three 'levels' of folklore (where the participants do not consider themselves to be 'doing' folklore) you may be forgiven for expecting this chapter to deal with level two (what most people would think of as folklore). Instead we are going to mostly leapfrog to level 3, and come back to level 2 later in the book. Level 3 is folklore self-consciously incorporated into entirely modern activities. This chapter will be dealing with *narratives* that self-consciously incorporate folkloristic elements, which means mostly novels and films, although video games also get a look in too.

The problem with looking at the links between folklore and popular culture is that the genres reflect back on each other like a kaleidoscope. Chapter 5 looked at the way literary adaptations of oral lore started in the fifteenth century and became a recognised literary genre by the end of the seventeenth century. By the middle of the nineteenth century this genre had entered fully into the mainstream of publishing.

Some of these blends of folklore and literature were sophisticated. M.R. James (1862–1936) raised standards far higher when he published *Ghost Stories of an Antiquary* in 1904. Jacqueline Simpson has painstakingly pieced together how James combined previous approaches to literary ghost stories (such as those by Charles Dickens and Sheridan LeFanu) with a detailed knowledge of folklore sources (principally Scandinavian material collected by the Danish folklorist E.T. Kristensen). James was an accomplished writer of short stories with a powerful imagination. Nevertheless, he used the folkloric material in a manner that remained 'folkloric'; his skill was to transform these tales into masterpieces of the horror short story (Simpson 1997).

Horror and fantasy

The horror fiction genre routinely draws upon folklore – where would the goosebumps come from without assorted werewolves, vampires, cursed Egyptian mummies, and a multitude of things unseen that bump, creak or moan at the midnight hour? Indeed, where would *The X Files* be without plots based on contemporary legends? But folklore supplies more than shivers. Folklore also infuses the fantasy genre too. Fairies, trolls, dragons, nasty witches (and sometimes nice ones too), magic swords, not to mention magic rings – from J.R.R. Tolkien to Terry Pratchett and a multitude of imitators in between, the realms of fantasy are populated from folklore. Few of these writers have the understanding of folklore of, say, M.R. James. Indeed, when Pratchett said 'I am not a folklorist, but I am a vast consumer of folklore – an end user, if you like.' (Pratchett 2000: 159) a great number of other fantasy authors might add 'Me too'.

Pratchett's 'consumption' of folklore has been regurgitated in various ways, such as references to the Horseman's Word (in *Witches Abroad*) and morris dancing (in *Reaper Man*). The latter book closes with an account of the *other* dance – done not at dawn in May but at dusk in the autumn, not dressed in white but in black, and with silent bells. And, lo and behold, this imaginary form of morris has been enacted by various morris teams 'One gentleman said it was a very strange and chilling experience which he would not willingly repeat.' (Pratchett 2000: 164)   As Pratchett cogently notes, 'It's traditional in a way that modern folklorists will readily comprehend: it's been done once before.'

Wicker men and megalithic monuments

As a begetter of folk customs, Pratchett has a long way to go before he matches Anthony Shaffer, the author of the book, *The Wicker Man*. The 1973 film rose to cult status in America, as the British film distribution oligarchy of the day consigned it to obscurity.   Only recently has *The Wicker Man* begun to be regarded in Britain as a classic of the *If...* and *Clockwork Orange* era of British film making. The UK still has nothing to offer to match the annual Burning Man festivities that started on a San Francisco beach in 1986 and now take place in the Nevada desert every August, where the Wicker Man inspiration has been subsumed within a 'fringe theatre festival' where everyone present (up to 25,000 people) is seemingly both performer and audience.

The folkloric and mythic elements that have been borrowed to make up the pagan festivities of Lord Summerisle in *The Wicker Man* are easy enough to spot – a beheading game at the culmination of the morris dancer's sword dance; naked girls jumping over a fire in the middle of a stone circle; and the eponymous burning effigy. If this suggests an 'unbroken pagan tradition', then the film itself informs us that these rituals were reconstructed by a Victorian botanist with anthropological interests. In any event there is clearly a 'larger than life' emulation of Gerald Gardner's 'borrowings' in putting together Wicca rituals in the 1940s and 50s. (For a useful analysis of *The Wicker Man* see Jones 1998: 211–13; in 1999, *Nuaða* a fan 'zine devoted to the film, was founded.)

Stone circles – usually but not always Stonehenge – appear in a wide range of films, from the Beatles *Help!* (1965) to Spinal Tap's *Stone'enge* (1984) via various episodes of *Quatermass, Dr Who* and a host of thankfully-forgotten 'B' movies. Leslie Ellen Jones has attempted to catalogue and assess megaliths in movies (Jones 1998, 2000, 2001). In at least one of these movies 'there is no explicit reason for Stonehenge [to be included] … it must be functioning as an icon, a symbolically-packed image operating as a shorthand for a whole raft of associations.' (Jones 2001: 7) Alternatively, as in John Boorman's *Excalibur* (1981), 'anonymous small scale local stone circles can carry the generalised legend motifs required by the plot.' (Jones 2001: 11)

Folklore, magic and science

Referring to *Dr Who,* Jones notes that 'Particularly in the Tom Baker years, it seems that the Doctor constantly encounters examples of British folklore which invariably turn out to derive from the machinations of hostile aliens bent on world domination.' (Jones 1998: 223). But folklore also runs deeper in the scripting. 'Much of *Dr Who* is based on the Frazerian premise that magic is misunderstood science …' (Jones 2001: 12). One of the creators of *Dr Who,* Chris Bidmead (who took over from Douglas Adams as script editor in the early 1980s) observed: 'The initial hypothesis of *Doctor Who* had been to alert children to the fact that science – knowing real stuff about real things – is a powerful force in the world and well worth getting to grips with.' (Bidmead 2002).

Bidmead notes that towards the end of the 1970s this initial hypothesis had been inverted – magic had taken over from science, creating a realm of fantasy where nothing was impossible. Perhaps respecting Arthur C. Clarke's famous aphorism 'Any sufficiently advanced form of science will appear indistinguishable from magic', Douglas Adams ('in real life a huge fan of science' reports Bidmead) extracted a lot of fun from this silliness – and went on to weave embellished science deeply into *The Hitchhiker's Guide to the Galaxy* (1979). Philip Pullman's Dark Materials trilogy – *Northern Lights* (1995), *The Subtle Knife* (1997) and *The Amber Spyglass* (2000) – also melds a sophisticated understanding of science with mythology and magic. Whereas J.K. Rowling's *Harry Potter* (1997) is all magic and 'wizardry', with neither science nor folkloric aspects noticeable.

Yet magic and wizardry have their roots in fairy stories and wonder tales – think of L. Frank Baum's *The Wonderful Wizard of Oz* (1900) – or, as most us will, think of the film version. And fantasy of quite a different genre can be built 'from the ground up' with deliberate 'mythologising' of the heroes, as when Joseph Campbell contributed to the characterisation of *Star Wars* (1977).

Filmmakers can produce such gems of self-consciously 'invented folklore' as *Shrek* (2001), based on William Steig's 1990 children's story. Other animators can take robust folklore material and remove its paradoxes and ambiguities of 'closure', leaving us with endings of trite reconciliation, as the Disney Studios have repeatedly demonstrated, exacerbating such errors with implicit and explicit elitism (see Stone 1975). Indeed, some would argue that America has 'Disneyfied' its entire culture, and is rampantly inflicting this monster on the rest of the world.

The 'rational' materialism of Western culture is proving to be an avid consumer of irrational fantasy and myth. As science increases the sense of certainty of how the universe seemingly works, it simultaneously enhances our sense of wonder at the 'magic' of it all. The increasing interest in mystery and fantasy is perhaps as much *complementary* to popular awareness of modern science as contrary.

Fantasy literature based on adoption and fabrication of folk narratives dominates the non-fiction sections of both adult and childhood reading. Countless children's stories rely on princesses, dragons, frogs and other 'usual suspects' pursuing escapades that comply with the intuitively-understood 'rules' of folklore. Even the dark and rather unpleasant original 'wonder tales' collected by the Grimm brothers, before they were increasingly 'bowdlerised' into nursery tales, seem to have found their successors in Raoul Dahl's scary humour.

Adapting to the times

Folk tales have always adapted to their times. Between the end of the First World War and the start of the 1930s, idealistic modern day 'fairy tales' were generated by Hermann Hesse - in such novels as *Siddhartha* (1925) and *Steppenwolf* (1927) – to contend 'what he perceived to be the sinister threat of science and commercialism.' (Zipes 1999: 183) Sadly Hesse's utopian idealism was followed in the 1930s by numerous examples of German fairy tales embodying the idealism of fascism. But, while we might raise our eyebrows at the idea of fascist fairy stories from the 1930s, racist stereotypes following the rules of folklore have been so thoroughly acculturated in the vast number of novels and films of 'cowboys and indians' that most readers and viewers fail to see the far-from-liberal agendas.

Idealism of a different denomination inspires the writings of C.S. Lewis in the 1940s and 1950s. Louis Markos notes that Lewis's precision on theological issues was matched by a sense of wonder and a respect for the 'significant stories' of who we are, from whence we came and where we are soon to go. Lewis warned against the loss of wonder, although a walk through a wardrobe into a witch-infested land where a lion is Lord may now seem to many readers too thin a makeover of chauvinistic Christianity. (Markos 2001, cited in Lazell 2001)

And, since the 1960s, non-sexist and 'politically correct' fairy tales have abounded. Some, such as James Garner's *Politically Correct Bedtime Stories* (1994), are intended as satires but others, such as the work of Angela Carter, Emma Donoghue, Anne Sexton, A.S. Byatt, Tanith Lee, Robin McKinley and others are works of serious literary merit. (Zipes 1999: 25–6 provides a concise summary of modern 'nonsexist' fairy tale writers; Canepa and Ansani 1997:21ff assess some of this work.)

As an example of these approaches, Emma Donoghue's *Kissing the Witch* (1997) subtly subverts thirteen traditional European fairy tales. The emphasis of her tales is on the relations between women – familial, sexual and sometimes treacherous. Her playful and impressionistic approach belies a masterly use, almost re-invention, of the literary genre. Far less subtle example, although not without interest, is Mitzi Szereto's *Erotic Fairy Tales* (2000) – where Prince Charming has a foot-fetish, and Grandma has had previous encounters with stray wolves passing in the night.

Paradox might be thought of as an especially 'postmodern' literary device. But 'fairy stories' and 'wonder tales' have always been rife with paradox; perhaps this is why a number of post-modern novelists have been drawn to the genre. For instance, Lewis Seifert kicks off the introduction to his 1996 book *Fairy Tales, Sexuality and Gender in France 1690-1715* (1996) with the statement 'Paradox is no stranger to fairy tales. They are at once among the most marginal and the most central of all cultural forms.' Marginal because they are deemed inferior to 'high' literature, central because these stories were powerful instruments of socialisation and acculturation (Seifert 1996: 1–2).

Seifert also notes the paradox in the way that concepts of sex and gender are created by and bound to specific contexts, and as such are fundamentally unstable and susceptible to change, but at the same time they are ideological formations that legitimise themselves as 'natural' and 'commonsensical'. There is also ambivalence in the way fairy tales accommodate 'revolt' against 'reality'. Yet, in the end, everything conforms again, so even the revolt is passed off as conformity. (Seifert 1996: 3; 12–13).

Despite Seifert's 'privileging' of fairy tales, as noted in Chapter 6, it may be more accurate to regard contemporary legends as at least as important to modern popular culture. In any event popular culture is eminently amenable to folkloristic analyses along the lines of 'form, function, transmission'.

Us and Them

For instance, the stereotypes of outlaws versus 'good guys', and of 'nationhood' versus an 'alien other' that are rehashed endlessly in Westerns and war movies have migrated to the sci-fi genre where a wide variety of aliens present greater or lesser challenges to the American Ideal. Sophisticated scriptwriting surfaces in *Men in Black* (1997) where both the sinister human secret agents and their extra-terrestrial counterparts share the eponymous dress sense – 'they' have become, superficially at least, indistinguishable from 'us'. Reality followed fiction when in September 2001 America was awoken to the reality that the 'alien other', in this instance fanatical Moslems, could be assimilated by society sufficiently to be able to attack from within.

Indeed, as with *Alien* (1979), the alien in *Men in Black* is born from a human womb. Even with *ET* (1982), this less-threatening homesick alien takes up residence in an archetypal American home. As Kearney notes, paranoia and phobia thrive in such fuzzy frontier zones of identity (Kearney 2002: 112).

The standby of Western scriptwriters, the eleventh hour appearance of the Cavalry, first appeared in D.W. Griffith's pioneering (and seriously racist) film *The Birth of a Nation* (1915). Only in this instance it was not the Cavalry, it was the Ku Klux Klan who rode to the rescue. Their appearance was accompanied on the sound track by Wagner's 'Ride of the Valkyries' (although it would be another 20 years before this would acquire its associations with Aryan supremacism) - 'a fact of which [Francis Ford] Coppola could not have been unmindful when he cited it in the famous GI helicopter attack on the Vietcong village in *Apocalypse Now* [1979].' as Richard Kearney notes (Kearney 2000: 108) Kearney continues by noting that 'one of the Klansmen riding to the rescue in *The Birth of a Nation* was none other than John Ford, pioneer of the cowboy-and-indian 'Western' about to emerge as the dominant Hollywood genre.'

Role playing and zapping

Folkloric and mythic narratives have not only spilled over from literature into film. They have also flowed naturally into role-playing games and their computer-based successors. *Dungeons and Dragons,* created in 1974 by Gary Gygax and Dave Arneson is regarded as the father of role-playing games. Vast armies of fantasy figurines were inspired by its rather Tolkienesque characters and mythology (although purists note that *D&D* owes more to Fritz Lieber's *Grey Mouser* series).

The success of these board-based fantasy games has been greatly exceeded by computer-based games. Some are close to the *D&D* model but most draw rather loosely on mythology to beget hosts of macho phantasms to be 'zapped' with the joystick's fire button. Early examples of such games have been studied by Sharon Sherman both from the way classic folklore elements manifest, and from the different ways such games are played by boys and girls (Sherman 1997).

Other games, known as 'adventure games', require the player to solve arcane puzzles. They started out in the 1980s as text-only computer games but by the 1990s had acquired simple graphics too. One of pioneering graphical adventure games, *Myst* (1994), set a high standard of visual design. The puzzles centre around 'mystical symbols' in a sort-of-Classical 'grove' and Myst Island has many mythical qualities, although few overt references to traditional myths.

More recent games, such as *Tomb Raider* (1996) blend action and adventure genres so there is exploration, puzzle solving and combat. *Tomb Raider* invokes some of the mythology of the films featuring the swashbuckling archaeologist Indiana Jones, while also creating more complex gender 'interactions' with the players.

Games such as *Dungeons and Dragons, Tomb Raider,* and their many imitators and successors have spawned a vast number of Web pages from fans, a number of whom act as historians and analysts. The boundaries between these games-related sites and an even vaster number of fantasy-fuelled Web sites can be blurred at times, making for very fluid interactions between 'traditional' folkloric and mythic motifs and the constantly-evolving contemporary manifestations of these motifs. Indeed, the 'rational' materialism of Western culture is proving to be an avid consumer of irrational fantasy and myth. The Web, by its very nature, is the most post-modern of these deeply intertwined interactions.

(See King 2002 for a 'cultural history' of computer games.)

Postmodern folklorists

Eclectic and often intentionally ironic, postmodern narratives often borrow from folklore or contain strongly 'folkloric' aspects. They have deeply permeated into popular culture and, as Kearney suggests, can be expected to thrive:

> A postmodern cult of parody and pastiche is, the pessimists conclude, fast replacing the poetic practices of narrative imagination. We shall see. For my part I am convinced that the obituarists of storytelling, be they positivists who dismiss it as an anachronistic fantasy or post-structuralists who decry its alleged penchant for closure, are mistaken. Indeed, amongst such

prophets of doom, I hold that the new technologies of virtual and digitised imaging, far from eradicating narrative, may actually open at novel modes of storytelling quite inconceivable in our former cultures. One thinks for example other way that Beckett explores the electronic retelling of one's life in *Krapp's Last Tape* (where a 69-year-old man rehears and retells the story of his 39-year-old former self through a tape-recorder); or, more graphically still, the way in which Atom Egoyan renarrates the Beckett play through the more sophisticated technologies of cinema and DVD. The complex narrative relationship between memory and recorded memory, between imagination and reality, can be brought into especially sharp focus by the new and technically avant-garde media.

(Kearney 2002: 11–12)

Kearney's enthusiasm and optimism is, however, not matched by folklorists' interest in postmodernism. The earliest reference to postmodernism within folklore journals that I have discovered is Henry Glassie's Presidential Address to the American Folklore Society in 1989. John D. Dorst responded to the negative tenor of Glassie's closing remarks in an article that appeared in 1990 (although in an issue of *Folklore Forum* with the cover date of 1988); Glassie had the last word in print in a response in the same issue. Around the same time Mark Workman prepared an article titled 'Folklore in the wilderness: Folklore and postmodernism' (Workman 1989) that seems to have problems with understanding what postmodernism is and adopts a pessimistic stance, other than promoting the importance of folklore as 'performance'. Thankfully Gerald Warshaver was capable of clearer thinking about the subject and published a useful article under the title 'On postmodern folklore' in 1991.

Since then postmodernism has informed a number of folkloric studies, explicitly so in Cristina Bacchilega's *Postmodern fairy tales* (1997) and the insightful chapter seven, 'Druids in a postmodern world', of Leslie Ellen Jones' book *Druid, Shaman, Priest* (Jones 1998). However, to my knowledge there has been little, if any, published debate about the implications of 'po mo' for folklore studies. I have cited Richard Kearney's recent study of narrative a number of times in this chapter – but he labels himself as a philosopher with an interest in stories, rather than a 'folklorist'. Folklore researchers are happily recognising that contemporary folklore exists as part of a wider 'po mo' culture, but seemingly not considering folklore studies themselves from a 'po mo' perspective.

Modern storytelling

At the same time that folk lore is mutating and interbreeding into a number of new genres, the origins of folk tale transmission are alive and healthier than ever before. Storytelling has never before had as many different tellers or as diverse a range of listeners.

Although formal storytelling has never 'died', its revival can be attributed to several key factors, as Simon Heywood has discussed in his history of storytelling in England and Wales (Heywood 1998), published as part of his doctoral research. These key factors have, inevitably, strongly coloured the nature of the revival.

One of these factors can be dated quite confidently to 1890. In that year a teacher at London girl's school, Marie Shedlock (1854–1935), left her job and became a full-time professional storyteller. There was already a well-established tradition of teachers and other educators using myths and fairy tales; indeed storytelling was an established part of teacher training (Bone 1923, cited in Heywood 1998: 17). In both England and America, Shedlock taught large number of 'workers with children' in the art of storytelling. Her innovative achievement was to establish widespread storytelling in American libraries.

Storytelling in this milieu, like Cecil Sharp's parlour 'folksong' of the same period, was a formal, high-minded, and rather stilted-sounding activity:

> New York Public Library story hours ... were formal and dignified, with fresh flowers, a wishing candle, and books on the table [The supervisor, Mary Gould Davis:] 'Her voice was gifted, her timing perfect, her gestures controlled ...'
> (Baker and Greene, 1977: 8, cited in Heywood 1998: 18)

At the time it was generally assumed that a children's librarian would be a woman, so such storytelling was a natural extension of 'domestic' storytelling to children that has always been part of parenting. However Britain was slow to include children's literature in libraries and not until 1926 did library storytelling begin to develop here, when Eileen Colwell was appointed to Hendon Library. She was already a keen story enthusiast and, by the time she retired in 1967, had advocated and exemplified library storytelling on a wide scale. Colwell was assisted from 1956 by Grace Hallworth, a Trinidadian who had studied storytelling formally in Canadian and US libraries (Heywood 1998: 19–21).

From 1919 stories and storytelling took a more directly didactic role, becoming a central feature of Rudolf Steiner's Steiner Waldorf education system (Heywood 1998: 19).

Storytelling for adults was established in the UK in the 1960s, partly through the activities of the Poet Laureate, John Masefield (1878–1967), who founded a Guild of Storytellers, but his efforts failed to take hold. Only in the 1980s, with the efforts of the Anglo-Indian writer on Sufism, Idries Shah (1924–96), and his colleagues, was oral storytelling for adults reactivated in Britain. By this time storytelling was evolving within the 'folk club' scene, partly as a result of Ewan MacColl's seminal BBC *Radio Ballads* (1958–1964). In reality there had been an elaborate, sometimes professional, storytelling tradition surviving in working class settings from before 1820 until around 1948. But this tradition existed quite independently from the assiduously middle class library storytellers and their successors. (Heywood 1998: 9–12).

Another field in which storytelling took root during the middle of the twentieth century was psychotherapy. Therapists in turn influenced other practitioners who applied storytelling to a wider range of spiritual, healing and personal development contexts – Joseph Campbell's *Myths to Live By* (1973), R.J. Stewart's *Magical Tales* (1990) and Robert Bly's *Iron Man* (1991) were followed by a flood of examples from writers rooted in alternative spiritualities and counter-cultures. (Heywood 1998: 10–11; see also Leigh 1998).

These different strands inevitably intermesh – Heywood (1998: 16) cites the example of Robin Williamson, formerly of the 1970s Incredible String Band, who connects 1960s counter-culture with both the folk revival and storytelling movement. Indeed, he weaves in even more of these strands, as I was present when Williamson performed in 2001 for an alternative spirituality 'workshop' weekend.

Clearly this modern storytelling, although delivered orally, and increasingly reliant on memorised or improvised texts rather than on reading, is not an *aural* tradition. The key tales are shared in books and, increasingly, through Web sites. There are even a number of books offering advice on storytelling techniques (e.g. Colwell 1991; Mellon 1992) and annotated bibliographies listing sources of suitable tales. Furthermore, the storytelling movement has benefited greatly from 'supportive and insightful media coverage' (Heywood 1998: 15).

What distinguishes these modern storytellers from their traditional forebears is that their repertoire is drawn from outside their 'tradition of origin' – that is, they are acquiring tales that they did not grow up with. The repertoire is nothing if not heterogeneous. King Arthur and Robin Hood rub shoulders with Irish Cuchullin myths, the Finnish *Kalevala*, Russian wonder tales, Caribbean Anansi tales and native American stories. The lack of personal tradition is further betrayed when, as is typical, storytellers refer to their activities as a revival, reawakening or renaissance (Heywood 1998: 16).

The tales and their tellers hark back in time to a tradition which is assumed to have once existed. The British tales that are favoured are the 'romantically medieval' ones such as the Arthurian Grail cycle and *Sir Gawain and the Green Knight*. Classical myths and those from non-Western contexts are stripped of their unique cultural identifiers and come across as 'anonymously Other'. The 'recollection' of a 'lost idyll' permeates the tales, reinforced by the 'moral message' often implicit in the closure. This is a tradition where yearning for a 'lost utopia' (needless to say one that has never existed) interbreeds with a variety of notions of 'personal development'. It may be considered a rich tradition, but one that contrasts dramatically with the robustness of traditional tales that are, on the one hand, well-rooted in the difficulties of daily existence and, on the other hand, enriched by supernatural beliefs that were once taken literally.

Modern storytelling does, generally, preserve two aspects that hark right back to the oral origins of the genre – the use of 'formulaic' phrases and the *externalisation* of crises (usually through violent confrontations). This is in sharp contrast to the way in which novels and other literary narratives increasingly *internalised* dramatic tensions (Ong 1982: 44).

Organised storytelling creates a clear distinction between teller and audience – the teller is situated at the focus of the audience; the audience sit and listen without interrupting. Above all, the storytellers regard themselves as having crossed some personal threshold such that they are no long 'casual' storytellers. Kay Stone (1997) has investigated the creation of this 'social identity' as a storyteller and the personal 'empowerment' that usually arises. Perhaps inevitably, the almost one hundred American storytellers interviewed by Joseph Sobol for a PhD thesis (cited in Stone 1997: 234) 'communicated their formative experiences in narrative form'. Sobol and Stone refer to these as 'vocational narratives' and they cover a wide variety of experiences and rationales. Above all they reveal an 'ever-emergent quality'. This diversity and emergent nature makes storytellers distinct from other performance artists, although more typical of folklore performers.

So storytelling is an aspect of modern folklore, yet one that is surprisingly different from many other contemporary genres.

8: FOLKLORE AND BELIEF

This chapter will explore those aspects of folklore known as 'folk beliefs' in a somewhat 'stereoscopic' manner. Through one eye we see the 'overt' subject matter (often full of interest in its own right, such as ghosts or UFOs); through the other eye we will try to see the implicit 'beliefs' that such lore implies. Belief is never an 'on/off' scenario – it is always situated along a spectrum of possible scenarios, from out-and-out dismissal as 'just old wives' tales', to unquestioned literal truth. In reality, most people's views are somewhere in the wide range of 'middle ground', and often quite 'fluid'.

Folk beliefs are alive and abounding. They manifest in what people do as well as what they say. Some of these beliefs are about what happens after death, or what they believe about the 'supernatural'. Some are often termed 'superstitions', but this is only one part of the spectrum of such folk beliefs. Remember that folklore is all around us, and we are all folk. 'Superstitions' do not have to be bizarre, many are quite prosaic, such as avoiding walking under ladders, touching wood after making a risky statement, taking a 'lucky mascot' into an exam room, saying 'Rabbits' (or whatever) first thing on the first day of a new month, avoiding planning significant journeys or events on Friday 13th, throwing confetti or rice at a wedding, or not wanting to be alone in a certain part of the workplace after dark because of rumours of a ghost.

We are in the realms of 'customary practice' where the participants do not consider themselves to be 'doing' folklore self-consciously. There is a wide range of overlapping manifestations of such folk beliefs, but folklorists have failed to agree on a nomenclature. 'Superstitions' form a key part (but far from the only part) but the word has rather negative connotations, as the *Oxford English Dictionary* definitions confirm:

1. credulity regarding the supernatural
2. an irrational fear of the unknown or mysterious
3. misdirected reverence
4. a practice, opinion, or religion based on these tendencies
5. a widely held but unjustified idea of the effects or nature of a thing.

The etymology of 'superstition' suggests something 'held over', by implication a tradition. Indeed. But some of the commonest British superstitions today are not so much 'held over' as 'made up', implying that there are deeper-rooted *underlying* beliefs. Touching wood is first mentioned in 1805 as part of a children's chasing game where touching wood conferred immunity from being caught; the association with good luck only came later. Likewise, thirteen is rarely mentioned as unlucky until the 1890s (indeed a 'bakers' dozen' was associated with *good* luck in the medieval era, although avoiding having thirteen present at a table was mentioned in 1695 as this is a direct link with the Last Supper as described in the Bible); the idea of Friday the 13th being unlucky is less than a hundred years old. (Simpson and Roud 2000)

Superstitions, folk beliefs and belief legends

Modern folklorists consider themselves non-judgemental about the material they study and collect. Given the problems with the term 'superstition', the alternative term 'folk belief' is often adopted. But, apart from other folklorists, no one else will have come across this term before. And, confusingly, they may use 'folk belief' as a wider category than just superstition (as indeed I have used the term). To add further confusion, 'folk beliefs' are often an important aspect of what we encountered in Chapter 6 as 'contemporary legend'. Indeed, as noted then, some folklorists dubbed them 'belief legends'. Linda Dégh has summarised this thus:

> In the experience of folklorists, tellers state, explain, interpret or at least imply their personal attitude toward the belief content of the legend they tell. Attitude toward belief is the essence of the genre and can be expressed in diverse ways; whereby identical contents – variants of the same legend type, may likewise be developed differently, depending on diverse interpretations of similar extranormal experiences of individual tellers. This peculiarly pivotal position of belief in legend makes all legends belief legends.
> (Dégh 1989)

To further confuse this already confusing issue, Dégh has since gone on to retract this statement. In 1996 she wrote 'folk belief is a part of any legend, therefore there is no need to maintain the term 'belief legend'. Belief is the stimulator and the purpose of telling any narrative within the larger category of the legend genre... ' Needless to say, other folklorists have ignored Dégh's suggestion to drop the term 'belief legend'.

So for this chapter to get underway I need to impose some terminology. As the term 'superstition' is not only pejorative but also carries a problematical payload about whether the folklorist shares the 'truth', 'rationality' or 'believability' of the belief, I will generally use the term 'folk belief'. Superstition is one part, but not the only part, of 'folk beliefs'.

The sort of 'folk beliefs' that have been studied include:

>**lore about plants and animals**, including the curative abilities of plants; the reputation for cats and hares being witches' 'familiars'; and anomalous animals such as the Loch Ness Monster; and unsubstantiated sightings of long-extinct species

>**folk cures and medicines**; 'herbalism' overlaps with plant lore, but cures and 'charms' cover a wide range of other ingredients and practices

>**weather lore** and related topics including 'wisdom' derived from bird flight patterns, phrases about why the fish aren't biting, etc.

>**legends about places** such as prehistoric stone circles that are dancers or soldiers turned to stone; improbable underground tunnels; and the widespread attributions of 'holiness' to certain wells

>**beliefs about the afterlife** including ghosts, premonitions of death, contact with the dead, etc

>**beliefs about fairies** in the widest sense of 'little folk', encounters with the 'Old Hag', etc

>**visions of saints and deities** and other 'anomalous experiences' with a religious context or interpretation

>**modern beliefs** e.g. UFOs and what have been termed 'Fortean phenomena' such as 'earth lights'; also abductions by aliens. In addition there is the wide range of beliefs implicit in the contemporary legends explored in Chapter 6.

As we will go on to explore, these are not exclusive categories. For instance, several writers have approached ghosts, fairies, UFOs and visions of saints as part of a 'spectrum' of anomalous phenomena.

Beliefs are basic

Long before reaching school age, young children understand that other people possess beliefs, wishes and intentions that operate, unseen, inside their heads. Children's understanding of their own and others' mental states shapes their most basic understanding of the world around them (Carpenter 2001). Through schooling and other processes of 'acculturation', these basic beliefs become more sophisticated, so there are few adults who 'step outside' these implicit beliefs that are an everyday – almost every moment – part of our lives.

We are so accustomed to forming beliefs about the mental states of other people that we have also 'projected', with varying degrees of literalism, similar beliefs onto animals and even inanimate objects. There can be few of us who have never treated a recalcitrant car or computer to a blast of verbal abuse. Most of us, if challenged, could state which beliefs about other people and things we consider to be 'real' and which, like cursing a computer, we recognise simply make us feel better but do not require a 'literal' belief in our computer having a mind of its own. Nevertheless, there may be a surprising divergence between different people's opinions on what is 'true' and what is not. And such divergence is most discernible when it comes to aspects of the 'supernatural', such as ghosts, fairies, UFOs and the whole realm of superstitions.

Plants and animals

Understandably, research on folk beliefs has taken the form of studies of specific beliefs, usually within a specific folk group. Folk beliefs regarding plants and animals form quite a substantial literature. Plants lore include traditional beliefs about a wide range of curative properties; Nicholas Culpeper's famous seventeenth century compilation of herbal remedies, *The English Physician*, remains a steady-selling book.

There have been several 'compilations' of plant lore, such as T.F. Thistelton Dyer's 1889 study *The Folk-lore of Plants*; Margaret Baker's *Discovering the Folklore of Plants* (1st edn 1969; 3rd edn 1996) and Roy Vickery's *Oxford Dictionary of Plant-lore* (1995).

One of the most comprehensive folklore 'projects' of the 1990s culminated in the publication in 1998 of Richard Mabey's *Flora Britannica* (probably the most significant folklore collecting project in Britain for many decades). The project's basis is set out thus:

> Our children still make daisy chains, whack conkers, and stick goosegrass stems on each other's backs. Despite being one of the most industrialised and urbanised countries on earth, we cling to plant rituals and mystical gestures whose roots stretch back into prehistory: holly decoration for the winter solstice, kisses under mistletoe, the wearing of red poppies to remember the casualties of war. We name our houses, streets and settlement after plants, and use them as the most prolific source of decorative motifs on everything from stained-glass to serviettes. From the outside, it must look as if we are botanical aboriginals, still in thrall to the spirits of vegetation.

But it is just the dying stages of an obstinate habit, the outward signs of a longing for the rural life that most of us have lost? Do we really still believe in the bad luck that may-blossom can bring into a house, and in the efficacy of the increasing numbers of herbal nostrums crowding onto chemists shelves? Or is our seeming respect now a touch tongue-in-cheek? [...] we didn't know whether... [British people] could still be said to have intimacy with wild plants that was not purely nostalgic and backward-looking. Did people still meet under meeting-place trees? Were children inventing new games for the new, exotic species constantly escaping into wild, as they did centuries ago for horse chestnut sycamore seeds; and was that two-way traffic of wild and cultivated plants over the garden wall still busy? Did plants continue to play any role in our senses of place and season, those fundamental aspects of everyday life that seem everywhere to be under threat from regimentation and the ironing out of local differences?

... what we have found in the field research for *Flora Britannica*, and in the multitude of public contributions to it, is that Britain still has a lively popular culture of plants... What is fascinating is how they are now informed by popular ecology and a sense of social history.

(Mabey 1998: 8–9)

The thousands of contributions sent to *Flora Britannica* project reflect a much wider 'folk relationship' with plants than revealed by more conventional folklore research.

Although modern minds still have rich associations with plants, our thinking about animals is not as rich as the mythology and deeply-rooted religious beliefs about all manner of creatures than evolved at an early stage of human development. We can only speculate what Palaeolithic painters had in mind about 30,000 years ago when creating the masterpieces of Lascaux and other caves. By about 2,500 years ago we have a better idea, as Miranda Green's authoritative study, *Animals in Celtic Life and Myth* (1992) explores. However these ideas are some distant in time that they are the realm of mythologists and archaeologists more than folklorists.

Birds have generated more than their fair share of superstitious belief, as Edward Armstrong's 1958 book *The Folklore of Birds* summarises (although it is far from a paragon of folklore research, as Armstrong was primarily an ornithologist). Some animals have so much mythology and folklore associated with them they led to book-length studies, as with George Ewart Evans and David Thomson's *The Leaping Hare* (1972).

But then, hares are an odd sort of creatures altogether. I was once out walking in Purbeck, crossing the downs above Lulworth, when a jack hare came lolloping down the farm track towards me, staring at me. In the moment before he darted off into the stubble I had the queer feeling that it was the hare who had right of way, and it was I who should have turned aside. The other creatures which one disturbs when out walking always fly away or scuttle into the bushes, but when an animal stops and looks at you, it is uncanny. At any rate, I am not the only person to feel this. In the thirteenth-century charm, "The Names of the Hare", he is the brodlokere and the make-agrise – the starer, the one who makes you afraid: and he has seventy-five other names, too.
(Harte 1997c; citing Evans & Thomson 1972: 202–5)

Hares and cats share a reputation for being witches' 'familiars'.

Both these animals seem to be singled out as humans-in-disguise because they are usurping the human right to stare… People in authority look unflinchingly at their subordinates, who must not stare back at them – but the cat is a heretic to this system of belief, because a cat can look at a king... In the army, where all the outward forms of power have to be carefully conserved, this business of staring back is forbidden. Queens Rules make it a punishable offence, under the name of Dumb Insolence…
(Harte 1997c)

As Jeremy Harte has explored in his article on witches' familiars, not only animals are supposed to be dumb. A talking hare or cat stands metonymically for the talking woman, or more specifically, for a woman who talks too much in the opinion of her menfolk (Harte 1997c, citing Le Guin 1987: 10–13).

'It's nature breaks through the eyes of a cat', say the Irish. 'Someways they would put a dread on you. What company do they keep? When the moon is riding high and the wind tearing the trees, and the shadows black with cold, who is it calls them from the hearth? Tell me that'
(Glassie 1985: 178).

Modern day beliefs may run counter to talking animals and the notion that witches have supernatural powers, especially the idea of 'shape shifting' from human to animal form and back at will. Yet modern minds have no

*Witches and their familiars from a sixteenth or
seventeenth century woodcut.*

difficulty in accepting that all these things can be believed in the context of
a 'folk tale'; they may not be 'true' but they are nevertheless perceived as
plausible. By 'nesting' plausible beliefs one inside the other the mind's
judgmental processes are somehow 'overloaded' and 'underlying' belief
systems can be pursued within this 'suspension of disbelief'. Only a
deliberate effort to 'deconstruct' the implicit meanings, such as Harte's
approach to witches' familiars, reveals more fully the contrast between
widely-held folk beliefs in the supernatural and what the consensus of
modern society believes to be 'real'.

Anomalous animals and cryptozoology

Folk beliefs abound when it comes to anomalous animals such as the Loch
Ness Monster or unsubstantiated sightings of long-extinct species, or just
well-known species in the 'wrong place'. The Beast of Bodmin might be
considered pure folklore, but sightings of large cat-like creatures leads to
speculation that unscrupulous owners of pumas or other large feline
species have released their pets into the wild, where they have survived or
even bred. *Fortean Times* has an annual round up of 'alien big cats' (ABCs)
– in 2000 nearly every county in England had at least a couple of such
sightings, with Cornwall, Gloucestershire, Leicestershire and Somerset

being especially prolific. ABCs also seem to be alive and well in many parts of Wales and Scotland too (Sieveking 2001).

As researchers into such matters need to be both astute zoologists and informed folklorists, the subject has acquired its own appellation, cryptozoology. Janet and Colin Bord compiled a pioneering book-length study, *Alien Animals*, in 1980 (revised in 1985). Every few months *Fortean Times* includes a major article about the activities of cryptozoologists. At the time of writing the most recent was Adam Davies' account of his travels to Lake Tele in the Congo, looking for what the locals call a *mokele-mbembe*, which the descriptions suggest may be a 'living dinosaur' related to the sauropods (Davies 2001), although more sceptical researchers claim the locals are describing rhinoceroses (which lived in the region until the mid-twentieth century). Each month *Fortean Times* includes a dozen or so snippets of news relating to cryptozoology.

As with so many aspects of 'folk belief', there is a range of beliefs and scepticism about the 'reality' of what is being studied. Only a few years ago the notion of pumas living wild in England was regarded as nonsense. Now there are several sightings every week and they are hit by cars (though rarely fatally; in 2000 one driver wrote his Range Rover off by swerving into a lamppost to avoid an ABC). Most folklorists look at the origins of the tales of the Loch Ness Monster in the early twentieth century (see Magin 2001) and conclude that this was an exceptionally successful publicity stunt that has generated an enormous folk belief.

Folk cures and charms

The official lists of *materia medica* in London and Edinburgh were revised in 1746. Out went cures based on human bones, cobwebs and unicorn's horn, although woodlice, vipers and the bexoar stone survived until 1788. Mice, toads and spiders were not so easily dismissed. 'The nature of mice is not to be despised' write Pliny the Elder in *Natural History* 29:15, adding that a mouse cut in two and placed on the wound would cure snakebite. Although Pliny died in 79 CE, 'Within living memory, children throughout the British isles were being treated for whooping cough with fried, stewed or roasted mice.' (Harte 2000: 32)

If the efficacy of mice is unknown to modern science, then this cannot be said for a common folk remedy for infections, dosing with garlic – the strongest antibacterial agent to be found in a kitchen cupboard. The 'active ingredient' in willow bark was commercialised as aspirin. Likewise eating spiders was also a common folk cure; interestingly, spiders do contain a fever-reducing substance. As already noted, folk beliefs about plants include a wide range of curative properties and compilation of herbal remedies have proliferated on bookshop shelves in recent decades.

All cures have a success rate of about 30 percent (Buckman and Sabbagh 1993, cited in Harte 2000) – this is the so-called 'placebo effect', combined with the tendency for most illnesses to abate with time. Going to an NHS doctor for a consultation and a prescription is often as valuable as a 'curative ritual' as anything in the tablets. Changes in mental state can trigger the body's healing processes – while traditional cures favour shock or revulsion, modern day 'alternative' therapies might promote 'visualisation'.

Grinding up dead men's bones into pills seemingly has suitable shock value, although is arguably less revolting than transplanting hearts and other organs from the recently-deceased. But perhaps it was not the 'active ingredients', or even the 'shock value' of traditional cures that was most important. Alongside the *materia medica* and the informal 'folk' ingredients for cures was a whole industry of charms and 'charmers', who survived into the twentieth century, at least in the West Country. Some charms were Biblical: 'The verse to stop nose-bleeding is the 6th verse of the 16th chapter of Ezekiel which must be repeated by one of the opposite sex to the patient', according to information collected in Cudlipton, Devon during the nineteenth century. Others were archaic formulae along the lines of 'Bone to bone, vein to vein, sinew to sinew'; these date back to Anglo-Saxon England and even older instances have been found in Europe, Russia and India (Davies 1996). Such formulae are entirely characteristic of the ways in which preliterate cultures transfer knowledge from generation to generation (Ong 1982).

Charms link directly to the power of religion belief to cure illness. Ælfric (c.955 to 1020), in his *Homilies*, asserted that God is the true 'leech' or doctor, the one who controls all sickness and health – ultimately one must appeal to God or use God's creation properly to achieve any well-being (Jolly 1996). Matthew Dillon has noted that in the Classical Greek era temples to Asklepion were thriving at the same time that medicine was developing. '… the doctors and the god do not seem to have been in competition, and the development of Hippocratic medicine did not mean the end of temple healing in the Greek world.' (Dillon 1997) Indeed, as the number of pilgrims to Lourdes adequately attests, modern medicine has not meant the end of 'temple healing'.

Günther Lottes has argued that 'The Protestant refusal to attend the magical needs of the people through an offer of licensed and hence controllable magic proved fertile soil for superstitious practices.' (Lottes 1984: 179) This runs somewhat contrary to the idea expressed earlier in this chapter that Protestants denigrated Catholic beliefs as 'mere superstitions'. It also points to the way boundaries between 'magic' and 'religion' have hanged over the centuries. Clearly the whole body of beliefs that can be considered, pejoratively or otherwise, as 'superstitions' has a complex history of change and adaptation. From the point of view of those practising such 'superstitions' there must clearly be an element of belief in the efficacy of the activity. Perhaps this belief is, in itself, a key aspect of the curative powers – which enters the realm of 'faith healing'.

The power of 'faith healing', in its broadest senses, perhaps lies in its ability to re-affirm the way we 'structure' the world about us. William Doty has observed that:

> Ritual exorcists or shamans encourage a patient to experience fully "the other world" into which the specialist takes him or her. Upon return to everyday reality, the person treated will be able to operate more effectively because he or she now recognises the actual contours of the world's powers as interpreted by society and is no longer controlled by fearful personal projections... By its behaviours – which may include disapproval or laughter – the ritual audience reinforces societal understandings about how the two worlds are to be related: "The doctor said I was not to worry"; "The priest gave me the benefit of the doubt"; "Our section manager says we were ready to tackle new projects".
> (Doty 2000: 70–1)

The modern mind has great difficulty assessing health objectively. We seek clearly-defined distinctions between sickness and health, perhaps endorsed by a doctor's sick note. Yet each of us is constantly shifting along a spectrum of physiological fitness. Furthermore, 'good health' is often relative to an individual's expectations – a good day for an arthritic pensioner would be a bad day for an athletic twenty-something.

While historical studies of folk remedies throw up colourful insights into seemingly-lost beliefs, the reality is that modern day beliefs about cures are every bit as rich, and perhaps even more 'exotic'. Although most of us are unlikely to eat fried mice or pills from dead men's bones, there a plenty of takers for the wide range of 'alternative' and 'complementary' therapies that have thrived in recent years. Traditional British herbalism has been augmented by homeopathy and 'exotic' imports, such as Chinese traditional medicines. Chiropractioners, osteopaths, various types of massage from reflexology, shiatsu and reiki, are among a wide range of more 'physical' therapies. And, as so many illnesses might be psychosomatic or brought about by 'stress' and other mental woes, there is enormous scope for the counselling too. In another place and another time we may have consulted a ritual exorcist instead. Indeed, from the perspective of the objective gaze of an anthropologist, perhaps counselling is a sub-set of ritual exorcism?

Weather lore

Just as belief in the efficacy of folk remedies is obscured by the propensity for illnesses to alleviate themselves spontaneously and for the 'placebo effect' to suggest that almost any 'cure' has its merits, so too the vagaries of the ever-changing weather system have meant that a wide variety of observations have been 'interpreted' as forecasts. Even with powerful computers helping meteorologists, the accuracy of their forecasts is still no better than chance (they are getting better at the 'broader picture', but the timing of events still eludes accurate prediction).

There may be some basis as to why a red sky a night may, indeed, mean that the next twelve hours or so may be dry. There may even be a correlation between cows lying down and imminent rain. 'Mare's tails and mackerel scales Make tall ships carry low sails' is based on the accurate observation that altocumulus ('mare's tails) and cirrus ('mackerel skies') clouds precede stormy changes within 12 to 36 hours. Some lore predicts the greater consequences, such as 'Rain in May makes bread for the whole year' – which alludes to May being the time when wheat needs plenty of rain to help it grow.

Unsurprisingly, a good deal of lore draws upon such 'magical' phenomena as the moon ('The moon with a circle brings water in her beak'), dew and rainbows. Other lore relates to observations of animals, fish – especially why they aren't biting! – ('Fish bite best before rain'; 'Trout jump high When a rain is nigh'), and bird's flight patterns ('Swallows high, stay dry, Swallows low, Wet 'twill blow').

As with folk remedies, the vast number of sayings themselves have interest. But, more interesting perhaps, are the complexities of the underlying beliefs. Which sayings are regarded as 'just old superstitions', which as perhaps credible, and others 'always right'? Sadly, despite great interest in collecting such 'folk sayings', questions about associated folk beliefs have rarely been asked by folklorists.

Legends about places

Prehistoric stone circles and standing stones throughout Britain are associated with legends that the stones are dancers or soldiers turned to stone. Prehistoric burial mounds are said to contain treasure, perhaps protected by a dragon or malicious elves. Throughout the country there are tales of improbable underground tunnels. And if all this is rather far-fetched, what about the widespread attributions of 'holiness' to certain wells and springs?

Perhaps as a counter to the overly-materialistic and reductionist professional archaeologists of the 1960s and 1970s, the 1970s and 1980s saw the awakening of a rather romanticised popular view of prehistory. A combination of John Michell's mystical idealism, expressed in *A View over Atlantis* (1969), and Alexander Thom's hard-nosed mathematics on ancient astronomy, *The Megalithic Sites of Britain* (1997), were melded together to give the impression of a Neolithic 'lost wisdom'. Michell's reactivation of Alfred Watkin's concepts of alignments of ancient sites, or 'leys', (first published in *The Old Straight Track* of 1925 but, despite a considerable popular following in the 1930s, all but ignored in the post-War era) conjoined with a series of books by the photographers and folklore researchers, Janet and Colin Bord (starting with *Mysterious Britain*, 1972) to create what became to be known in the 1980s as 'earth mysteries' or 'geomancy' (but, contrary to the dictionary definition of this word, as a synonym for 'earth mysteries' there is no implication of divination).

A quarterly magazine, *The Ley Hunter* (for many years edited by Paul Devereux, who also wrote a series of notable books and continues to write on related matters) acted as the main forum for debate on all 'earth mysteries' (EM) matters (not only the eponymous leys). *The Ley Hunter* was accompanied by a fairly fluid number of regionally-based EM periodicals, often quite short-lived. As a one-time editor of such a 'fringe' 'zine, I feel it appropriate to say that the enthusiasm of the authors and compilers was rarely matched by their ability to critically assess their sources. With hindsight much of the content of these 'zines can best be seen as popular folk beliefs being repeated and mutated – although the exceptions, such as the contributions of Jeremy Harte and a few others, often stand up to the test of time as valid assessments of their subject matter.

Harte has compiled an annotated bibliography of folklore related to places, *Research in Geomancy 1990-1994* (Harte 1999) and a further bibliography, *Alternative Approaches to Folklore 1969-1996* (Harte 1998d), that summarises folklore published in twenty-two of the often-obscure EM magazines. If 'annotated bibliographies' sound a tad dreary then Harte demonstrates that they can make lively reading, interwoven with his trenchant humour. Together these bibliographies highlight a large body of research mostly 'invisible' to researchers who rely on the resources of academic libraries. Although the quality of this 'grey' literature is variable, it represents one of the largest manifestations of folklore about places during the last 30 years.

Rollright Stones, Oxfordshire. Legends tells that a witch transformed a king and his army into these stones. Other legends say that the stones cannot be counted accurately, and of misfortune befalling anyone who tried to move the stones.

But research into the lore and legend of places in the 1970s and 1980s was not restricted to the sometimes dubious activities of EM researchers. Leslie Grinsell's comprehensive study of the *Folklore of Prehistoric Sites in Britain* was published in 1976 to the general disdain of academic archaeologists of the day, but has proved to be a timely record. Jennifer Westwood had an even more ambitious scope with *Albion: A guide to legendary Britain* (1985), and her approach still remains an exemplar of modern folkloric research. Katy Jordan looked in detail at the folklore, ghosts and legends of Wiltshire in *The Haunted Landscape* (2000); the first impression is of one of those county-based studies that proliferated about a hundred years previously. But closer reading reveals that the tales and lore have all been collected by Jordan in recent years, proving the vitality of this tradition despite the absence of many other such 'collectors' and researchers.

Holy wells and springs

One specific aspect of place-related lore has its own coterie of researchers. Holy wells and springs resist exact definition but are based around wells named after, indeed originally dedicated to, Christian saints. Other named wells, and unnamed wells in or on the boundaries of churchyards, also form part of the corpus. A further substantial corpus of 'holy' wells concerns those reputed to have healing properties; the ailments recorded as being cured are exceedingly varied, with 'eye complaints' being frequent, although now-rare illnesses such as scurvy and scrofula (a form of tuberculosis also known as the King's Evil) are also quite common. With the advent of piped water, many of such wells have been capped over or lost during the last 80-or-so years, revealing how quickly something as commonplace yet important can be elusive in documentary records and readily erased from popular memory.

Some holy well enthusiasts are specifically interested in the Christian associations of the wells, while many others are actively involved in modern paganism and hold that these are instances of Christianity taking over prechristian sacred sites. Important as wells and springs undoubtedly were until piped water, it is hard to find any evidence of prechristian veneration of springs. Indeed, the Old English *halig wella* (holy well, with the word 'well' having the modern sense of 'spring') may have come to Britain as part of a 'cult of saints' imported on a large scale from Mediterranean Christianity in about the eighth century (Tristan Hulse, pers. comm.). This cult initially took hold in Wales and Ireland, then spread throughout other parts of the British Isles.

Springs that have undoubtedly been venerated since the Iron Age are the unique, for the British Isles, hot waters at Bath. Marion Bowman (1998) has summarised the legends and beliefs associated with Bath, including both historic lore and some aspects of modern paganism that flourish there (Bowman 1994, 1998).

Bowman is one of a small number of folklorists who have taken an interest in wells; she also brings to bear her academic career in the study of contemporary religion. Holy wells research more typically is undertaken either by historians with a penchant for detailed documentary research, or by a more active breed of researcher who is willing to undertake fieldwork to locate the forgotten sites and, as is often necessary, remove rubbish and

The 'holy well' at Ashwell, Rutland.

overgrown vegetation. A number of county-based studies have been published a as result of such fieldwork, of which Phill Quinn's 1999 study of the *Holy Wells of Bath and Bristol Region* and Edna Whelan's *The Magic and Mystery of Holy Wells*, (2001) are excellent recent examples. So far there has been only two wider surveys of British holy wells. *The Living Stream* by historian James Rattue (1995) gives only exceedingly brief mention of the folklore of holy wells. This is counter-balanced by Janet and Colin Bord's *Sacred Waters* (1985b), which is devoted to the folklore related to such wells and springs in Britain and Ireland.

Archaeologists and place-related folklore

Professional archaeologists have largely been dismissive of folk beliefs about the sites they study and excavate. However one PhD student, Amy Gazin-Schwarz, took an anthropological approach to the folklore of Scottish archaeological sites. She wanted to see how folklore might aid archaeological research – not in any simplistic way, but rather to

> understand the differences and similarities in how folklore and
> archaeology construct ideas about the past. What aspects of
> history, time, and space are remembered and retold in folklore,

and how may these memories inform archaeological
interpretations of history, time, and landscape.
(Gazin-Schwarz's PhD proposal cited by Wade Tarzia, pers.
comm., 1997).

Gazin-Schwartz co-edited, with Cornelius Holtorf, about ten augmented
conference papers under the title *Archaeology and Folklore* (Gazin-
Schwartz and Holtorf 1999). Sadly all the contributors were
archaeologists, somewhat restricting the success of the exercise. The key
aspects of their approach to the relevance of folklore to archaeology are
contained in an article titled 'On archaeology and folklore (Gazin-
Schwartz and Holtorf 2000). For a far more nuanced assessment of folk
beliefs about ancient sites, some of which implausibly suggest that
memories have been maintained for millennia, see Harte 1998c (see also
the section on continuity in Chapter 4 of this book).

At about the same time Gazin-Schwarz was researching her PhD, another
doctoral candidate, Kathryn Denning, was assessing the different
approaches of 'fringe' and 'orthodox' archaeologies, and regarded them as
competing 'belief systems' (see Denning 1999). In particular the
academics, perhaps understandably, were having difficulty accepting that
the 'self-evident truth' of their interpretations of the past do not necessarily
have epistemological primacy to other people interested in the past.
Cornelius Holtorf has published a number of relatively theoretical papers
attempting to extend awareness of the need for academic archaeologists to
recognise that their beliefs about the past exist alongside a wide variety of
'alternative' beliefs. The heated arguments resulting from the discovery of
'Sea Henge' on the north Norfolk coast in 1999 revealed more dramatically
the conflict over ancient sites. When professional archaeologists and
English Heritage refer to 'sacred sites', their belief system is markedly
different from, say, a modern pagan who uses the same phrase.
Furthermore, there is a great range of beliefs within the modern pagan
movement.

Some may regard the arguments over Sea Henge as relevant to
archaeologists and pagans, but remote from folklore. Far from it. Although
archaeologists can establish certain 'facts', such as construction dates, with
reasonable certainty – their *interpretations*, even when supported by high-
handed calls to science and rational argument, are every bit as much 'folk
beliefs' as those of their pagan adversaries. Indeed, over the last 30 years
or so, the archaeologists' *beliefs* have evolved and adapted far more than
those typical of public perceptions.

The afterlife

The way we think about ghosts, premonitions of death, contact with the dead, and other aspects of the 'afterlife' form a fascinating field of folklore, albeit one that in Britain before the 1980s was merely 'collected' rather than studied. If anyone took any interest at all, it was simply assumed that 'superstitions' had more-or-less died out in modern Western cultures, except for remote rural areas or among recent immigrants from less modern societies.

Since the 1960s there has undoubtedly been extensive secularisation of British society (Brown 2001 provides an excellent analysis based on what people are saying rather than what 'statistics' purportedly tell us). Yet popular 'secular' belief is based on an underlying Christian 'world view', although that world view is derived more from popular belief than any officially-promulgated ideology.

To understand this modern 'world view' we need to step back to the later medieval and early modern periods when the Church was creating an abstract concept of the Otherworlds – wherever heaven, purgatory and hell might be, they were places distinct from the physical Earth. However, such notions were too abstract to be assimilated into popular belief. The majority of the European population of the time, in common with most preliterate societies, considered that the spirits of the dead continued to share the physical world with the living. (Devereux 2001: 90, citing Gordon (2000) and Caciola (2000).) A broader analysis of the problems of medieval popular beliefs, including those of the Otherworld, can be found in Gurevich (1988).

The survival of 'medieval' world views into folk beliefs of the late twentieth century has attracted some notable folklore studies. Gillian Bennett's *Traditions of Belief* (1987) is based on her field work among Lancashire women. At the time of its publication it was one of a very small number of British folklore studies that had a solid academic basis, and still remains as an exemplar of folkloric research.

Bennett notes that there is a huge difference between popular stereotypes of the supernatural, trivialised by mass media 'ghost busting' and the like, and the beliefs that emerged during her interviews. On the one hand there is the widespread 'haunted pub' scenario, where a 'friendly' (or entirely fake) phantom boosts trade. On the other there are a variety of 'friendly apparitions of dead members of the family, personal to the percipient rather than peculiar to any location.' Bennett continues in a passage that resounds with the medieval popular world view outlined in the previous paragraph:

> These supernatural "witnesses" of earthly life are expressions of an
> unchanging need for an effective, organised and unified Cosmos
> where both the dead and the living, both the divine and the
> mundane, can exist side-by-side in mutual harmony.
> (Bennett 1987: 211)

However this should not be taken to suggest that her fieldwork revealed a
consistent pattern of belief. Far from it; respondents expressed a wide
range of belief and disbelief in various aspects of the supernatural.
Nevertheless, she was able to conclude that 'supernatural belief is still alive
and well and living in the hearts of ordinary people...' (Bennett 1987: 212).
Indeed a 1990 Gallup poll concluded that one-quarter of Americans
believe that 'ghosts or... spirits of dead people can come back.' And,
contrary to expectations, this belief was held by 28 percent of those with
college education and merely 9 percent of the *least* educated sector (cited
in D. Hufford 1995a: 17). So much for Keith Thomas's opening statement
in *Religion and the Decline of Magic* (1971) that belief in ghosts is now
'rightly disdained by intelligent persons'. Frank Muir was nearer the mark
when he reputedly said 'The modern superstition is that we're free of
superstition.'

A unified theory of anomalous phenomena?

The suggestion that anomalous and supernatural experiences might be
similar phenomena 'explained' in terms of different belief systems is
pursued by Janet Bord in her 1997 book, *Fairies: Real encounters with little
people*. As the subtitle suggests, her approach might be termed
'phenomenological' or 'experience-centred' and she suspends disbelief
about whether the purported events are 'true' or 'false'.

Bord asks us to consider how much encounters with fairies have in
common with other 'anomalous' or 'supernatural' encounters, such as
ghosts, will o'the wisps and other 'earthlights', UFO sightings, and visions
of saints. There had been a previous attempt to link together various
supernatural apparitions from ghosts through 'will o' the wisps' to UFOs.
There is Paul Devereux's 'earth lights hypothesis' which was first argued in
1982, with major updates in 1989 and 1997 (Devereux 1982; 1989;
1997b; Devereux and Brookesmith 1997). Bord's contribution was to
extend this further, into the realms of fairies and the like. Patrick Harpur
made similar links in *Daimonic Reality: A Field Guide To The Otherworld*
(Harpur 1994) where traditional and modern entities, from fairies to
phantom social workers, are combined in a unified theory of the
Otherwold.

As these attempts at a 'unifying theory' cover a wide range of disparate topics, each of which is problematical, I will deal with each of the topics in turn. (Most of the following sections of this chapter are based on Trubshaw 1998.)

The Old Hag

Bord was not the first to adopt an 'experience-centred' approach to supernatural encounters. Such an approach had been successfully adopted by David Hufford when, between 1971 and 1974, he was working at the Folklore Department of Memorial University on the Canadian island of Newfoundland. As he notes, 'the conservative influences of isolation have left intact in Newfoundland elements of traditional culture no longer functioning in most of the English-speaking world.' (Hufford 1982: xviii)

If most people think they know what a ghost would look like if they happened to encounter one, there is another kind of supernatural encounter that, although surprisingly widespread, has not acquired a consistent name. As a result of Hufford's study, published as *The Terror that comes in the Night* (Hufford 1982), folklorists at least know the experience by the name 'the Old Hag' (although just to confuse them, Hufford now prefers the term 'Mara').

He first encountered the Old Hag while researching these 'isolated' Newfoundland traditions.

> Many Newfoundlanders are familiar with the Old Hag tradition
> and define it as did a university student about twenty years of age:
> "You are dreaming and you feel as if someone is holding you
> down. You can do nothing only cry out. People believe that you
> will die if you are not awakened.
> (Hufford 1982: 2)

Hufford notes that such definitions are not the natural form of living traditions and are rarely found except when a folklorist, or other outsider, asks for an explanation. Rather, the tradition is expressed in a variety of narratives. These may start with such expressions as 'I was hagged last night.' (Hufford 1982: 2) Despite the term 'the Old Hag', the attacker could be male or female. Hufford was able to show that what Newfoundlanders called the Old Hag was part of a consistent experience underlying belief traditions in widely separated places. In Southeast Asia it is known as *da chor, dab coj, poj ntxoog* or *dab tsog*, in China *bei Guai chaak* (the sitting ghost), and *Mara* in Sweden (in the same *original* sense of the Old English term 'night mare'). Even the Salem witch trials refer to 'witch riding' (and Old Hag attacks by male assailants are commonly attributed to hostile witchcraft).

Hufford's analysis of the Old Hag tradition in Newfoundland is an excellent example of folklore research. He is able to show that the experience probably corresponds to medical literature describing a combination of sleep paralysis and hypnagogic hallucinations (experienced by about twenty percent of people worldwide) but, nevertheless, does not adopt a 'Nothing but... ' dismissal of the traditional narratives.

In recent years Hufford has developed his study of folk beliefs about spirits, again based on the *experiences* of individuals, and regarding these folk beliefs as rational and reasonable explanations. This is *not* the same as suggesting that such beliefs are 'true' from a scientific standpoint, but rather that the inferences used are commonly accepted as valid among those sharing the folk belief. As such, Hufford stands apart from many academics who assume that folk beliefs about the supernatural are 'false', non-rational or non-empirical (D. Hufford 1995a: 11).

Hufford notes that there is a potential confusion between *belief* and *knowledge*. *'Belief* is a certainty that something is true... Knowledge is a particular kind of belief, that is, belief that has met customary criteria of justification. ... knowledge is justified true belief.' But the usage of these terms by the folklorist may not correspond to those being interviewed. '... in ordinary conversation people choose the strongest term that conforms to their own level of certainty.' Therefore if a folklore researcher asks for *belief* the response may exclude what the respondent *knows*. And, if the folklorist uses the term *belief* to describe what the respondents consider *knowledge,* those being questioned are likely to be offended. However, Hufford resolves this dilemma by accepting that, between folklorists, the term 'belief' should include 'knowledge' (D. Hufford 1995a: 19; see also Hufford 1995b for an informative and easily-digestible discussion of reflexivity in belief studies).

Ghosts

Ghosts have a history that goes back at least as far as classical Greece; indeed the oldest-known ghost story appears in the earliest 'book' – the Sumerian *Epic of Gilgamesh* written around 2000 BCE but based on already-mature oral traditions. Most of the dead in ancient Greece, such as those who died in 'normal' conditions and had funeral ceremonies properly done on their behalf, were led by Hermes to cross the river Styx in Charon's boat and then passed into the realms of Hades. But some of the dead (such as those who died untimely or violent deaths, or where the funeral ceremonies were not properly performed) remained trapped between two worlds, and were attracted to the realm of Hekate. They roamed with her during the night and were to be seen at crossroads and near their graves. However, the Greek word *phásma* or *phántasma* was a wider concept than our 'ghost', as the invisible demons associated with Hekate were called *phásmata* when they appeared in the visible world, as were also some liminal 'undead' beings such as Lamia (Gonzalez 1997).

Ghosts are known by a variety of names in the Anglo-Saxon era, of which 'boggart' is the main survivor. 'In medieval England it was fully accepted that dead men might sometimes return to haunt the living' states Thomas (1971: 701), noting that the Catholic Church rationalised this belief by regarding such apparitions as the souls of those trapped in Purgatory. Early Protestant preachers treated the belief in ghosts as a Popish fraud. To ask someone in the sixteenth century whether or not they believed in ghosts was akin to asking if they believed in transubstantiation or the papal supremacy. (William Shakespeare's inclusion of ghosts in *Hamlet* and *Macbeth* was exceptionally contentious at the time.) Needless to say, this clear-cut theological issue became greatly diluted in subsequent centuries, suggesting that popular belief in ghosts was not easily passed off as a popish superstition.

We should not assume that previous generations believed in ghosts in the same way that modern day journalism still reports on 'haunted pubs' and the like. In medieval times ghosts were either demons and malevolent spirits, or they were people known to the witness who had died recently. Ignoring the obvious marketing ploys, the nature of modern ghosts simply conforms too closely to a narrow range of 'idealised scripts', as Jeremy Harte showed convincingly for Civil War ghosts (Harte 1997a). And why do tales of pre-Reformation monks, sixteenth century Elizabethans and seventeenth century Civil War ghosts predominate over those from later eras? Why so few ghosts from the much more heavily populated twentieth century? More crucially, why do people only start seeing ghosts of people from earlier periods after about 1680? Indeed such sightings are rare until the late nineteenth century. As Jeremy Harte observes, 'nobody saw the ghosts of Roman soldiers in Dorset until the arrival of mass education taught the public hat there had been such things as Roman soldiers and then they started popping up all over the place' (cited in Devereux 2001: 187).

The 'hands on' paranormal investigator, David Taylor, has observed that haunted houses and their occupants need to be approached quite differently from the assumptions of many 'ghost hunters' (Taylor 1998).

Preliminary ideas on a 'social history' of ghosts were put forward a decade earlier by Peter Rogerson (1987), who observed that 'The traditional Victorian haunted house was the short-lease house where the servants came with the property. The archetypal modern haunted house is the council house. Such house literally "belong to someone else"... There is a greater likelihood of a failure of bonding between the occupant and the house.' (Taylor 1998)

Whatever people who claim to have seen a ghost have actually experienced (and I for one would not suggest that it was 'all in the mind') it seems clear that the anomalous experience is 'understood' by the witnesses in terms of ideas that are already familiar to them (Devereux 2001: 188). Similar remarks could also be made about encounters with fairies, as the next section hopes to show.

Fairies and their kin

The term 'fairies' is problematic. As has been noted in Chapter 5, the image of 'gracefulness, refinement and snobbery in miniature' (Harte 1998b) is a Victorian fantasy that confounds our understanding of the already-complex issue of what people meant by 'fairies' before the mid-nineteenth century.

And the further back we go, the sense of distinct fairy entities becomes increasingly chimerical. Chaucer puts fairies on the same footing as elves and hags. Indeed, there seems to be no systematic mythology of fairies before 1380. 'Elf' related place-names are common in northern England, but absent from the southern part until the seventeenth century. Conversely, in the south the term *puca* (not necessarily the same sort of character that Shakespeare gave to Puck in *Midsummer Night's Dream*) is common, but absent in the north.

The *puca* haunts cliffs and holes, according to Deasun Breatnach's study of Irish *puca* lore (Breatnach 1993). He will knock down a wall that stands in the way of his path; often he pushes a traveller to one side, out of the way of a dangerous invisible presence. In Leinster he has become a household spirit of castles. But, reports Breatnach, generally *pucas* are no longer seen.

Only in the eighteenth century do place-names incorporating 'fairy' begin to appear in England, suggesting that fairies were part of literary lore (such as the romances of Richard II's late fourteenth century court and his Tudor successors) but took several centuries to enter popular lore (Harte 1998a). Indeed the origin of the word 'fairy', from the Old French *faerie* (itself from the Latin *fata*, 'fate'), confirms the Romance origins. Other terms for fey little folk, such as 'pixie' and 'gnome' have entered the English language and consciousness during the last two hundred years from Continental fairy tales.

Prior to the eighteenth and nineteenth century synthesis of fairies with previous traditions, there were a number of distinct 'species' of otherworldly folk. Elves and dwarves seem to come to Britain from Scandinavia. The Anglo-Saxons brought *puca, grima, scucca* and *thyrs* to these shores, where they lived on as Pucks, Church Grims, Black Shucks and Hobthrusts. The Irish maintained beliefs in the *sidhe*. Interestingly *none* of these, apart from the dwarves, were short in stature until the melting down of all the traditions by nineteenth century folklorists (not the folk themselves), who also marginalised the Germanic Pucks, Church Grims, Black Shucks and Hobthrusts (Harte 1998a). Indeed, it was folklorists who made the Irish *sidhe* into 'little folk'. In recent decades Edmund Lenihan has collected a remarkable quantity of fairy stories 'from the firesides' of older people in County Clare in Ireland (so far little of this has been published to my knowledge). These tales have revealed anew the original 'dark side of fairie', rather than the widespread cutesy popularisations of earlier folklorists misunderstandings.

While the fairies of Victorian nurseries and their prolific progeny may be kindly and cute (at least in the eyes of the pre-Pokémon generation), this might be regarded as an exceptionally successful spin-doctoring campaign. In the tales collected by folklorists up till this time fairies and their kin were neither particularly small nor kindly. They were spirits against which people guarded themselves by ritual precautions. John Penry reported that, around, 1770, the country people of the British Isles continued to show an 'astonishing reverence' for the fairies and dared not 'name them without honour' (Penry c.1773, cited in Thomas 1971: 726). In 1911, Jonathan Caredig Davies published his *Folk-lore of West and mid-Wales*. No less than 60 pages are devoted to detailed accounts of fairy beliefs. Although he is poor at citing his sources, we must assume that most of these were still current as folk tales in the second half of the nineteenth century.

Also in 1911, W.Y. Evans Wentz published his better-known book, *The Fairy-Faith in Celtic Countries*. This took its place alongside Robert Kirk's *The Secret Common-wealth* (first published 1815 but written in 1691) and Thomas Keightley's *The Fairy Mythology* (1828) as the leading works of reference on fairy lore. Despite a substantial volume of fairy-related literature, the next major study of fairies did not appear until 1959 when Katherine Briggs' *The Anatomy of Puck* was published, which lead in due course to her better-known *A Dictionary of Fairies* in 1976. Few folklorists have looked for fairy encounters in the mid-twentieth century (after all,

A sixteenth century woodcut showing what may be meant to be 'little people' dancing in a ring. Note the door into what appears to be a hollow hill and the prominent Fly Agaric mushroom.

nobody believed in fairies any more...), but they kept on appearing for all that and are chronicled by David Lazell (1993).

On a different tack, magical human-fairy relationships recorded as part of seventeenth century Scottish witch trials (and these are testimonies usually provided voluntarily without torture) have been assessed academically by Lizanne Henderson and Edward Cowan's book *Scottish Fairy Belief* (2001)..

Another book in Heart of Albion's 'Explore' series by Jeremy Harte, *Explore Fairies* (Harte in press), provides a more detailed history of fairies. In the next sections I want to explore the 'phenomenology' of fairy and fairy-like encounters. Janet Bord's 1997 book, *Fairies: Real encounters with little people*, brought together for the first time a surprisingly wide range of possibly-related phenomena. However this 'phenomenological' or 'experience-centred' approach had been used to good effect in the 1970s by David Hufford in his study of the Old Hag, and in the 1980s by Gillian Bennett in her study of supernatural beliefs among Lancashire women (both discussed earlier in this chapter). Bennett's work showed that an individual's belief/ disbelief is not just 'on' or 'off', but rather is more akin to part of a spectrum of belief on any one topic - and with complex inter-relationships of beliefs on more-or-less related topics.

As a further example of how 'fairy lore' links to other phenomena, Emma Wilby's study of witches' familiars shows how the widespread belief in fairies provided the 'foundations' for other, apparently unrelated, beliefs. She suggests that popular beliefs in fairies interacted with an 'élite demonological theory' to provide the beliefs that underlie the varying accounts of witches' familiars in Scottish and English records (Wilby 2000).

Saints and deities

There is one category of anomalous phenomena that is inherently described in culturally-specific terms. Visions of saints are commonest in Catholic societies – it is self-evidently improbable that Chinese Buddhists would aver to having encountered the Blessed Virgin Mary, although such Buddhists could quite probably consider that their lives had been blessed by coming upon Kuan Yin, the Goddess of Compassion. But what do Protestants claim to encounter in such situations? The nearest I can find to an answer to this question is David Blackbourn's study of *Marpingen: Apparitions of the Virgin Mary in Bismarckian Germany* (1993) which describes a 'complete medieval experience' – with holy well, pilgrims and all – but dating to 1876.

In Britain, the shrine and holy well at Walsingham in Norfolk were restored in 1931 by the Anglican church on the site of the original twelfth century shrine to Our Lady of Walsingham, founded following a vision of the Virgin Mary. Even if the restoration owes less to folk belief than to an 'Anglo Catholic' faction within the Church of England, the numbers of 'pilgrims' attending this shrine attest to a substantial 'folk belief', although I doubt that few visitors arrive with the least expectation of seeing a vision of the Virgin Mary. Fairies, ghosts and UFOs might conceivably creep unexpected into the edges of our perceptions, but somehow visions of saints seem altogether 'un-British' – have we been Protestants too long?

Will o' the wisps and 'earthlights'

Will o' the wisps have often been rationalised as 'marsh lights' – methane produced by rotting vegetation that spontaneously ignites. In 1810 the poet James Jennings wrote:

Search the Truth when, down the dark lane,
Spirits glide and Blue Lights gleam.

(From *Poems Consisting of the Mysteries of the
Mendips etc,* cited in Quinn 1997b).

Yet anomalous lights appearing from the earth also occur in places that are far from marshy. Paul Devereux has dubbed these 'earth lights'. In bare outline, Devereux argues that tectonic strain in rocks – especially those near to active geological fault lines – can cause anomalous light phenomena. Such phenomena have been recreated under laboratory conditions and there has been sufficient evidence to support his suggestions. For instance, 'tadpole-shaped' lights were seen before an earthquake in Leicestershire on 11th February 1957, and anomalous lights appeared before the earthquake centred on Mounts Bay in Cornwall of 10th November 1996 (Devereux 1997a). According to a Japanese scientist, Yoshizo Kawaguchi (1996), many people reported seeing red and blue lights an hour or tens of minutes before the 1995 Kobe earthquake.

David Clarke has provided evidence for both 'earth lights' in the Pennines and for a continuity with folk lore predating any of this theorising (Clarke 1998). A detailed study of folklore and anomalous lights around Bristol (Quinn 1997b) provides equally convincing independent data linking 'earth lights' with, in this case, both fairy and ghost lore. Reports of anomalous lights are certainly not recent. At Mount Athos, Greece, monks have had visions of light around sacred places on the mountain; these are interpreted through the symbolism of Hesychast meditation. Colchester Abbey was founded after a similar vision (Collins 1987). In Lincolnshire, a prophecy from Gedney Church End, dated 1745, refers to apparitions of lights and fire above the church and the raising of ghosts (Dickinson 1993).

Devereux suggests that poltergeist activity and ghosts, especially the vague white shape types, are another manifestation of the same earth light phenomena. In *Places of Power* (1990: 32–4) Devereux provides clear evidence for links between fairy lore and anomalous lights in Ireland and Cornwall. He has also suggested that earth lights are capable of triggering temporary brain 'dysfunctions' (such as temporal lobe dissociation).

Temporal lobe dissociation has been studied extensively by Professor Michael Persinger and his colleagues at Laurentian University in Canada. They have spent many years researching 'sensed presence' phenomena (otherwise termed 'ego-alien intrusions') from a neurophysiological perspective. In the search for brain correlates to the experience of 'presences', their studies have focused primarily on the deep temporal lobe structures of the brain, the amygdala and hippocampus, which Persinger characterises as the most electrically-unstable structures in the human brain. By using electrodes to stimulate the temporal lobes, Persinger is able to induce a variety of deeply disturbing mental experiences (some readers may recall a BBC2 *Horizon* programme from 28th November 1994 when Susan Blakemore interviewed Persinger and underwent temporal lobe stimulation). Such 'temporal lobe dissociation' generates strange visual and other sensations which the brain finds difficult to 'process' – subjects will often describe the sensations as being like someone pulling at their limbs, or even as a sequence of events which resemble aspects of so-called 'alien abduction' experiences. A 1998 issue of *Fortean Times* (No.108) included a useful overview of temporal lobe research and its relationship to anomalous experiences.

Elf-infested spaces

Devereux and Persinger have collaborated to explore the possibility that the anomalous energy seen as earth lights might have sufficient electrical energy to cause temporal lobe dissociation. Perhaps more relevant to folklore studies is the recognition that many of the sensations induced by temporal lobe stimulation are akin experiences with some types of psychoactive plants and drugs. According to Dr Horace Beach (1997), auditory hallucinations – closely resembling experiences generated in Persinger's experimental subjects – are a common experience with high doses of psilocybin ('magic mushrooms'). As many readers will be aware, magic mushrooms and some other psychoactives, such as DMT, also readily lead to visions of little people – not for nothing has Terence McKenna (1992) described these imaginary worlds as 'elf-infested spaces'.

Other researchers have indicated that such experiences are cross-cultural. Julia Phillips (1998) reports that Australian Aborigines from New South Wales recognise traditional 'guardians of place' whose descriptions tally closely with her first-hand encounters with the modern 'archetypal' British elf or fairy in 'old' south Wales. Kevin Callahan at University of Minnesota claims Ojibwa indians of the American Midwest see 'little people' for about thirty minutes during hallucinations induced by atrophine-containing plants from the Deadly Nightshade family. Callahan also notes that those in the second stage of alcohol withdrawal (i.e. two to three days after stopping drinking) report similar encounters with 'little people' (Callahan 1995).

Although never known to drink more than a small sherry, my grandmother, when in her early nineties and suffering from the combined effects of long-term crippling arthritis, failing eyesight, and the relatively limited social stimulation of living in an old people's home where the fellow residents were almost all senile (whereas my gran was not senile, although beginning to have slight problems with short-term memory) began to report seeing a 'little boy' who came into her room at various times – often at night, when he would curl up in a chair or at the foot of her bed. Needless to say, children were infrequent visitors to the home and none stayed overnight.

Taken together, there is a variety of evidence to suggest that 'elf-infested spaces' are more common than rational twentieth century thinking would normally accept. Could it be that, as with the Old Hag of Newfoundland, folklore is providing us with direct evidence of subtle mental states that we are too quick to dismiss as pure fantasy?

Hollow hills and abductions

As if this 'experience-centred' approach to anomalous phenomena has not covered enough territory already, there is also a claim on the contentious waters of 'close encounters' with aliens and alien spaceships. Janet Bord (1997: 94–7) shows that the various tales of being 'abducted' to take part in fairy parties inside hollow hills have many similarities to the recent literature relating to 'alien abductions'. The curious similarities between hollow hills and the interiors of Spielberg-like space craft so suggest that the 'pre-technological' age experience is a close match for modern-day 'close encounters'.

This is hardly a new suggestion – back in 1984 Ian Cresswell examined the subjective nature of 'close encounters' and their similarity to dream and trance states. Peter Rogerson (1988) picked up on similar themes four years later.

Jeremy Harte has questioned the folklore of hollow hills and found curious inconsistencies (Harte 1997a). And the lure of hollow hills has been retained in modern times, as confirmed by popular culture as successful yet disparate as the Teletubbies and *Lord of the Rings*.

For similar reasons Phil Quinn's 'Toast to the recently departed fairy folk in the Bristol region' (1997a) concludes that 'it is not hard to wonder whether the fairies have in fact not left us but rather undergone a change in identity more in keeping with an eclectic modern world'. Perhaps this should be turned around to ask if certain 'altered states of consciousness' have for millennia regularly lead to visions of 'little people'? Today we might prefer to 'justify' those imaginary experiences in terms of 'alien abductions' or even the neurological-speak of 'temporal lobe dissociation', but in previous centuries the same range of experiences were discussed in terms of fairies and a host of names relating to other diminutive beings – and were kept alive in the copious folklore.

Close encounters with UFOs and their occupants

So far in this chapter I have suggested that ghosts, fairies and earth lights are all examples of anomalous phenomena that are 'explained' by their witnesses according to ideas familiar to them. This means that anomalous phenomena are 'explained' in terms of the popular beliefs of the society in which the observer is based. Novel explanations are rare. Indeed, the only major example in the last fifty-or-so years has been the 'invention' of UFOs, when the mass media picked up on a report by private pilot Kenneth Arnold, who reported seeing nine silvery objects travelling at high speed near Mount Rainer, Washington State, on 24 June 1947. The subsequent 'UFO flap' and the vast literature it has generated is a wonderful example of folklore and mass media interweaving (see Evans and Stacy 1997 for an overview of history of UFO sightings and their interpretation since 1947).

But, assuming that similar phenomena date back before the late 1940s, how were these experiences 'explained'? Matthew Graeber has discussed the similarities between UFO sightings and Biblical accounts of visions and miracles, such as Ezekiel's encounter with a mysterious flying wheel. Whether such Biblical exegesis is valid, Graeber does catalogue a wide range of nineteenth and early twentieth century 'aerial anomalies' that prefigure the coining of the term Unidentified Flying Object in 1947 (Graeber 1995). Martin Kottmeyer has looked in detail at sightings of 'improbable' aerial objects around 1896 and 1897. As might be expected at this date they were described as anomalous airships. Even more intriguingly at least thirty-six witnesses described the occupants as being 'extraterrestrial' (Kottmeyer 2002). So it seems *ET*'s great-grandparents stopped by to phone home too.

In 1970 two ufologists, Jacques Vallee and John Keel, independently published books that equated the occupants of UFOs with the elves and fairies of folklore. This has become so widely known within ufological circles that in 1993 a cartoon by Hunt Emerson in *Fortean Times* (No.71) could 'mischievously suggest … that ufonauts were indeed really fairies, flying about in fake spaceships in order to avoid the humiliation of dressing up in butterfly wings and gossamer.' (Sivier 2000)

Indeed, by the mid-1980s a whole chunk of fairy lore – abduction, abnormal sexuality, rape, substitution of babies, had been subsumed into UFO studies. 'Alien abductions' were on the lips of all ufologists. Peter Rogerson (1993a; 1993b) notes that common folklore themes of amnesia, time-loss, lampless lights and seduction had been incorporated into narratives of alien abduction since the 1940s. Later developments include the prophetic status of abductees, and several prominent American researchers who have used hypnosis to 'recover' memories (see Chapter 6) of alien abductions. Proponents of the 'literal belief' in alien abductions have rarely entered into meaningful debate with their 'psycho-social' opponents, as the two belief systems are all but exclusive.

It is beyond the scope of this book to explore the heavily-promoted claims for alien abductions. A steady series of articles in *Magonia* (Rottmeyer 1988; Ellis 1991; Rogerson 1990; 1994; Goss 1996; Rimmer 1997) have built up a well-argued case for both 'alien abductions' and 'ritual abuse' allegations being the consequences of 'false memory syndrome' induced by what might be regarded as 'leading questions' asked under hypnosis. A summary of this work appeared in *Fortean Times* (Brookesmith 1996). In 1997 Kevin McLure launched a newsletter entitled *Abduction Watch* that deals specifically with 'the irrational muddle of faith and belief that typifies [alien] abductions'. A clear 'deconstruction' of an ostensible alien abduction is reported by Devereux and Brookesmith (1998).

David Hufford notes that:

> Having listened to many who have memories of these terrifying events [i.e. 'the idea that extra terrestrials are repeatedly abducting humans and subjecting them to bizarre experiments aboard spaceships'], I have no wish to dismiss or debunk the subject. I do not pretend to have a clear idea of what lies behind all of these reports. However, within the past two years I have had it repeatedly called to my attention that many accounts of abduction begin with "waking up paralyzed with a sense of a strange person or presence or something else in the room". (Hufford 1995, citing Hopkins 1992.)

This blurs the boundaries between alien abductions and the 'Old Hag' that Hufford had investigated in detail, suggesting that 'alien abduction' experiences are 'invented' by the brain in a similar way 'Old Hag' encounters are ways to 'rationalise' either temporal lobe dissociation or a sleep paralysis experience.

And that's not all...

This survey of folk beliefs is far from comprehensive. There is a wide range of other anomalous phenomena that has generated both popular beliefs and a healthy diversity of 'interpretation myths' by their investigators. The term 'Fortean phenomena' is an umbrella term, after Charles Hoy Fort (1874–1932), the pioneer researcher of experiences that science of the day was ignoring, discrediting or suppressing.

More conventional folklore subject matter has also been approached for insights into popular belief, such as Gillian Bennett's study of premonitions among Lancashire women (Bennett 1995) and Owen Davies article on healing charms used in England and Wales between 1700 and 1950 (Davies 1996).

There seems to be little in common between people who touch wood for luck and those who believe they have been abducted and subjected to intimate body examinations by aliens. Yet, in their varying ways, these and the other topics touched upon in this chapter all show the fabrication and adaptation inherent in contemporary folklore. More interestingly, the ideas are linked to a wide range of 'implicit' beliefs that also betray a great deal about modern thinking. Far from there being neat and tidy categories separating the 'rational' from the 'irrational', the reality is that most people occupy a complex 'middle ground'. The implications of this extend well beyond the interest of folklorists, although have rarely been studied, even by folklorists.

9: FOLK CUSTOMS AND SEASONAL FESTIVALS

For many people 'folklore' means folk customs and folk dancing, in the way morris dancing is, rightly or otherwise, seen as synonymous with English folklore. So, as this the ninth chapter of a thirteen chapter book, some readers may feel that discussion of folk customs is long overdue!

The reason for holding back so long is that 'folk customs' are not as easily defined as the popular imagination might think. Moreover, what is often held up as 'timeless tradition' rarely has roots deeper than a hundred-or-so years and, for all the flourishing of folk customs in recent decades, most of the growth has involved substantial 'grafting'. But then again, 'timeless traditions' have always mutated and adapted surprisingly frequently. The previous chapters should have helped prepare us for the slipperiness of the subject matter, and the attempts over the last hundred years to equate 'folk customs' with an imaginary rural idyll and/or prechristian religion.

Yet again, think of Gerald Warshaver's distinction between three 'levels' of folklore:

Level 1 or 'customary practice', i.e. customs where the participants do not consider themselves to be 'doing' folklore, such as weddings and funerals. In other words it is not 'self-conscious' folklore.

Level 2 is what most people would thing of as folklore – whether it is morris dancing, mummer's plays, folk singing, fairy stories or folk crafts.

Level 3 is where folklore is self-consciously incorporated into entirely modern activities. Examples include a host of 'invented' folk customs from Penzance Mayday celebrations to numerous National Trust 'activity days'. In some cases there is an intentional irony in the incorporation of 'archaic' folklore.

The folk customs to be discussed in this chapter fall into all three of these levels, although we will explore Level 2 examples first. All the problems of modern folklore discussed in Chapter 4 abound. Infinite recycling of Sir James Frazer via Robert Graves, Margaret Murray, Gerald Gardner and a huge number of lesser-known popularisers of folklore has led to a widespread belief that folk customs are survivals from a pagan, prechristian past, based on a 'secret wisdom' focussed on the fertility of nature.

Led by Roy Judge's book on the Jack in the Green (Judge 1979), a series of studies by folklorists (notably Smith 1981; Buckland 1982; Boyes 1987 and

1993; Buckland and Woods 1993) revealed that apparently-archaic customs had not only been created in the last two hundred years, but had altered repeatedly during that time. The falseness of popular beliefs about the 'timelessness' of folk customs has been clearly demonstrated. However this research has, so far, failed to penetrate into popular awareness.

At the risk of only slight exaggeration, a defining feature of traditional folk customs is that the original reasons for doing the activity have long been forgotten and later explanations have been foisted upon it, possibly a number of times.

Seasonal festivities

Thanks to eighteenth and nineteenth century speculation, fuelled by the equally-unsubstantiatable writings of several eminent archaeologists in the 1960s and 1970s, not to mention the beliefs of modern pagans of both Druidic and Wiccan persuasions it is now widely thought that prechristian pagans celebrated eight seasonal festivals (Samhain, Midwinter, Imbolc, Spring Equinox, Beltane, Midsummer, Lughnasa and Autumn Equinox), each approximately six weeks apart. Sadly, just about every aspect of this ritual year has no substance in history, and the exceptions are different in character to the nature of modern day pagan beliefs. Ronald Hutton has published a major book discussing the ritual year (Hutton 1996) and a number of associated books and articles (e.g. Hutton 1994a, 1995). Hutton supplements his detailed research on customs of the seventeenth century with the work of a surprisingly substantial number of other historians whose work is little known except to fellow academics (for instance Hill 1975; Cunningham 1980; Bushaway 1982; Underdown 1985; Cressy 1989 and 1997).

Hutton's conclusions are that British customs suffered drastic reformulation in the Civil Wars and Revolution of the 1640s, when the newly-installed Puritan regimes were relentlessly hostile to popular pastimes. Many simply disappeared; those that did reappear did so in a different manner.

This seventeenth century hiatus had been preceded by substantial disruption to popular customs during the Reformation (Hutton 1995). Given all these changes in the last 600 years, we should be surprised if any popular traditions go back a further 600 or more years to the prechristian era. But Hutton suggests that ritual bonfires at Maytide and midsummer have pagan antecedents, as does the custom of decorating churches and houses with greenery at midwinter. 'Christmas presents' and Yule logs may also have such ancient origins. And that is it, so far as British folk customs that could plausibly have prechristian precursors.

Although such historical delvings into the origins of folk customs clear the mind of the false suppositions of popular beliefs about these activities, in the end what is most interesting about folk customs are the ways they adapt and mutate. To illustrate this, I will discuss two well-documented examples from north Derbyshire and south Leicestershire.

Castleton Garland Ceremony

Garland Day in Castleton is 29th May (or the preceding Saturday if the 29th falls on a Sunday). We know that before the Commonwealth celebrations took place on May Day. The custom was revived at the Restoration, being transferred to May 29th, otherwise known as Oak Apple Day, to mark the occasion in 1648 when Charles II hid in the Boscobel Oak in Shropshire.

The first written reference dates to 1749 but the ceremony seems to have been developed by the church's bell ringers sometime after 1648 to reinforce the customary bell ringing on Oak Apple Day and to their right to largesse for their efforts. Sidney Oldall Addy has left us a detailed account of the Castleton Garland celebrations in the late nineteenth century (Addy 1901); from Addy we know that until 1897 the bellringers organised the ceremonies and performed morris dances, while carrying oak sprays. In 1897 dancing girls were substituted for the morris dancers. Since 1916 younger children have danced around a maypole in the village square.

The main characters, the Garland King and his lady, ride shire horses while dressed in Stuart costume. But the local museum has an old costume worn by the Garland King, which is a red hunting jacket (Green 1993: 54). And until 1955, the King's Lady was a she-male (i.e. a man dressed as a woman) – a common aspect of popular festivities. She is now an attractive young woman. The Garland King also has a widespread counterpart, at last in pre-Reformation customs, of the election of Summer Lord to rule over the Whitsun ales (Bushaway 1982: 57).

In 1955 new costumes were made for the King and Lady. Since then, little has changed, informs a booklet about the ceremony published in 1972 (Lester 1972). However the King and Lady are secondary to the Garland itself. This is a cone-shaped wooden frame covered in greenery and flowers. The total weight is about 56 pounds – and the King bears this on his shoulders for about two hours while he and his retinue process slowly around the village. He and his Lady are followed by the Castleton band and then a bevy of schoolgirls dressed in white, carrying white flowers. Behind them walks a troop of Boy Scouts.

Since the late 1980s the procession starts from a different public house each year, although earliest records suggest that until 1974 the Nags Head was consistently the starting place, when the Peak Hotel took over for about ten years. There are five more pubs to stop at, where the girls perform a dance. When the procession arrives at the Market Place the girls dance the Castleton morris dance, which includes a song reminiscent of the Cornish Floral Dance. Finally the King rides to the churchyard and the garland is lifted from his shoulders and hauled to the top of the church tower. There it remains for about a week until the flowers fade when it is taken down.

A development clearly datable to the first half of the twnetieth century is the removal of the posy from the top of the Garland (known as the 'Queen') before it is lifted. The Queen is placed at the War memorial, accompanied by the Last Post, in memory of the village men who lost their lives in the Wars; the man who had been King for many years in the 1930s was killed in the Second World War. Prior to the First World War, the local gentry paid for the privilege of having this posy presented to them.

Castleton Garland Day has few, if any, parallels in the English Midlands. Indeed, as the echoes of the Cornish Floral Dance confirm, the whole ceremony may have been brought to Castleton by Cornish miners who came to work in the extensive lead mines of the region. Georgina Boyes suggests that the ceremonies may have been based around local rushbearing festivities although she admits that there is no evidence for this (Boyes 1993b). She does however provide a detailed account of the changes to the costumes and what she terms the 'social dynamics' of this custom.

Popular folklorists write of 'Druidism' (the oak leaves), 'human sacrifice' (the lifting of the Garland from the King suggesting ritual decapitation) and other 'pagan survivals'. The reality is somewhat more prosaic but nevertheless intriguing as the custom adapts and mutates.

Hallaton Bottle Kicking and Hare Pie Scramble

Just as Sidney Addy provides a detailed late nineteenth century 'datum point' for the study of the Castleton Garland ceremony, so Charles Billson's 1895 account provides the first detailed description of the Hallaton Bottle Kicking and Hare Pie Scramble.

As the name suggests, this event, now held on Easter Monday, may have originated as two distinct customs brought together on the same day; the joining together of the two events appears to have occurred in the early nineteenth century.

The Bottle Kicking has its nearest equivalents in the Shrove Tuesday 'street football', as survives at Ashbourne (Derbyshire) and Atherstone

(Warwickshire). The Hare Pie relates to a piece of land, known as 'Hare Crop Leys' that was bequeathed to the rector (probably in the eighteenth century) on condition that he and his successors provided 'two hare pies, a quantity of ale, and two dozen penny loaves, to be scrambled for on each Easter Monday at Hare Pie Bank'. After the enclosure of 1771 another field was substituted for Hare Crop Leys, but Hare Pie Bank remains the same. In 1790 the rector of Hallaton attempted to suppress the ceremony but on the walls he found chalked the slogan 'No pie, no parson and a job for the glazier.' Traditionally the pie and ale was collected from the Rectory at 3 p.m., but this too has changed.

Billson (1985) described the ceremony thus:

'On Easter Monday in every year a procession is formed in the following order:

'Two men abreast, carrying sacks full of hare pies.

'Three men abreast, carrying aloft a bottle each, two of which are filled with beer and the third is a wooden dummy.

'A hare (if it can be procured) in a sitting posture, mounted on top of a pole.

'The procession was also formerly accompanied by a man carrying a sack full of bread, which he threw out to be caught by the company.

'This little troop, followed by the townspeople and a band of music, marches to an ancient earthwork about a quarter of a mile south of the town, consisting of a small oblong bank with a narrow trench round it and a circular hole in the centre. This is known as 'Hare-pie Bank'. The pies are here tumbled out of the sacks and scrambled for by the crowd. Then begins the well-known 'Hallaton Bottle-Kicking'. The bottles containing the beer are first thrown into the circular hollow, and then the dummy bottle, for which all scramble, and the men of Medbourne or other villagers try to wrest it from the Hallatonians' grasp, and try to force it over the brook which forms the parish boundary.'

My first opportunity to observe this event was Easter 1989 (the following account is based on Trubshaw 1990). At the appointed time (1.45 p.m. that year, although subsequent years have varied) a procession formed outside the Royal Oak public house (since closed and converted to a house) comprising the Air Training Corps band, then three sturdy lads holding aloft the three wooden casks or 'bottles'. Right up in the front were two young women carrying a large pie between them.

They marched off towards the churchyard, to be received by the parson. At this point the grey clouds turn to light rain. 'The eighth year running it has rained while the vicar blesses the pie', noted a local. After a simple ceremony the Hare Pie was cut and eager hands reached out to grab small portions. The meat was indeed hare (although mutton, veal or bacon has often been substituted), mixed with potatoes and vegetables. Some of the pie was placed in the bottom of a sack and saved for later on in the day's proceedings.

The rain ceased and everyone moved over to the village green where, at the base of one of the two crosses, the parson decorated the 'bottles', that is, tied red, white and blue ribbon around the wooden casks. This caused a little difficulty, but was eventually completed, Most people went off to the pubs again. After time for another pint or three and a bit of cheering and shouting, the ATC band reformed outside The Fox (the pub furthest from the centre of the village) and the three serious-looking lads carrying the bottles lead the procession right through the village and out along one of the lanes until the gate to the field known as Hare Pie Bank was reached.

A large crowd followed, some of the young bucks dressed in rugby shirts, old jeans and heavy boots. The almost non-existent rules were announced and the remains of the hare pie taken from the sack and scattered in the air over the crowd. The dummy bottle which is played for (the other two are full and saved to be awarded to the winners) was thrown in the air three times and when it touched the ground the third time, a free-for-all scramble commenced.

The scrum of 20 or 30 heavily-built lads took the contest seriously and what ensued made rugby look effete. How the two sides identified each other was entirely unclear but such ambiguity probably contributed little to the general confusion. Every so often the bottle broke loose and the scrum rapidly ran after it, scattering the surrounding crowd and allowing bruised and sometimes bloodied combatants to sprawl on the ground and recover.

The aim is for the Hallatonians to carry the bottle about 200 yards down the hill and across the ditch, or for the neighbouring villagers from Medbourne to carry the bottle several fields away in the other direction. The distances involved are quite unequal, but traditionally the Medbourne side is supported by all comers.

The previous preoccupation with prodigious beer consumption was probably an essential part of team tactics. Not only would no sober person enter such an affray but, to some extent, the alcohol would have a medicinal effect in deadening the inevitable pain. Not for nothing did one of the bottle bearers take up his position in the parade with the words 'This is where the beer does the talking.' The 'bottles' hold nine pints of beer and, as many wags have suggested, this is about how much beer the participants need to have inside them too before contemplating taking part.

After about two hours of uninterrupted and hard-fought combat, the first game was won when the Hallatonians carried the bottle over the ditch. The second game was quicker, with mostly just village lads keeping up the contest. This too was won by Hallaton and the third game was conceded to allow a much needed return to the village green to open the two winner's 'bottles' and celebrate. As custom dictates, the first drink was taken by the captain of the winning team and then the contents of the 'bottles' shared by both teams.

Hallaton Hare Pie Scramble and Bottle Kicking procession, Easter Monday 1989.

Hallaton adapts

However, at Hallaton, as with other 'traditional' British folk customs, nothing remains static. In 1994 the 'hare on a pole' mentioned by Billson was reintroduced – albeit in the form of a half-life-size bronze sculpture that is leaping rather than sitting on top of the pole.   This introduction was accompanied by a first for the Hallaton parade – people in 'fancy dress' costume. The man who holds the hare aloft and a woman with a basket of small bread rolls (since 1982 the penny loaves mentioned by Billson had been dispensed with) are dressed in finery of an indeterminate 'oldness', which is in marked contrast to all the other participants, who are dressed in old clothes suitable for the rough-and-tumble of the bottle kicking.

In 1999 I saw for the first time (although the practice may have started anytime after 1995) the use of 'team shirts', with a contingent from the Medbourne side sporting rugby shirts – with some interestingly self-deprecating nicknames on the back!

Sadly there was the first known break in the tradition in 2001, as a result of the restrictions resulting from foot and mouth disease. Villagers report that the tradition was maintained throughout the twentieth century as, during the World Wars, the women took over from absent men (although there seem to be no photographs or other documentary evidence of this significant, if temporary, adaptation).

For a detailed history of Hallaton Hare Pie Scramble and Bottle Kicking see John Morison and Peter Daisley (2000), although neither of these authors are folklorists so their work includes some full-on support for the 'pagan origins' of the event (on the premise that the hare indicates the event was once sacred to the purported prechristian goddess Eostre, which Billson had promulgated (Billson 1911)). Morison is the costumed 'bearer' of the hare sculpture and clearly enthusiastic about Hallaton's annual custom, revealing a clear example of how enthusiasm about 'restoring' lost aspects of the custom leads to adaptation and mutation. These may be inaccurate form a historical perspective but encapsulate modern day ideas of how the past 'ought to have been' with an eye for pageantry not entirely inappropriate to such a popular event.

The growing calendar of curious customs

Every county in the country yields its own calendar of 'curious customs' that are maintained by local people and, in many cases, attract large crowds. J.D.A. Widdowson has looked at the commercialisation of such customs (Widdowson 1993). As with the Castleton and Hallaton examples I have discussed, most seem to have their origins in the later eighteenth century and have adapted and mutated at least as much, and continue to do so. Many of the leading examples – Abbots Bromley Horn Dance and Padstow Mayday come immediately to mind – were 'paganised' in the early twentieth century, as the popularity of Sir James Frazer's speculations spread through the country. Indeed the present day success that has made these customs into 'leading examples' may be a result of the popularity engendered by *The Golden Bough*.

In addition to these old customs adapting and mutating, new traditions are abounding. There is almost a sense of 'it's been done like this once before so it's traditional'. By the time it's been done since your grandma was a baby, it certainly has 'always been done', and the reasons for doing it have been forgotten and reinvented many times. All Spanish people living today know that it is traditional to eat twelve grapes at midnight on New Year's Eve. This undoubted tradition was started in 1909 in a imaginative, if not desperate, attempt to respond to the glut caused by an exceptionally good grape harvest (*El Sur Semanal* 17 February 2002: 58).

Coming closer to home, the tradition of pancake racing on Shrove Tuesday started in 1945. Father's Day was created by the greetings card industry in 1970s. The reintroduction to Britain of 'Trick or Treat' and other Hallowe'en activities since the 1980s has clearly been imported through American television, as indigenous children's visiting customs had died out nearly a hundred years before while thriving among American settlers (perhaps because they had no reason to sustain Guy Fawkes' celebrations). Hallowe'en may be a safer alternative to Fireworks Night but, as Simpson and Roud note:

> There have been howls of protest in this country against the Americanization of British culture, the danger to children out at night, and/or alarm caused to the elderly. Most vociferous is the backlash from fundamentalist Christians, and even many mainstream clergy, arguing that celebrating supernatural evil forces is morally dangerous, and the fact that it is "fun" makes it worse. Neo-pagans added fuel to this fire by claiming Samhain is older than All Saints, and was hijacked by the Church. (Simpson and Roud 2000: 164)

Edinburgh's spectacular 'Beltane Fire Society' celebrations on Mayday Eve started in the mid-1980s. Fire-eating Red Men take the streets with Blue Men, Green Men, White Women and a May Queen, all seemingly inspired by Mediterranean Carnival Queens. Penzance Mayday celebrations are equally modern (presumably inspired by the over-successful celebrations 'down the road' at Padstow). So why should not the dubious custodian of the heritage of England and Wales, with its emphasis on the (re)creation of the glories of life in stately homes with none of the ghastliness of the lives of the workers who sustained them, not also get in on the act of inventing a few traditional folk customs too:

> At Badbury Rings in Dorset, you can celebrate the winter solstice on 22nd December by meeting at dawn for some Celtic tales, before a downhill walk to Home Farm at Kingston Lacy for a big cooked breakfast, a demonstration by the Bourne River Morris dancers and a Christmas mumming play. [...] Finch Foundry, near Okehampton, Devon, holds blacksmiths' competitions, and celebrates local traditions such as clogging the bellows and firing

the anvil, when blacksmiths dance on the bellows and fire
gunpowder in the anvil.
(*The National Trust Magazine* No.79 Autumn 1996 p13–14.)

Somewhere in the last few paragraphs we have shifted from Gerald
Warshaver's Level 2 to his Level 3, where a motley collection of popular
conceptions of folklore are teamed together into 'fantasy folklore', built on
the shifting sands of self-conscious eclecticism but without the reflexivity of
full-on postmodernism. Is this one step from the Disneyfication of British
culture or simply the latest manifestation of the processes of mutation that
have always been the heart of a living tradition? This same question could
be asked of the next two chapters, so I will leave the question hanging in
the air until the conclusion of this book.

Folklore in social customs

I want to drop back for a moment to Warshaver's Level 1, customary
practice that is not considered to be folk customs by the people involved.
The remit is vast: funerals, weddings (secular and religious), stag nights,
hen nights, office parties, Tupperware / lingerie / Ann Summers parties;
football / rugby / sports events (think of the difference between the customs
of football 'hooligans' and those of attending horseracing at Ascot);
children's playground games; and even the rituals of 'what we do on our
holidays' (from a widow on a Saga holiday seeking 'companionship', to an
18–30 'clubber').

Indeed, there is considerable folk custom in holiday behaviour. Somehow
being in a 'liminal space' between land and sea makes acceptable what is
not acceptable elsewhere (indeed, the very act of taking a holiday is itself
'liminal'). Topless sunbathing (or, increasingly in recent years, nudity in
designated areas) is acceptable on beaches in a way that is not on
adjoining streets. Seaside resorts have also encouraged other 'liminal
behaviour'; Brighton had a long held reputation among Londoners as the
destination for 'dirty weekends'; in the 1960s it was one of the destinations
chosen for the ritual encounters of 'Mods' and 'Rockers' between each
other and the constabulary; in the mid-1970s gay culture developed from
an alternative to seemingly-dominant trait of the town's nightlife. (For a
fuller discuss of Brighton as a liminal location, see Rob Shields 1991 Ch.4.)

Royal rituals

Changing tack, think of the large number of civic, charitable and
commercial organisations in Britain who are visited each year by various
members of the Royal Family. Much is ritualistic – receiving bouquets,

unveiling plaques, shaking hands and making polite conversation with lined-up delegates, visiting the sick and elderly (usually selected to make suitably photogenic opportunities for the local press), cheering crowds behind barricades and police adopting 'friendly bobby' body language, plus behind the scenes preparations (such as special attention to a loo that HRH just might need). One the one hand there is a high level of 'organisational formalisation' and on the other a high level of consistency (I am tempted to say 'informal formalisation') of the way crowds and passers-by contribute. This consistency of 'spontaneous' behaviour is, partly if not greatly, mediated by television reporting. Some further insight into aspects of such behaviour can be gleaned from Anne Rowbottam's study of a diverse group of people who regularly travel around the country to attend royal visits (Rowbottam 1998).

Spontaneous ritual behaviour with a high level of formalisation arose during the mourning following the sudden death of HRH Princess of Wales and her funeral procession from Westminster Abbey through north London to her final resting place in Northamptonshire. (Marion Bowman, Margaret Evans, George Monger, Jennifer Chandler and Juliette Wood all made contributions to *Folklore* 109 (1998) about what the editor dubbed 'The Diana Phenomenon'.)

Wayside memorials

Popular funerary rituals in Britain have been diversifying in recent years. Diana's death led to floral tributes being left, in vast quantities, in public places. Other tragic deaths, whether murders, deaths in house fires or traffic accidents, also lead to bouquets (rather than wreaths which, perhaps because more expensive, still seem to feature only at funerals) being left on the pavement nearby. Such public sharing of grief is particularly notable when children have died suddenly.

Having spent the last fifteen years travelling on business throughout England, I am aware that since the mid-1990s there has been a marked increase in the presence of flowers at the site of fatal motoring accidents. Some of these become more or less permanent memorials. The plastic flowers left at the site of the death of a motorcyclist a few miles to the east of where I live also incorporated parts of the bike left on site, such as the speedometer. Another such death in 2001, a few miles to the west, has led to the placement of a permanent cross on the verge. In 1994 Susan Drury was the first contributor to *Folklore* to document this tradition in Britain; Tony Walter (1996) and George Monger (1997) drew attention to further examples; Smith (1999) and Everett (2000) drew comparisons with Australian and Texan examples, respectively.

Imported customs

Not all diversification of British folk customs is homegrown. 'Imported' traditions such as Chinese New Year celebrations, the Notting Hill Carnival (and its various imitations nationwide), or the Diwali street celebration organised by Leicester City Council (said to bring together the greatest number of people of any Asian festival in Britain) all add considerably to the folk customs that are adapting and evolving in Britain today.

However, to the best of my knowledge, there has been little attempt by folklorists to study these events, still less the more private customs of immigrant cultures, such as weddings and funerals. Not only do they introduce a colourful and 'exotic' element compared to their traditional British counterparts but, for the folklorist, there are intriguing blends of 'imported' and British customs – especially among second- and third-generation descendants who live their lives in a truly multicultural manner. For instance, brides of south Asian descent prefer Western formal white wedding dresses rather than saris, despite the associations between white and death in Asian traditions.

Children's playground games

Play is a universal human characteristic and invariably incorporates customary behaviour. However, unlike many other 'folk customs', it is done self-consciously. '[W]e play when we know we are playing... If we could not conceive of acting by a set of rules that are different from those to which we have learnt to adapt, we could not play.' (Csikszentmihalyi 1981). Play is also an essentially social phenomena – even a child playing alone is usually conversing with a fictionalised character or make-believe playmate – or, increasingly, with the characters of a computer game.

Play inherently incorporates fantasy – play actions are never quite what they seem to be (Miracle 1992: 60). This is carried through from the playground to adult games where 'bluffing' can be an inherent part of the play, overtly so with card games such as poker or bridge, or more subtly with games such as golf and football.

Peter and Iona Opie are indelibly associated with the study of British children's games, publishing numerous papers and several books (notably *Children's Games in Street and Playground*, 1969). The pioneering study, with an emphasis on singing games, was Alice Gomme's *The Traditional Games of England, Scotland and Ireland*, published in two volumes in 1894 and 1898. Despite the great diversity of rhymes collected, by the 1970s most of these singing games had died out. While 'folkloristic' aspects of children's games appear to have greatly diminished in the last 40 or 50 years, the 'mythological' content has increased greatly as children base their fantasies on the myth-rich popular culture of cartoons, children's TV dramas, films such as *Star Wars*, and computer games. Modern-day counterparts to the Opies must cast a wider net to ensnare the elusive but thriving playground 'lore'.

Adapting and mutating healthily

Clearly the examples discussed in this chapter are but a small selection of topics that could have been considered. The selection here is unashamedly based around customs of which I had at least a partial prior awareness. What I hope comes across is that folk customs at all three of Gerald Warshaver's levels are adapting and mutating healthily in Britain today. Sadly, there are too few British folklorists documenting and studying any but a small proportion of these. Fly-on-the-wall docusoaps 'incidentally' capture Level 1 folk customs, although the purposes of such films are usually remote from the interests of folklorists. Some of these areas of activity are being studied by social historians, but their approach tends to be more at the level of 'this is what happened' whereas folklorists might be expected to bring a more 'nuanced' approach, perhaps along the lines of form, function/context, and – perhaps most importantly – transmission (see Chapter 3).

Would it be too much too hope that someone writing an introduction to British folklore in, say, ten or fifteen years time will complain about the *excess* number of studies of contemporary folk customs? Compared to the current dearth of research, it would seem a welcome problem to have to deal with …

10: FOLK DANCE AND DRAMA

The last chapter was about 'folk customs and seasonal festivities'. This chapter is titled 'Folk dance and drama', and the next 'Folk song'. Clearly, these are fairly arbitrary divisions between genres. The common ground is 'performance'. But then, the telling of stories is equally 'performative'. Indeed, everything about folklore, apart from the study of folklore, is really what happens when folklore 'happens' (Warshaver's Level 1) or when it is 'performed' (Levels 2 and 3).

However the sense of 'performance' here is more fluid than might be used by a stage dancer or actor. For them there is a contrast between rehearsal and performance that does not exist to the same extent in folk performance. Indeed, a great number of 'folk performances' (especially those fitting into Warshaver's Level 1) have no rehearsal. Seasonal customs, such as the Castleton Garland ceremony and Hallaton Bottle Kicking described in the previous chapter, 'just happen' each year. Clearly considerable planning is needed, but this is quite distinct from 'rehearsal' in the sense that a morris side might meet in between more public performances. Even folk dance teams rehearsing have a different emphasis to rehearsing for a staged dance or drama. With rehearsals for stage performances the aim is to learn something new (typically for all performers) then perform 'properly' in public. Except for major West End shows, the number of performances may be less than the number of rehearsals. With folk dance rehearsals there is much more a sense of developing and maintaining a repertoire; once a side is established only a minority of those rehearsing will be learning from scratch. Compared to stage performances there is less distinction between rehearsal and public performance. I suspect that the same is also true for traditional story tellers.

I have combined folk dance and drama into the same chapter largely because the predominant forms, morris dancing and mummers plays, are nowadays frequently performed by the same groups of people. As noted in Chapters 4 and 9, in the last hundred years a widespread belief has developed that these folk customs are pagan survivals. Since 1979 it has been increasingly clear that these 'timeless' customs have been repeatedly altered during the last two hundred years, although this has not entered into popular awareness.

At this stage of the previous chapter I noted that the defining feature of traditional folk customs is that the original reasons for doing the activity have long been forgotten and later explanations have been foisted upon it, possibly a number of times. Mummers plays provide a good example.

They have a small range of plots and characters. One of the best-known includes St George and the Turkish Knight. So mummers plays must date back to the Crusades. Not so. Mumming appears as a seasonal 'begging' custom in the eighteenth century and, as Jacqueline Simpson and Steve Roud observes (Simpson and Roud 2000) 'as that period is not noted for its fertility rituals or pagan customs, a "literary" origin is most likely.'

The mirage of morris

A more complex example, but central to both English folk and to folklore studies, is morris dancing. Since the Elizabethan era morris dancing has been the best-known English dance performed by experts for an audience (as opposed to a wide variety of 'social dances').

> As such it was studied by the 18th and 19th century antiquarians Francis Peck, Joseph Strutt and Francis Douce, who traced [the Morris dance] back to a late medieval courtly entertainment. Nobody doubted this until 1903, when Sir Edmund Chambers published his popular book *The Medieval Stage*.
>
> Chambers was a civil servant with a passionate amateur interest in the history of theatre; a good research scholar but one who leaned heavily on others for interpretations. In this case he was intoxicated by the work of Sir James Frazer, and proceeded to apply his theory of survivals to the morris, without any actual evidence, by declaring that it was descended from an ancient ritual to induce fertility.
>
> Chambers' idea came as a wonderful gift to the musician Cecil Sharp, the man who effectively inspired the English folk dance revival. By the 1900s the morris was dying out, and it was Sharp, by collecting over 150 examples of it and publishing and teaching a selection, who established it at the centre of the new folk dance movement.
> (Hutton 1994)

Chambers' views greatly strengthened the arguments of Sharp in an intense personal battle with Mary Neal (who had first asked Sharp to collect morris dances and taught them to a girls' club in London's East End). Sharp wanted to conserve morris in its timeless purity (which, among other things, he said meant it could only be danced by men). Sharp's views held sway for over sixty years and Barbara Lowe's entirely-contrary 1957 study of the history of morris was simply ignored.

Lowe found that morris had appeared around 1450 as a fashionable craze in the courts of western Europe. It was a Christmastime entertainment in which a lady was wooed by a group of men wearing bells that tinkled as they danced frenetically. But the dancing was in vain, as she pledged her heart to a fool. In the sixteenth century this pastime spread from the royal palaces along the Thames to nearby towns and then the rest of the country; along the way it migrated from wintertime to part of the widespread summer games.

It took until 1978 for folklorists and historians to pick up on and confirm Lowe's work. By the mid-1980s it emerged that the dances that Sharp collected in the Cotswolds in the 1890s had been devised by local antiquarians a few decades before (Hutton 1994a; 1996; Chandler 1993). If morris dancing before Sharp was characterised by continual adaptation (both the form of the dances and their audiences), then twentieth century morris dancing has proven to have maintained this tradition of adaptation. Even if morris dancing was not originally a pagan fertility rite, it undoubtedly is now, at least in the eyes of a great proportion of performers and their audiences.

There are a number of other problems with Sharp's impact on morris dancing, as Georgina Boyes summarises:

> Sharp privileged the dances from the area which had provided his
> introduction to the genre. His personal experience dictated what
> was to become the dominant form both in the Revival and
> nationally. A marginalised, rural and anachronistic Folk were
> maintained as the source of culture; white-clad, handkerchief-
> waving teams of men dancing on the village greens of the South
> Country were assured a role as the embodiment of lower-class
> Englishness. The ideal provided by Sharp's south Midlands
> archetype offered no conceptual or physical space for the male
> factory workers and teams of girls who performed non-ceremonial
> urban morrises at wakes and Rose Festivals in the industrial north-
> west. Vital and popular English dance traditions were thus
> unrepresented or misrepresented in the Revival.
> (Boyes 1993: 102)

Elsewhere Boyes notes that the English folk dance revival did include dances from the industrial north-west – but only the men's sword (or 'rapper') dances. She goes on to note how Sharp and other leading figures in the English folk dance revival, such as Douglas Kennedy, would 'correct' the position of morris dancers' arms and determine the 'artistic expression' of all dances. 'The predilections of Revivalists, rather than reference to historical usage, were soon accepted as setting the terms for all types of performance.' (Boyes 1993: 105).

In the last twenty years some of the original variety and vitality of early twentieth century folk dancing has been restored. Border morris, women's clog and morris dancing teams and molly dancers (see below) take their place alongside a wide range of male morris teams, from sides still venerating the ideals established by Cecil Sharp to those adopting a self-consciously post-modern stance toward costumes and dance steps.

Social dancing

Morris dancing may have been the predominant English dance performed by 'experts' for an audience, but was certainly not the prevailing participatory dance style. Every age has regarded dancing as a leading social event. Modern night clubs may have entirely different social customs to, say, Elizabethan church ales, but the underlying similarities are greater than the superficial differences. Innumerable fashions in dance styles and steps come and go all too quickly, quickly rendering the fashions of a previous generation seriously uncool.

Cecil Sharp and others in the English folk dance revival collected dance styles from the rural villages that, in their metropolitan eyes, were already 'seriously uncool'. They seemed so out of date that, to them, they must have been 'traditional country dances'. And for the next fifty or more years, 'country dancing' was taught to children and young women. Sadly Sharp and his followers did not normally look at the dancing in the newly-emerged industrial towns and cities, where they would have found that these dances had adapted and mutated into far more dynamic styles. These days researchers bring together the 'country' and 'urban' dance styles under the title 'social dancing'.

If one of the main reasons for sustaining morris dancing, plough plays and mummers plays in the pre-revival era was to provide agricultural labourers with an opportunity for raising money during 'quiet times', then we should not be surprised to find that such money-making schemes also encompassed other dance forms too. Elaine Bradtke has researched the way parodies of current 'social dance' styles were combined with costume (such as cross-dressed she-males) in East Anglian 'molly dancing' (Bradtke 1999); 'molly' was a common term for transvestites in the eighteenth and nineteenth centuries.

As molly dancing did not get swept into the English folk dance revival it was extinct by 1940; although since the 1970s an increasing number of teams have revived the genre. Pre-revival molly dancers had close links with plough gangs (teams of young men who went around during the Christmas season with a plough, threatening to plough up the property unless money or drink was forthcoming). The accepted form of revived molly dancing, although there are exceptions, is for mixed sides (with some of the males and females cross-dressing) performing specially-composed dances with exaggerated arm and leg movements.

Revival versus tradition

Nigel Pennick has observed (1998: 229) that modern day ballroom dancers performing the foxtrot or tango are not regarded as 'revivalists'. Indeed, the differences between 'authentic' Argentinian tango of the early twentieth century and the forms displayed on *Come Dancing* are substantial, and might reasonably be considered as evidence that this is a 'living tradition' rather than misguided 'revival'. That modern day morris or molly dancing also differs substantially from what we know about the 'authentic' forms is, however, less rarely seen as evidence of a thriving tradition and more frequently castigated as inappropriate revival. Unravelling this contrast of views perhaps says more about the prejudices introduced during the folk dance revival than it does about the nature of transmission and mutation of folk traditions.

If Sharp seems to be getting all the stick for inflicting his prejudices on English folk dancing, then he has his counterparts in Irish and Scottish folk dance. Indeed the Irish folk dance tradition has suffered especially badly, with the dictates of revivalists imposing absurd stiff arm and upper body postures. (There are comparisons here with the way the rules of piping competitions and the malign influence of the military marching bands have both seriously stilted Scottish bagpiping; a comparison with the way Scottish emigrants to Cape Breton have developed their piping traditions reveals just how different 'genuine' folk traditions are from traditions burdened with rules and regulations.)

Mumming and mummers' plays

I have deliberately put these two similarly-named customs together, not because they have a common origin, but to emphasise the differences in their history.

The word 'mumming' comes from the Greek *mommo,* meaning 'mask'. It first enters English language and culture in 1347 when Richard II invited groups of masked revellers to enlive the court's Christmastide festivities (Hutton 1996: 11). By the time of the Elizabethan court 'mumming' was part of the Christmas tradition, but by then had become more formal masques. Mummers also became part of popular entertainment, or more probably had entered into the strategies for seasonal begging. In 1616 Ben Jonson described a typical mummer's costume as being a pied suit and a mask (Hutton 1996: 21). A hundred-or-so years later, cross-dressing she-males were part of the mumming tradition too.

Disguise, cross-dressing and blackened faces were part of eighteenth century popular culture, and frequently encountered in civil disobedience, such as that associated with enclosure. 'Female rioters were often joined by men disguised in women's clothes. The practice had protective purposes, but it also involved elements of ritual inversion', that is the protesters symbolically turn the customary world upside down in order to turn it right-side up. (Underdown 1985: 111). Such 'ritual inversion' is usually now encountered only in the more harmless contexts of pantomime and carnival. And, of course, cross-dressing 'she-males' (usually known as 'Bessie' which, like 'Molly', was a common term for transvestite) entered into the motley collection of characters of mummers' plays.

Masks and disguises are, of course, part of many seasonal festivities throughout Europe, as Nigel Pennick has explored in detail in his book *Crossing the Borderlines* (Pennick 1998).

> The typical Mummers' Play opens with a narrative introduction in
> which one of the performers craves the spectators' indulgence,
> asks for room and promises a fine performance. When this is
> concluded that two protagonists appear, and after each has
> boasted of his valour they fall to fighting. In this duel one or the
> other is wounded and killed. A doctor is then summoned to
> vaunts his proficiency in medicine and proceeds to revive the
> fallen hero. Here the main business of the play ends. It is now
> the turn of minor characters to enter and provide irrelevant
> amusement of a simple sort. One of them collect money and the
> performance finishes with the song.
> (Tiddy 1923)

Actually, referring to them as 'mummers' plays' is one of convenience. At the turn of the nineteenth and twentieth centuries when these plays were being 'collected' by folklorists, the protagonists referred to themselves as guisers, guizards, tipteerers, Johnny Jacks, seven champions, as well as mummies or mummers. The tradition had all-but died out in the pre-First World War era (Tiddy was one of about six collectors). Fortunately it found favour with the folk dance revival coterie – and the influence of Sir James Frazer seriously 'paganised' mummers' plays more-or-less simultaneously with their revival.

There are two distinct 'strands' of mummers' plays. One is the combat between St George and the Turkish Knight (with innumerable local variants of name). The other is found only in parts of the East Midlands and is a 'wooing play' (which echoes early forms of morris dancing), otherwise known as the 'plough play' because of its performance on Plough Monday. Sword dancing features in early forms of both variants.

The origins of mummers' plays are quite distinct from mumming. Whereas mumming is fourteenth century, the origins of mummers' play lay between 1700 and 1750 (Hutton 1996: 78), and the 'wooing play' seems to have come later in the second half of the eighteenth century (Hutton 1996: 129–30). In the north-west of England a variant form, the Pace-Egging play, was common at Eastertime during the nineteenth century.

See Eddie Cass and Steve Roud's *An Introduction to the English Mummers' Play* (2002) for an up-to-date overview of this topic.

Punch and Judy

Although now considered a children's entertainment, Punch and Judy are direct descendants of sixteenth century puppet shows. However only in the 1660s did a new character – Pollicinella or Punchinello – arrive from Italy to join the sundry collection of Biblical characters, St Georges, Dick Whittingtons, Guy Fawkes, Fausts and other more-or-less legendary protagonists. Mr Punch's squawking voice seems to have been an early feature, but his main adversary seems to have been the Devil (who, contrary to modern plots, seems to have usually had the upper hand in the end), although his shrewish wife (then known as Joan) also incurred his wrath.

In 1828 the text of a 'Punch and Judy' show performed by an Italian puppeteer, Giovanni Piccini, was transcribed and published with illustrations by George Cruikshank. This plot is the one that has come to dominate to the exclusion of earlier variants: Punch gets angry with his baby and kills it; he then fights his wife and kills her too. He then fights and kills a variety of other characters such as a clown, ghost, beadle or crocodile depending on the puppeteer. Punch next beats a policeman, then tricks an executioner into hanging himself although Punch is the intended victim. Finally he takes on the Devil and kills him.

Until the end of the nineteenth century the Punch and Judy show was performed by itinerant showmen at fairgrounds and street shows. The escapades were intended for adult audiences. Then, rather improbably given the audacious violence of the plot, Punch and Judy became a children's entertainment associated with seaside holidays and Christmas parties. Until the outbreak of the Second World War, Punch and Judy booths were ubiquitous on English seaside beaches. The dialogue of the traditional plot was adapted to include topical characters and events. In the last forty years puppeteers have introduced considerable audience participation, along the lines of that associated with pantomimes, perhaps to mask the perversities of the plot. But the handmade 'swazzles' that give Punch's voice its screech is a consistent feature that dates back to 1699 or earlier. (Simpson and Roud 2000: 286–7)

Mr Punch appears to have little in common with mummers' plays, and morris dancing may seem to share little with the fashion for salsa dancing. Yet these distinctions arise mostly from how we are accustomed to 'categorise' such customary practices. Folkloristic eyes reveal the processes of adaptation and mutation that confirm these genres of popular culture are less the victims of revivalist dictates than yet another example of traditions that can be categorised as adopted and fabricated. Long may they continue to transform!

11: FOLK SONG

One, two or three?

It is conventional to speak of the folk song revival instigated by Cecil Sharp in the late nineteenth century. But it would be better to speak of the folk song *revivals* as the initiatives of Sharp and his contemporaries themselves were in urgent need of revival by the 1950s. This second revival was fuelled by the considerable energy and passion of A.L. Lloyd (1908–82) and Ewan MacColl (1915–1989). Indeed, British folklore in the second half of the twentieth century is indelibly stamped with their influences.

Likewise the audiences for this music are equally stamped – it is reality not cliché that leads to the 'bearded, beer-gutted, shapeless Arran-sweatered' epithet. This audience was young when MacColl and Lloyd were at their most active in the 1960s, but is now mostly fifty-something or greater. There is a younger 'market' interested in folksingers, but this is the current American usage of the term 'folksinger', that is, a singer/songwriter inspired (consciously or, more usually, seemingly unconsciously) by such 1960s and 1970s luminaries of the genre as Bob Dylan or Joni Mitchell.

Thankfully there is the possibility of a third revival in British folk music with a whole new generation of seriously talented young musicians looking anew at the folk music heritage. Despite the undoubted success of a number of these twenty-something musicians with the fifty-something aficionados, there remains plenty of scope for reducing the average age of folk music audiences.

Ye hae broken the charm noo

The history of folk song revival has been well-documented by Dave Harker (1985), Maud Karpeles (1987), Georgina Boyes (1993a) and Neal Mackinnon (1993). With good reason Harker titles his book *Fakesong: The manufacture of British 'folksong' 1700 to the present day*. Likewise Boyes' title is *The Imagined Village*.

One problem is the way pioneering nineteenth century folk song collectors defined their quarry. Any songs learnt from by the singer from broadsides or other printed forms were out, as were songs sung to a popular or well-known tune (for instance, music hall songs were generally well-known to the singers). The extent to which this distorted the repertoire is difficult to assess but the available evidence suggests that 'substantially' would be an understatement (Harker 1985: esp. 164–5; 193–4).

Tampering with the texts was entirely allowable. Collectors edited different versions of songs together, happily marrying with broadside versions if they considered their aural sources to be corrupt, and omitting verses not essential to the story. There was a confident assumption that there was an 'original' version that had been corrupted in the transmission from singer to singer, or that singers were imperfectly remembering the 'original' broadside versions (although, of course, the broadsides were themselves based on aural sources). (Harker 1985: 167; 195)

Textual manipulation was especially notable with ballads. Ballads are distinguished from other folk songs by the extent to which narrative dominates their content.

> The ballad develops an episode in which action takes place and is concluded, whereas the other folk songs focus on articulation of feelings, ideas, fantasies, and attitudes without utilising a narrative thread to achieve their ends. In the ballad, the story itself carries much of the meaning, and we as audience "watch" and "listen" to the characters as they interact meaningfully.

So summarises Barre Toelken in his overview of ballads and folk songs (Toelken 1986: 152–3). But it is not simply a case of ballads 'telling a story'. They often do so in a more 'literary' manner, with subtle references to cultural traditions and beliefs, often expressed through subtle metaphors.

The literary aspirations of ballads were recognised by their early collectors and editors. This lead to manipulation of their sung forms into printed versions of the texts that *read* well too. These manipulations were not necessarily subtle. As one Scottish collector's mother told him:

> ye he spoilt them awthegither. They were made for singin' an' no for readin'; but ye hae broken the charm noo, an' they'll bever [be] sung mair. An' the worst of a', they're nouther richt spell'd nor richt setten down.
> (Cited in Harker 1985: 70)

The standard collection of ballad texts is still the five volumes of Francis James Child's *The English and Scottish Popular Ballads*, originally published between 1882 and 1898. Child was Professor of English at Harvard University. Dismayed by the poor standard of editing of ballad collections, he built up a massive collection of original manuscripts and early printed forms. His influence is extensive, although the editing of the texts is frequently below the standards of modern scholarship and, despite including 305 examples, there are inexplicable omissions.

As a literary scholar, Child was more interested in the texts than the tunes. This was put to rights with Bertrand H. Bronson's *The Traditional Tunes of the Child Ballads*, which appeared in four volumes between 1959 and 1972. The timing was perfect and the phrase 'Child ballad' has become an integral part of the 1960s folk revival (even though more than one librarian has catalogued the collection under 'Children's stories'...). When brought to life by a powerful voice, such as Frankie Armstrong's, these ballads convey a forceful yet fully nuanced intensity, proving that they have not necessarily suffered too badly at the hands of their collectors and editors.

Ballads reassessed

Modern scholarship has highlighted the unfortunate distortions that early ballad collectors introduced. Tessa Watt enquires:

> In what way did a broadside's status as song restrict and shape what could be said with it? We need to know how the medium of song was used in ways specific to early modern England. The same ballad might have had quite different meaning when chanted by a vagrant ballad singer, or drunken dancers on the village green, from that it acquires within the repertoire of the twentieth-century 'folksinger'. It would appear that the ballad was once performed in a wider variety of circumstances, including minstrelsy, dance, theatrical jigs, three-man-songs and other recreational forms now extinct. [...]

> Like a modern 'folksong', the early modern notion of a 'ballad' concealed a wide variety of song types, from courtly wooing songs to Scottish battle legend. Such distinctions were constantly breaking down as a natural result of the process of oral dissemination. "Once the ballad style had crystallised in the late Middle Ages, it was the cumulative variations over decades and centuries that remade all manner of diverse poetry – carols, episodes from romances, debates, coronacts, and the multifarious poetry of the minstrel repertory – into ballads."

> The advent of print must have accelerated to divorce of a song's form and content from any specialised social function. The broadside ballad publishers borrowed tunes and stories from court, city and country without discrimination, and distributed them to an equally varied audience.
> (Watt 1991: 13, citing Albert B. Friedman 1983: 218)

Ballads are an important aspect of the history of popular culture, and there has been a correspondingly substantial quantity of academic publications. Sadly no one has attempted to provide an overview of recent scholarship.

Sharp's stamp

If Child's 'academic' interest in folk ballads ultimately led to their revival, then Cecil Sharp's stamp on British folksong ranks less as revival than invention. Sharp was not the only folk song collector at the turn of the nineteenth and twentieth centuries – Mary Neal, George Gardiner, Sabine Baring-Gould and Vaughan Williams were also notable – but Sharp imposed his elitist and far-from-liberal views so forcibly on the others that it is his opinions that shaped the revival and, in the process, created a serious distortion of the previously-prevailing traditions.

Sharp preferred publishing songs collected in small villages, rather than larger ones. And any village was to be preferred over towns (Harker 1985: 195). So the seriously declining and already-anachronistic rural traditions were privileged over the thriving urban traditions. Once collected the songs were transformed from solo performances into stilted versions for small groups of singers 'as though they were hymns in Sunday School' (Boyes 1993: 102), suitable for teaching in schools and for polite Edwardian drawing room performances. Although Sharp demanded reverential treatment of the tunes by collectors, needless to say, the variation and embellishment of tunes inherent in solo singing was lost in a single 'tidied up' version. The rhythmic vitality of the originals was excised in favour of four-square rhythms that fitted into the bar lines of notated music. Worse, there was no indication that traditional musicians put the emphasis on the 'down beats' (as is the case also with blues, jazz and pop music since rock'n'roll) so classically-trained performers accustomed to playing 'what is written' sound strained. Likewise Western 'serious music' requires chords – so Sharp provides them, shifting the music far from its original strengths. And the instrument most suited to chordal accompaniments in the school and parlour was the piano – so its equal temperament tuning supplants the subtleties of just intonation, or even the 'wayward' scales of unaccompanied singing.

Furthermore, Sharp made sure the words conformed to his high literary standards – excising and bowdlerising anything he considered unsuitable or betraying the poor education of the singers. Dialect and poor grammar were unsuitable for the middle-class singers who would purchase and perform his collections of song, so such distinctive signs of social status were suppressed. And the homogenised end result is what Edwardians thought of as folk song. Is it any wonder that 'serious' composers of the day could get away with such travesties as Vaughan Williams' arrangement of *Greensleeves* or Percy Grainger's *Sea Shanty Settings*? Whatever their merits as 'serious' music, works of this genre demonstrate that folk music performance cannot be reduced to the simplicity demanded by conservatoire-trained composers and performers without sounding like a bad parody.

In 1935 about 21,000 people were actively pursuing the revival of folk song and dance in the manner prescribed by Sharp (Boyes 1993: 1). But the early twentieth century generation of collectors had all but died out by 1929 and no comparable collectors came forward to replace them (Harker 1985: 198). Despite the middle-class enthusiasm for performing folk songs in the 1920s and 30s, by the Second World War the folk song traditions that did not fit in with Sharp's prejudices had withered and died.

Sharp has undoubtedly had a great energy and influence. But just how different would the evolution of British folk song and dance in the twentieth century have been if Sharp had not been so determined to impose his own prejudices and definitions? Certainly this is a hypothetical question that can never be answered with confidence. Suffice to say that Sharp's contributions to song and dance are almost as alien as rhododendrons and sycamores in ancient woodland.

Folk protest

Understandably and perhaps thankfully, the Sharp-led revival of British folk song was transformed in the years after the Second World War. American service men stationed here brought their popular culture to these shores. 'Big bands' were wowing the younger generation, and jazz and blues were available to those who knew where, providing a more 'exotic' influx of popular music.

American music had a direct effect on British folk music. Young singers were learning American songs from Kingston Trio and Weavers records. In 1951 Alan Lomax and Ewan MacColl decided that a thorough revival of British folk music was necessary. About 1957 the famously passionate Ewan MacColl decreed that musicians performing at the folk club he organised, then called the Ballads and Blues Club, could only play music from their own country. The response was somewhat explosive and the echoes still resound today. Yet it succeeded in encouraging a new generation of musicians to investigate their own traditions. MacColl, ably assisted by his wife, Peggy Seeger, A.L. Lloyd and others, had triggered the second revival of British folk music. Of these 'others', the passionate and kindly Scot, Hamish Henderson (1919–2002), least deserves to be consigned to anonymity; his School of Scottish Studies survives his recent death.

Folk revives

However MacColl's influence did not 'fossilise' folk song. Far from it, a whole new generation of folk song writers emerged. And they emerged into a new type of venue for folk music – the folk club. MacColl's Ballads and Blues Club, founded in 1956, led to at least once such club in every town and city (Boyes reports approximately 1,700 folk clubs in Britain by 1979; Boyes 1993: 1). By the end of the 1970s annual 'folk festivals', such as Sidmouth and Cambridge, augmented the opportunities for folk music enthusiasts to share their interests and repertoire.

Around this time the folk music movement acquired a belief that folk music was a form of working-class expressive culture, 'evidence of the artistic creativity of the proletariat' (Boyes 1993: 3). Sharp's fantasy of preserving a never-existent rural idyll was supplanted by the fantasy of idealised industrial urban 'underdogs'. However shallow the historical truth, some thirty-or-so years later we now have a deep and rich tradition of British folk song, 'evolved, adapted and fabricated' as with all thriving folk genres.

The folk doth protest too much

With the hindsight of history the shadow of one person looms large – Bob Dylan. A Jewish American, in the early 1960s (before he became famous) he visited the folk clubs in London, sleeping on the floor of a near-exact-contemporary in the British folk scene, Martin Carthy (not the only claim to fame for Carthy; around this time his version of *Scarborough Fair* was to provide Simon and Garfunkel with the inspiration for their hit). British folk music made its way into Dylan's mental melting pot, finding its place alongside the metaphysical poet John Donne and his latter-day emulator, T.S. Eliot, and the more folkish 'outsider', Woody Guthrie, among many other influences. Dylan found fame, fortune and, soon afterwards, controversy in the form of the loudest electric backing band of its day. In homage, or simply in search of the same fame and fortune, late-1960s West Coast American bands such as Jefferson Airplane transformed themselves from Pentangle-like politeness to the prototypes of heavy metal.

For all that Dylan and The Band provoked the electric rock revolution of the late 1960s and 1970s, the influence of his lyrics was at least as great. The acoustic folksingers who had venerated his early records may not have responded well to his electric reincarnation, but Dylan had demonstrated that potent protest songwriters had not died out with Woody Guthrie. Undoubtedly the most popular 'singer songwriters' of the 1970s were more spiritual than political (such as Joni Mitchell and Neil Young) or, all too often, overly attentive of their navels. Indeed, Dylan's own song writing took on new heroin-preoccupied directions before entering a maudlin maturity.

British folk song reacquired a strong political focus from the 50s onwards, gaining strength over the years such that by the Thatcherite 1980s a substantial body of finely-wrought politically-aware songs appeared. While the 'Mersey beat' helped revitalise American pop music in the mid-1960s, none of the British folk musicians ever shared the level of success of their American and Canadian counterparts. Martin Carthy, in collaboration with Dave Swarbrick, steadily re-invented folk guitar and fiddle playing. Various bands, starting with Fairport Convention and Steeleye Span, explored performing traditional folk songs and ballads with an electric rock band line up, without ever seriously threatening dominant pop music genres of the day.

Folk music by the folk

Then, in 1977, a segment of the 'street culture' of London exploded into popular awareness. Spiky 'Mohican' haircuts and safety pins inserted through both clothes and facial tissues gave the media an image to ridicule. A clothes shop owner with a penchant for media sensibilities, Malcolm Maclaren, gave these punks the icon that had so far eluded them. The Sex Pistols were nothing like any folk group that had gone before; certainly their rendition *God Save the Queen* owes nothing to Cecil Sharp.

Improbable as it is that Sid Vicious was inspired by *Strawberry Fair*, or had heard of Martin Carthy and his compatriots, still less likely of Ewan MacColl, punk has many of the characteristics of folk music. Although there is little apparent continuity between punk and other folk music, punk rock has its origins purely in popular culture. The vehemence of the views expressed in many of the lyrics are considerably closer to 1960s protest singers than to the prevailing pop music massaged by mid-1970s record-company A&R men with a fixation on glam rock. Most punk rock was badly performed, but there were notable exceptions – with The Clash, Britain belatedly found the combination of energy and anger to match Dylan's excursion into electric amplification over a decade before. The Pogues showed that punk could be successfully combined with at least two Irish traditions – folk music and serious drinking. The squeaky-clean established ambassadors of Irish music, The Dubliners, were now counterbalanced by these devilish envoys. Then, when the Oysterband took the Padstow Mayday song *Hal-an-Tow* by the scruff of its neck in 1994, 'folk rock' finally rocked. Their repertoire increasingly included some of the more powerful protest songs from the dark days of

Thatcherism side-by-side with covers of New Order songs. Nevertheless the politically-aware genre of those days is best remembered by the exceptional incarnation of the angry-young-man-with-guitar archetype, Billy Bragg, who took his brand of 'folk' out of its ghetto, and up to the barricades of the miners' strike and the poll tax protests. I'd like to think that the ghosts of A.L. Lloyd and Ewan MacColl were smiling then.

You can never expect the unexpected

Punk came and largely went. With the exception of the seriously exceptional, such as Billy Bragg, folk music with its roots more deeply in tradition seemed destined to survive ghetto-like in folk clubs and folk festivals. As ever, the unexpected happened. Who would have expected that a kid playing the Northumbrian bagpipes ('The *what?*') would trigger a revival. Well, Kathryn Tickell also played the fiddle and was good enough to seemingly win every local competition she entered but, in 1988 when her first recording, *The Common Ground*, appeared on an obscure label, few crystal balls foretold the events of the next few years.

By dint of much hard work and excesses of enthusiasm, Tickell not only made a name for herself among the folk aficionados, but inspired a new generation of talented youngsters to come to the fore. Ireland's Sharon Shannon went out on stage in black leather to give accordions a long-lost 'street cred'. Eliza Carthy, daughter of Martin Carthy and diva of the folk scene Norma Waterson, showed what prodigious talent and youthful enthusiasm could do for English folk song and dance. Soon after came another youngster brought up in folk clubs whose winsome singing combined innocence and aptitude, Kate Rusby. Along with them are a significant number of contemporaries who have yet to achieve the same recognition.

The freshness and vitality of these twenty- and thirty-somethings goes down well in the now-traditional venues for folk music such as folk clubs and festivals. These musicians have also coped much better than many of the older generation of folk performers with the entirely different 'dynamics' of performing to people in rows of seats in generally rather characterless arts centre theatres and small concert halls. This may be bringing the music to a wider audience (although not necessarily a younger one) but such audiences are accustomed to passively listening, so the enthusiastic joining in with the choruses typical of folk clubs is rare.

Eclectic excesses

No matter how much convenient terms of reference tend to imply 'pigeonholing', thankfully British folk music does not exist behind barriers.

Indeed, anyone with an interest in British folk music would probably be exposed to what, for want of a better term, is known as 'world music'. The leading folk music monthly magazine, *Folk Roots,* has always concerned itself with music from around the world. It has a somewhat fluid definition of the music, but the emphasis is on popular music that is not primarily a product of the music industry. And, since the mid-1980s, Andy Kershaw's national radio programmes have provided listeners with a wide-ranging selection of music of the kinds covered in *Folk Roots.*

The consequences for British folk music and many and varied. It would take a full-length book to describe the fusions with Scottish music alone. Hip hop, rap, reggae and various 'techno' genres all feature. Mouth Music devised a refined combination of African rhythms with Gaelic song and *puirt a bail* (literally, 'mouth music' but specifically the syllabic mnemonics used to teach Scottish *piobroch* or classical bagpipe tunes). Much less refined are the antics of Bloco Vomit, several heavily-built Glaswegian lads blending bagpipes with belting samba rhythms, while dressed in drag. Martyn Bennett has taken a droll approach to Scottish traditional music and shaped it, using the techniques of techno dance, for the dance clubs. A similar straddling of dance club and folk festival audiences is achieved by Shooglenifty.

English folk dance tunes with a full-blown reggae backing were the speciality of a group who started out as Edward II and the Red Hot Polkas; greater excesses of such fun-seeking mix-and-match mentalities followed with the bands Blowzabella and 3 Mustaphas 3. Senegalese and British musical styles are seamlessly combined by Baka Beyond. Suns of Arka, an ever-changing succession of musical collaborations led by Wadida, have been mixing every kind of musical tradition with just about every other since 1983, although the accolades for eclectic excess should perhaps be shared with the dance club maestros, Transglobal Underground.

However the introduction of 'exotic' elements into folk music can be both more subtle and more pervasive. As Ian Anderson, editor of *Folk Roots,* observes, this is what 'traditional music' is about:

> A few hundred years ago, an unknown person might have
> brought a foreign instrument to an island and over a period of
> time radically change a local tradition. Because of improved
> communication and recording, we *do* know that in the 1960s,
> Johnny Moynihan and Andy Irvine introduced the [Greek]
> bouzouki to Irish music and it's now pretty much standard kit for
> 'Celtic' fans everywhere. The djembe, a West African drum, has
> spread worldwide in the past few decades (because, like a guitar,

it can be adapted to so many different musics), and even the didgeridoo is getting about a bit. Digital sampling technology is just another instrument in the right hands, and rap is just another musical form sweeping the world like the polka did... if it works in a way that roots musicians like, it'll all get integrated. Elements, speed and opportunity change, the process doesn't.

The thing is, nobody can make traditions do anything. They either evolve, mutate and survive their own accord or they don't. Turning a deaf ear to where music is going in these interesting, multi-cultural times is as misguided as those old folk song collectors who ignored big chunks of the repertoire of their sources because, in their blinkered, it 'wasn't traditional'. Sorry, in traditional music the only thing that is constant is that musicians have a mind of their own!
(Anderson 2002)

Bhangra and beyond

As may be expected, second- and third-generation British Asians have evolved an essentially 'home grown' popular culture, resulting in a substantial number of bhangra bands in the last fifteen or so years. Bhangra's origins combine Punjab folk dances with 'Bollywood' film music and mainstream Western pop. In the mid-1970s, a West London band, Alaap, blended the complex cross-rhythms of traditional bhangra with 'disco' idioms and found themselves with a recording contract in 1978. Birmingham's Bally Sagoo is one of the pioneers and has had some support from a major label but has failed to find wider appreciation. Although bhangra bands have achieved substantial record sales, they are sustained with little national radio airtime or support from major labels.

Bhangra has also been blended with a wide range of other 'world musics'. Joi, Talvin Singh, Nitin Sawhney, Fun>da>mental and Asian Dub Foundation have explored these opportunities for cross-fertilisation and all have been nominated for the Mercury Music Award and other such prestigious accolades, but this 'insider awareness' is not matched by a wide appreciation or 'top ten' success. (See Ritu 1999 for an overview of bhangra and related styles).

Afro-Caribbean cultures in Britain have also generated a healthy reputation for music-making. But, in contrast to the British Asians, their inspiration is much more rooted in Jamaican reggae and urban American hip hop and rap. British musicians in these genres have certainly put their own 'spin' on these styles, but musical fashions pioneered outside Britain have a far greater influence than in bhangra, which is 'pioneered' from Britain and generally distinct from any trendsetting in south Asian popular music.

The range of ideas and ideologies in today's British folk music is vast – from Asian Dub Foundation's bitter anti-racist anthems to Kate Rusby's self-penned wistfully-romantic ballads. This brief overview is, inevitably, based on personal preferences and omits far more than is included. 'Evolved, adopted and fabricated' cogently summarises all the different styles, confirming that British folk music remains rich territory for anyone who adopts a folkloristic approach.

12: FOLK CRAFT AND ART

Previous chapters in this book have drawn upon the work of various researchers. Indeed one of my problems has been to concisely summarise shelf-fulls of monographs and articles. For the first time I find myself dealing with an important aspect of folk activities but one largely ignored by British folklorists, with the exception of popularising accounts of specific crafts.

American folklorists are different. For them 'material culture' (the term used by both anthropologists and archaeologists) or 'folk art' is an integral aspect of folklore studies. Indeed, seemingly it is not possible to be an American folklorist without taking an obsessive interest in native American basket weaving traditions – although Barre Toelken musters a longer roll-call:

> Material folklore includes vernacular houses and barns (designed and made by those who use them rather than by trained architects), fence types, home-made tools, toys, tombstones, foods, costumes, stitchery, embroidery, tatting, braiding, whittling, woven items, quilts, decorations (Christmas trees, birthday party decor), and culturally based musical instruments and rhythm makers – insofar as they are learned by example within an ongoing tradition shared by people with something in common.
> (Toelken 1996: 9)

Predictably, most of these have, or at least had, their British counterparts. Once again I find Gerald Warshaver's three levels of folklore applicable to folk craft. There are many 'Level 1' folk crafts that can be considered to be 'customary practice', that is where the practitioners do not consider themselves to be doing folk crafts. There are relatively few examples of folk crafts at Warshaver's Level 2, that is what most people would thing of as folk craft and art; although carving Welsh 'love spoons', making so-called 'corn dollies', and decorating hardware in the 'castles and roses' style of canal folk are perhaps best considered as Level 2. Self-conscious incorporation of 'folk crafts' and 'folk art', that is Warshaver's Level 3, is widespread although the most frequent manifestations are in souvenirs of dubious tastefulness and other mass-produced tourist 'tat'.

Level 1 activities have, as may be expected, changed significantly in the second half of the twentieth century. For instance, until the 1960s most women would expect to make their own clothes, to spend their evenings hand-knitting, and be well-practised at darning socks and patching the elbows of jackets and cardigans. Those skilled at needlework would add to these chores the time-consuming production of embroidery and crochet pieces. With the availability of affordable mass-produced clothes, combined with an ever-increasing pace of change in fashions and greater wealth, home-made clothes quite quickly became the exception. Needlework is now a minority 'specialism' and, while hand-knitting, embroidery and crochet are still practised, alongside them has been a revival of cross-stitching (which had remained popular in America) and hand lace-making. In the 1980s the prevailing 'back to nature' ethos took the meaning 'homespun' literally and led to a resurgence of hand-spinning wool and dyeing the yarn using natural pigments. Indeed, there is an implicit distinction between 'traditional crafts' which, almost by definition predominately use natural materials, and other handicrafts where a greater variety of resources are acceptable.

Sometimes fashions move full circle. Until the 1950s making 'peg rugs' from old rags was commonplace. Then pegged rugs became considered rather too plebeian and a fashion for making 'hooked' woollen rugs was promoted by commercial organisations, although this did not survive long after the 1960s. In the late 1990s the pervading interests in nostalgia saw a minor revival of peg rugs, although I suspect far more were bought ready-made than pegged at home.

Some crafts have died out entirely. In the East Midlands during the mid-seventeenth century a tradition started for carving tombstones in locally-available slate (from quarries at Swithland in the Charnwood Forest area of Leicestershire). Initially these were comparatively small and inscribed with just a few lines of text. Within fifty years the slabs had grown to about five feet high and the biographical information was augmented with epitaphs and elaborate decorative scrolls and bas-relief 'vignettes'. So far as can be ascertained they were designed by local schoolteachers and other literate members of the middle-class although, initially at last, they were executed by illiterate carvers (as attested by anomalies of 'typography'). With the advent of the railways easier-to-work and cheaper Welsh slate was available and, although the tradition flourished, the pioneers of specialist 'monumental masons' took over from the part-time craftspeople.

Some crafts have survived despite all expectations. When piped water was introduced in the 1930s, traditional wells and pumps were neglected. Within a few decades they had, to all intents and purposes, been lost. But in a dozen or so Derbyshire villages the tradition of creating pictorial floral 'well dressings' was sustained, even when piped water had been installed.

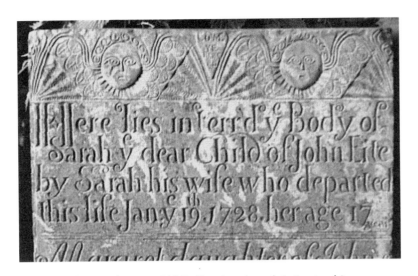

Slate tombstone, Old Dalby churchyard, Leicestershire.

Given that the images were almost invariably taken from popular Bible stories, it seems probable that deeply-rooted church and chapel social groups were responsible for maintaining the tradition. With the 1950s and the increase in private motoring (and, I suspect some 'cashing in' by coach tour operators) the well dressings grew into tourist attractions and raised useful funds for charities. Neighbouring villages increasingly 'revived' their well dressings to encourage visitors, even though in more than a few instances it would be more accurate to term them 'old kitchen sink dressings'.

Well dressing is essentially ephemeral – once the flowers have wilted the art lives on only in memory and, in the last hundred-or-so years, photography. As such there are close parallels to such ephemeral arts forms as Navaho sand painting and south Asian *rangoli*. Perhaps the most widely-practised ephemeral folk art in Britain currently is children's face painting. Contentiously, may I suggest that the newest form of ephemeral folk art is crop circles, which are first recorded in 1980 (see Schnabel 1993 for a sane approach to such circlemaking).

Ephemeral forms of folk art are mostly peripheral to folk crafts, largely because ideas about what constitutes 'folk crafts' are shaped by the type of objects in museum collections where needlework, kitchen equipment, farm implements and home-made toys predominate. Visiting the Welsh Folk Museum near Cardiff or the Ulster Folk Museum in Belfast enables an assessment of the varied domestic items and farm appliances that were produced according to established 'folk craft' traditions. The larger museums of this type include rebuilt timber-framed buildings and other examples of 'vernacular architecture' that are characteristic of a specific area.

Nigel Pennick suggests (Pennick 2002) that there are 'five precepts' which rule traditional crafts:

- suitability for purpose
- convenience in use
- proper use of materials
- soundness of construction
- subordination of any decoration to the four preceding principles.

Although these 'precepts' could also be said to apply to the architects of the worst of the 1960s and 1970s office blocks and the like, they were also the ideals of the Arts and Crafts Movement instigated by William Morris in the late nineteenth century. Morris was self-consciously emulating idealised medieval craftsmen; his influence continues to influence the design and manufacture of furniture and furnishings produced in workshops that distance themselves from mass-production factories.

The methods used in 'traditional' crafts, and the patterns and symbolism used for decoration, were all passed on by example, usually through apprenticeship. 'How to do it' books are a modern aspect of crafts; apart from pattern books of decoration written manuals for traditional crafts were rare, and always rudimentary.

Anthropologists have long recognised that artefacts are never merely functional; indeed complex studies of objects as 'signs' have developed in academe (see Babcock 1992 for a summary). In the final analysis, material artefacts can yield invaluable insights into aspects of a culture or folk group that might otherwise be invisible.

Tradition and revival

In the studies of folk crafts, as with folk customs and folk music, a contrast is made between 'traditional' and 'revived' activities. The intention is to privilege those styles, processes or customs that are believed to have been practised continuously since an unrecorded origin, and to subtly disparage activities that have been reinstated after a lapse, however brief.

This distinction appears to originate in two untenable assumptions: firstly that traditional craftspeople have always received their techniques and designs directly from those who taught them, and then reproduced them in an unchanging way; and secondly that their designs have been handed on without reference to outside influences. Examination of the historical realities shows something different. Where they could not be bettered, techniques and designs remained substantially the same over long periods of time. But conservatism for its own sake was never a guiding principle. New ideas considered valuable were always adopted and incorporated into the local milieu. The historical progression of the traditional arts and crafts is testimony to this.

(Pennick 2002)

Although the perceived distinction between 'traditional' and 'revival' is widespread, in practice there is no clear boundary separating the two. Unless they learnt their skills through an unbroken chain of masters and apprentices, all 'traditional' craftspeople can be considered to be revivalists, although such an extreme view is rarely helpful in practice. In reality the distinction is chimeral and the supposed prestige of the 'traditional' often illusionary. Approached from a different angle, what passes for 'traditional' is not rooted in the real past but rather in the nostalgia that derives from dissatisfaction with modernity.

A preliminary list of British folk crafts

In the absence of any other overview of British folk arts and crafts, so far as I am aware (excluding studies of specific skills or artefacts), I would like to make a provisional list. Outside the realms of folklore studies most people would *not* call these 'folk crafts' as the term 'handicrafts' covers many of them. In selecting or excluding I have looked mostly at the ways the ideas and skills are transmitted. There is a great irony here as most 'traditional' crafts are well-documented in 'how to do it books', whereas more recent practices are the ones more likely to be transmitted from person to person. Some readers might argue that this list verges on 'social studies' rather than folklore but that simply begs the wider question of how much difference there is between these two approaches.

Examples which seem to have no modern day survivals or revivals include the aforementioned slate tombstones. To this I would add such 1920s to 1940s phenomena as building crystal radio sets, and the widespread tradition during the first half of the twentieth century of keeping scrapbooks of postcards, greeting cards and other examples of early colour printing. Wickerwork was also once widespread but is now all but extinct. Home brewing also seems to be on its way from commonplace to comparative obscurity.

Cooking is a vast 'folk craft', both in the way key skills are passed on by example (even if the medium is now via television rather than at mother's elbow) and in what is served when. 'Sunday joints' served to the entire family may be giving way to pub 'carveries' but the tradition is maintained, however mutated. The absence of a Sunday joint has displaced the eating of the 'left overs' cold on Mondays. And fish on Fridays is now seldom observed, although the tradition had survived for over three hundred years even though, after the Reformation, it had ceased to be a mandate of the Church. Committed Christians give up a type of food for Lent – these days more likely to be a luxury such as chocolate rather than meat and eggs. 'Traditional' Christmas Day lunch and tea has evolved over the decades, and will no doubt continue to do so. No other seasonal festivity in Britain has quite such deeply-established fare, excluding Jewish and Asian families. Sadly, few British folklorists have taken a detailed interest in the customs associated with food.

As noted, a wide range of needlework skills have been transformed from commonplace to specialist 'hobbies'. In the late 1960s the exoticism of *ikibana* and *origami* augmented indigenous flower arranging and paper crafts. In the 1970s various small commercial operations promoted the home-assembly of costume jewellery and, a decade later, other such small-scale enterprises created a fashion for making and dressing china dolls. Hand-made greetings cards have ceased to associated with primary school children and are currently on the increase. Nevertheless a wide range of 'crafts' are promoted for children, many of which are manifestations of older forms. Indeed, there is scope for a detailed study of the changes in promotion of handicrafts suitable for children. Whereas projects in 1930s *Boys' Own* annuals famously required an empty cigar box (for making one-string banjos and a variety of fretwork projects), by the 1960s these had yielded to *Blue Peter's* fetish for empty washing up bottles and toilet roll cores.

Most male-orientated handicrafts since the 1950s – such as home woodturning, model railways, slot car racing, radio control cars/planes/boats, building live steam railway locomotives and traction engines, constructing plastic scale model kits, painting model soldiers, and the like – all seem a long way removed from most people's ideas of 'folk crafts'. Indeed, with the increasing promotion of materials, equipment and ideas for 'DIY' home improvements, most men with an aptitude for working with their hands find themselves with a lengthy list of 'projects' around the home. And now, as home décor becomes increasingly fashion-conscious, the perceived need for interior and garden 'makeovers' gathers pace.

As television-promoted 'makeovers' compete for leisure time, other DIY activities decline. For instance the increased complexity of modern cars, coupled with longer service intervals and greater reliability, means that home car maintenance is now rare.

If 'DIY' activities and the archetypal Sunday morning 'rituals' of car washing or lawn mowing are most certainly examples of Level 1 activities, then Level 2 examples include carving Welsh love spoons, 'castles and roses' decoration of canal boat hardware, well dressing, straw craft such as making 'corn dollies', and carving walking sticks. I am tempted to add making models from vast quantities of match sticks to this list, as this has its precursors before the invention of safety matches in the mid-nineteenth century in, say, modelmaking from bone, such as the exquisitely-executed ships-in-bottles produced by mariners and Napoleonic prisoners of war.

Making simple home-made toys was once a prevalent leisure-time activity for fathers but, now toy shops offer a vast range of moulded plastic, this tradition has its nearest modern day equivalents in the making of sophisticated rocking horses, dolls' houses and the like – quite specifically plugging into the fashion for 'nostalgia'. For this reason I would consider these, along with making and dressing china dolls, as Level 3 crafts (although this is somewhat tendentious as, in their heyday, rocking horses and china dolls were produced not as 'folk crafts' but in factories).

But there are many other leisure pursuits that could be considered either Level 1 or Level 3. Painting and sketching, especially using watercolours, is a 'folk art' with many significant differences in approach from either commercial illustrators or artists who have studied for art college degrees. We are now entering another realm of leisure activities, where the art or craft is pursued (or least learnt) with a group of like-minded enthusiasts. Practical 'evening classes' include such crafts as French polishing, upholstering, as well as the ubiquitous pottery making. Their origins in William Morris's 'Arts and Crafts' revival have long been forgotten, as have the origins of evening classes themselves as more 'intellectual' and less practical means of self-improvement, as promoted by the Workers' Educational Association. Indeed, the socialist-inspiration of the WEA as a provider of study groups is increasingly being eclipsed by the much more Conservatively middle-class, yet more intrinsically 'self-help', activities of the University of the Third Age.

There is also a whole field of popular religious art. There include tapestry kneelers and other needlework in Anglican churches, 'Jesus loves you' banners associated with more charismatic worship, and *rangoli* and other arts associated with Asian religions. Some of these overlap with folk performances, as with more 'involved' preaching styles.

While sectarian rather than religious, the use of painted murals by both sides in the Northern Ireland troubles has added a new genre to modern folk art (for a study of the 'serious business' of symbolism in Northern Ireland see Buckley 1988).

Folk crafts and folk groups

In the quote at the start of this chapter Toelken defined folk crafts 'insofar as they are learned by example within an ongoing tradition shared by people with something in common.' (1996: 9). However (and I am sure this is as true in American as Britain) these 'people with something in common' are now more likely to be readers of 'how to' books, magazines and Web sites. Indeed, there is seemingly at least one monthly or quarterly magazine for the most obtuse interests. Learning by example is increasingly from books, magazines, videos and Web discussion boards, rather than the face-to-face learning that, almost by definition, is a characteristic of traditional crafts. The extent to which this will increasingly influence the ways folk crafts adapt remains to be seen.

Nevertheless the notion of a 'folk group', even if the members rarely if ever physically meet, is essential to the notion of these pursuits being in some way folk crafts. Implicit to the study of folk crafts is the assumption that distinctive designs and ways of using materials are passed on from one practitioner to another. These days the transmission of ideas, designs and skills may rely less on face-to-face tuition or discussions, but if there are shared underlying approaches (even if entirely implicit or otherwise unconsidered by the participants) then I consider it appropriate to consider the craft as a 'tradition'. Even where commercially-produced magazines and books are key to the dissemination of ideas, or commercial producers of specialist parts or equipment clearly have a vested interest in the promotion of the pursuit, we are still firmly in the realms of what may be regarded as a 'folk group'. Clearly a great many folk crafts are now self-conscious 'revivals', and the work created often risks being regarded as 'twee'. Nevertheless, these 'revivalists' can often be considered to constitute a folk group. So, although folk crafts are seemingly about artefacts, a more informed approach is that they are as much about the processes by which ideas, information and techniques are shared among a 'folk group', and the way that these adapt and mutate over time.

13: WHERE NEXT?

In attempting to provide an overview of British folklore studies in so few pages, inevitably this has been a partial and personal selection. The contents of this book overlap surprisingly little with various American introductions to folklore, although I hope this reflects some major differences in interests between Old World and New World folklorists rather than any major omissions on my part.

In the absence of any comparable activities by British folklore enthusiasts in the middle part of the twentieth century, the 'theoretical foundations' for the subject have been determined by Americans. Attempting to draw a consensus of their eclectic views is difficult, but I hope most of them would agree that to a large extent 'folklore' is an entirely artificial and 'made up' concept. Much of what has been done in the name of 'folklore studies' would have been better labelled 'ethnology of social customs'.

The nineteenth century British folklorists who adopted the term 'folk-lore' also created a more-or-less illusionary continuity to a 'once upon a time' idyllic rural past, indeed often to prechristian paganism. This illusion has remained a dominant aspect of popular understandings of British folklore, and is likely to continue. So, Britain is likely to always have certain social customs that are viewed as being 'traditional' rather than 'contemporary'. The notion of 'contemporary folklore', although almost tautological to an American folklorist, remains somewhat 'odd' to many with an interest in British folklore, especially those with limited contact with academic folklore activities over the last two decades or so. 'Contemporary folklore' sees the 'folk' of 'folklore' as a versatile way of labelling specific groups of people with some common interest, such as occupation or leisure pursuit. Even within folk groups, the *context* of the activity may be quite relevant.

I have frequently referred to Gerald Warshaver's three levels of folklore (Level 1 being unselfconscious activities not thought of by the protagonists as being folklore; Level 2 is what is commonly thought of as folklore or folk customs; and Level 3 is a deliberate attempt to mix and match folklore with more modern, or post-modern, ideas). I hope this book has shown that 'what we think of as folklore' (Warshaver's Level 2) is only a small part of the folklore in modern society. A good proportion of what interests folklorists is going on around us everyday, the unselfconscious 'Level 1' activities not thought of by the protagonists as being folklore. Another lively area is the self-conscious incorporation of folklore into entirely modern activities such as computer games and the more fanciful inventions of the heritage industry (Level 3).

The different activities that attract the attentions of folklorists are perhaps best regarded as *processes*, adapting and mutating according to external influences and the ways they are transmitted. Although the study of folklore cannot be reduced to a simple formula, the four main areas of concern to folklorists can be summarised as 'form, function, context and transmission.'

All aspects of folklore can be considered to be the process of transmission of *symbols*. While it is easy to get over-theoretical or reductionist about 'semiotics', there are times when thinking about folklore that we need to bear in mind that these symbols are metaphors or metonyms for wider ideas, such as notions of nationalism or disaffection with modernity. As such they are subject to relevant methods of analysis, such as those opened up in recent years by cognitive linguistics.

Today's folklorists on both sides of the Atlantic have developed an adequate theoretical basis for their collecting and analysis (without always being as 'theoretically aware' as their academic close-relations in anthropology and archaeology). Although there are American books offering helpful advice on such matters (such as Oring 1985; Georges and Jones 1995; Toelken 1996) these are of limited assistance to understanding British lore. Despite a steady flow of soundly-based 'monographs' and papers on specific aspects, there has been no attempt by leading British folklorists to create pedagogical material for their compatriots with an interest in folklore. As a result popular understanding of folklore is dominated by ideas that are many decades past their sell-by date. This book is an attempt to summarise academic developments in recent decades. If someone with a better pedigree in folklore studies thinks this attempt too rough-and-ready and is provoked to do a better job then I will be entirely satisfied! (In the meantime you might want to inform me of the worst of my errors so I can correct them in a future edition of this book.)

As the substantial bibliography at the end of this book indicates, I have attempted to leave sufficient 'footprints' in the text of this book for readers to follow up specific topics. Public libraries in Britain can obtain obscure books and copies of articles from academic journals for a moderate fee. However the bibliography is in no way exhaustive – the emphasis is on books published in the last couple of decades and ones about the study of folklore (as opposed to studies of specific instances of folklore).

The constantly-evolving content of the Web is an invaluable resource for folklorists. The better search engines, such as Google, readily provide useful links about the most arcane topics. Not all Web site authors can be said to adopt high academic standards, but anyone who has even part-digested the ideas in this book should be able to make an assessment of the 'quality' of the material.

Don't just sit there ...

Given its brevity, I am well aware that there are relatively few examples of actual folklore in this book. Generally this is not for lack of source material – the quantity of published information is vast, although all-too-often the very act of collecting or preparing for publication has been strongly coloured by preconceived ideas about what constituted folklore (i.e. the activities of rural 'peasants' but not their urban contemporaries) or its interpretation (chiefly the notions of a pervasive 'prechristian pagan tradition').

Even more importantly, folklore is very much alive; modern day culture abounds with examples. Sadly too little is being collected or analysed by the small number of folklore enthusiasts in Britain. Despite the wealth of material collected in the late nineteenth century, there is a relative dearth of material from a century later. This book is not intended to offer guidance for would-be collectors, as the three books by American folklorists previously mentioned (viz. Oring 1985; Georges and Jones 1995; Toelken 1996) offer considerable insights for the collecting of 'contemporary' lore. Their examples have strong American 'accents' but mostly can be readily translated into British counterparts.

Such study can beneficially be linked to other research. For instance, most of the local history societies throughout Britain are preoccupied with documentary sources (such as those found in county record offices), although some have also embraced 'non-documentary sources' (such as the study of ancient earthworks, surveys of hedgerows, or even archaeological fieldwork). Few chose to document current activities for the benefit of future historians, although there was something of an exception in 2000 when many groups decided to mark the millennium with a variety of accounts of life and times in that year. There is considerable scope for local historians to record 'Level 1' customs and lore in both urban and rural areas. While some cities may be overtly multicultural, the same dynamic processes of adaptation and mutation are also taking place in nearly every rural village too, as 'commuters' and 'townies' bring an equally multicultural (although rarely 'multi-ethnic') influx to indigenous ideas.

Likewise family history is seen by many as tracing ever more elusive ancestors back into the oblivion of early records. Few family historians are interested in documenting 'habitual customs' within the family. For instance, the type of food served at family celebrations, such as Christmas or children's birthdays, and the way it has 'evolved' within living memory. Likewise, most families have 'in jokes' and a handful of narratives about key events or people that are only heard at certain types of events, such as weddings or funerals. Despite the widespread use of video cameras to capture weddings, there has not, to my knowledge, been any attempt to analyse the information about folk customs and beliefs that these contain. Every family provides scope for detailed record-keeping; 'comparing and contrasting' a modest number of such records would yield a useful folklore project.

Other readers may have more creative interests in folklore and wish to incorporate a more informed approach into their dancing, storytelling, music, novel writing, computer-game creation, or whatever. Go ahead – it made Terry Pratchett a multi-millionaire!

One way or another, don't just sit there, make awareness of the folklore going on all about you into part of your interests.

BIBLIOGRAPHY OF WORKS CITED

ADDY, Sydney Oldall, 1901, 'Garland Day at Castleton (Derbyshire)', *Folklore*, 12, 394–428.

ANDERSON, Ian, 2002, 'Editor's *Box*', *Folk Roots*, 223/4, 11.

ARMSTRONG, Edward A., 1958, *The Folklore of Birds*, Collins.

BABCOCK, Barbara A., 1992, 'Artifact', in Richard Bauman (ed), *Folklore, Cultural Performances and Popular Entertainments*, OUP.

BACCHILEGA, Cristina, 1997, *Postmodern Fairy Tales: Gender and narrative strategies*, University of Pennsylvania Press.

BAKER, Augusta and Ellin GREENE, 1977, *Storytelling: Art and technique*, Bowker.

BAKER, Margaret, 1996, *Discovering the Folklore of Plants* (3rd edn), Shire (1st edn 1969).

BARNES, Daniel R., 1991, 'The contemporary legend in literature: towards an annotated checklist', *Contemporary Legend*, 1: 173–83.

BARRETT, John C., 1994, *Fragments from Antiquity: An archaeology of social life in Britain, 2900–1200 BC*, Blackwell.

BAUMAN, Richard, 1982, 'Conceptions of folklore in the development of literary semiotics', *Semiotica* 39, 1–20; reprinted in Richard Flores (ed), 1996, *Problems in Cultural Anthropology: The anthropology of performance*.

BAUMAN, Richard, 1986, *Story, Performance, and Event: Contextual studies of oral narrative*, Cambridge UP.

BEACH, Horace, 1997, 'Listening for the logos: A study of reports of audible voices at high doses of psilocybin', MAPS 7:1; posted to MAPSFORUM email list 16 July.

BELSEY, Catherine, 1980, *Critical Practice*, Routledge.

BENNETT, Gillian, 1987, *Traditions of Belief: Women and the supernatural*, Penguin; revised as *Alas Poor Ghost: Traditions of belief in story and discourse*, Utah State UP, 2000.

BENNETT, Gillian, 1993, 'Folklore studies and English rural myth' *Rural History*, 4, 1, 77–91.

BENNETT, Gillian, 1994, 'Geologists and folklorists: Cultural evolution and "The science of folklore"', *Folklore*, 105, 25–37.

BENNETT, Gillian, 1995, '"If I knew you were coming, I'd have baked a cake": The folklore of foreknowledge in a neighborhood group' in B. Walker (ed), *Out of the Ordinary: Folklore and the supernatural*, Utah State UP.

BENNETT, Gillian, 1997, 'Review essay: folklorists and anthropologists', *Folklore*, 108, 120–3.

BENNETT, Gillian, 1998, 'The vanishing hitchhiker at fifty-five', *Western Folklore* 57 No.1 (Winter) 1–17.

BENNETT, Gillian and Paul SMITH, 1996, *Contemporary Legend: A reader,* Garland.

BETTELHEIM, Bruno, 1976, *The Uses of Enchantment: The meaning and importance of fairy tales,* Thames and Hudson.

BIDMEAD, Chris, 2002, Futures column in *PC Plus* 186, 22.

BILLINGTON, Sandra, 1996, 'Preface: The life and works of Hilda Ellis Davidson' in S. Billington and M. Green, *The Concept of the Goddess,* Routledge.

BILLSON, Charles J., 1895, *Leicestershire and Rutland: County Folk-lore,* Folk-Lore Society.

BILLSON, Charles J., 1911,'Vestiges of paganism in Leicestershire' in Alice Dryden (ed.), *Memorials of Old Leicestershire,* George Allen (reprinted 1994 with an introductory biography, annotations and additional illustrations as *Vestiges of Paganism in Leicestershire,* Heart of Albion Press).

BLACKBOURN , David, 1993, *Marpingen: Apparitions of the Virgin Mary in Bismarckian Germany,* Clarendon; reprinted 1995 as *The Marpingen visions: Rationalism, religion and the rise of modern Germany,* Fontana.

BLY, Robert, 1990, *Iron John: A book about men,* Addison-Wesley.

BONE, Woutrina A., 1923, *Children's Stories and How to Tell Them,* Christophers.

BORD, Janet, 1997, *Fairies: Real encounters with little people,* Michael O'Mara.

BORD, Janet and Colin BORD, 1972, *Mysterious Britain,* Garnstone.

BORD, Janet and Colin BORD, 1985a, *Alien Animals: A worldwide investigation,* Granada.

BORD, Janet and Colin BORD, 1985b, *Sacred Waters: Holy wells and water lore in Britain and Ireland,* Granada.

BOWMAN, Marion, 1994, 'Religion in Bath: Beyond the façade', *Religion Today,* 9.3, 32–7.

BOWMAN, Marion, 1998, 'Belief, legend and perceptions of the sacred in contemporary Bath', *Folklore,* 109, 25–31.

BOYES, Georgina,1987, 'Cultural survivals theory and traditional customs', *Folk Life,* 26.

BOYES, Georgina, 1993a, *The Imagined Village: Culture, ideology and the English folk revival,* Manchester UP.

BOYES, Georgina, 1993b, 'Dressing the part: the role of costume as an indicator of social dynamics in the Castleton Garland ceremony', in T. Buckland and J. Woods, *Aspects of British Calendar Customs,* Folklore Society.

BRADLEY, Richard, 1991, 'Ritual, time and history', *World Archaeology,* 23, 2, 209–219.

BARDTKE, Elaine, 1999, *Truculent Rustics: Molly dancing in East Anglia before 1940,* FLS Books.

BREATNACH, Deasun, 1993, 'The puca: A multi-functional Irish supernatural entity', *Folklore,* 104, 105–110.

BRIGGS, Katherine, 1959, *The Anatomy of Puck.*

BRIGGS, Katherine, 1976, *Dictionary of Fairies*, Allen Lane.

BRIGGS, Katherine M., 1977, 'Symbols in fairy tales', in H.R. Ellis Davidson (ed), *Symbols of Power*, D.S. Brewer and Rowman and Littlefield.

BROOKESMITH, Peter, 1996, 'Do aliens dream of Jacob's sheep?', *Fortean Times,* 83, 27–30.

BROWN, Callum G., 2001, *The Death of Christian Britain,* Routledge.

BROWN, Theo, 1979, *The Fate of the Dead,* Folklore Society.

BUCKLAND, Theresa, 1982, 'English folk dance scholarship: an overview', in T. Buckland (ed), *Traditional Dance,* Vol. 1, Crewe.

BUCKLAND, Theresa and Juliette WOODS (eds), 1993, *Aspects of British Calendar Customs,* Folklore Society.

BUCKLEY, Anthony D. (ed), 1998, *Symbols in Northern Ireland,* Institute of Belfast Studies.

BURKE, Peter, 1978, Popular Culture in Early Modern Europe, Wildwood.

BUSHAWAY, Bob, 1982, *By Rite: Custom, ceremony and community in England 1700–1880,* Junction Books.

CACIOLA, Nancy, 2000, 'Spirits seeking bodies: Death, possession and communal memory in the Middle Ages', in B. Gordon and P. Marshall (eds), *The Place of the Dead,* Cambridge UP.

CALLAHAN, Kevin L., 1995, 'Rock art and lilliputian hallucinations', *TRACCE,* 2; downloaded from www.geocities.com/Athens/2996/trace2b.html#lil

CAMPION-VINCENT, Véronique, 1997, 'Organ theft narratives', *Western Folklore* 56 (Winter), 1–37.

CANAPA, Nancy L., and Antonella ANSANI, 1997, 'Introduction' in N.L. Canepa (ed) *Out of the Woods: The origins of the literary fairy tale in Italy and France,* Wayne State UP.

CARPENTER, Siri, 2001, ' Mindreading ability helps organize thinking', *Monitor,* 32:5 (May). Also online at: www.apa.org/monitor/mindread.html

CARR, Edward, 1964, *What is history?,* Penguin.

CARSON, Ciaran, 1999, *Fishing for Amber: A long story,* Granta.

CASS, Eddie and ROUD, Steve, 2002, *An Introduction to the English Mummers' Play,* English Folk Dance and Song Society in association with the Folklore Society.

CHALMERS, David, 1996, *The Conscious Mind: In search of a fundamental theory,* Oxford UP.

CHANDLER, Keith, 1993, *'Ribbons, Bells and Squeaking Fiddles: The social history of morris dancing in the English south midlands 1660–1900,* Hisarlik.

CHARTIER, Roger, 1987, *The Cultural Uses of Print in Early Modern France*, trans L.C. Cochrane, Princeton UP.

CHARTIER, Roger, 1988, *Cultural History: Between practices and representations,* trans L.C. Cockrane, Polity Press.

CLARKE, David, 1998, 'Peakland spooklights', *At the Edge*, 10, 28–33; online at www.indigogroup.co.uk/edge/peakland.htm

CLARKE, David and Andy ROBERTS, 1996, *Twilight of the Celtic Gods: An exploration of Britain's hidden pagan traditions*, Blandford.

COLLINS, Andy, 1987, 'Mount Athos', *The Ley Hunter*, 104, 15–23.

COLLIS, John, 1994, 'Celtic fantasy', in *British Archaeological News*, March; based on a paper given at the 'Celts in Europe' conference, Cardiff, December 1993.

COLLIS, John, 1997, 'Celtic myths' in *Antiquity* 71, 195–201.

COLWELL, Eileen, 1991, *Storytelling* (2nd edn), Thimble (1st edn 1980).

COOPER, Geoff, 1997, 'Textual technologies: New literary forms and reflexivity', in J.H. Collier and D.M. Toomey (eds), *Scientific and Technical Communication: Theory, practice and policy*, Sage.

CRESSWELL, Ian, 1984, 'What dreams might come', *Magonia*, 16, 3–7.

CRESSY, David, 1989, *Bonfires and Bells: National memory and the Protestant calendar in Elizabethan and Stuart England*, Weidenfeld and Nicolson.

CRESSY, David, 1997, *Birth, Marriage and Death: Ritual, religion and the life-cycle in Tudor and Stuart England*, Oxford UP.

CSIKSZENTMIHALYI, Mihaly, 1991, 'Some paradoxes in the definition of play', in *Play as Context*, ed. Alice Taylor Cheska.

CUNNINGHAM, Hugh, 1980, *Leisure in the Industrial Revolution c.1780–c.1880*, Croom Helm.

DARNELL, Regna, 1974, *Readings in the History of Anthropology*, Harper and Row.

DAVIDSON, Hilda Ellis, 1987, 'Changes in the Folklore Society, 1949–1986', *Folklore*, 98, 123–30.

DAVIES, Owen, 1996, 'Healing charms in use in England and Wales 1700–1950', *Folklore*, 107, 19–32.

DAVIES, Adam, 2001, 'I thought I saw a sauropod', *Fortean Times*, 145, 30–32.

DAVIES, Jonathan Caredig Davies, 1911, *Folk-lore of West and Mid-Wales*.

DAVIES, Owen, 1996, 'Healing charms in use in England and Wales 1700–1950', *Folklore*, 107, 19–32.

DE CARO, F.A., 1986, 'Riddles and Proverbs' in E. Oring (ed), 1986, *Folk Groups and Folklore Genres: An introduction*, Utah State UP.

DÉGH, Linda, 1986, *Folktales and Society: Story-telling in a Hungarian peasant community* (2nd edn), Indiana UP (1st edn 1969).

DÉGH, Linda, 1996, 'What is a belief legend?, in *Folklore* 107, 33–46.

DÉGH, Linda, and Andrew VAZSONYI, 1976, 'Legend and Belief', in Dan Ben-Amos (ed), *Folklore Genres*, University of Texas Press.

DENNING, Kathryn, 1999, On Archaeology and Alterity, unpublished PhD thesis, University of Sheffield.

DEVEREUX, Paul, 1982, *Earthlights: Towards an understanding of the UFO enigma,* Turnstone.

DEVEREUX, Paul, 1989, *Earth Lights Revelation: UFOs and mystery lightform phenomena: the Earth's secret energy force,* Blandford.

DEVEREUX, Paul, 1997b, 'Everything you've always wanted to know about earth lights', *Fortean Times,* No.103, 26–31.

DEVEREUX, Paul, 2001, *Haunted Land: Investigations into ancient mysteries and modern day phenomena,* Piatkus.

DEVEREUX, Paul, and Peter BROOKESMITH, 1997, *UFOs and UFOlogy: The first fifty* years, Blandford.

DEVEREUX, Paul, and Peter BROOKESMITH, 1998, 'The great brain robbery', *Fortean Times* No.107, p22–4.

DICKINSON, Bob, 1997 'An eighteenth century vision of a spirit line?', *Markstone,* 8, 9–10.

DILLON, Matthew, 1997, *Pilgrims and Pilgrimage in Ancient Greece,* Routledge.

DORSON, Richard M., 1968a, *The British Folklorists: A History,* RKP.

DORSON, Richard M. (ed), 1968b, *Peasant Customs and Savage Myths,* (2 vols), RKP

DORSON, Richard M., 1972, *Folklore and Folklife: An Introduction,* University of Chicago Press.

DORST, John D., 1988, 'Postmodernism vs. Postmodernity: Implications for folklore studies', in *Folklore Forum,* 21:2, 216–220.

DOTY, William G., 2000, *Mythography: The study of myths and rituals,* University of Alabama Press; 2nd edn (1st edn 1986).

DRAKE, Carlos C., 1969, Jungian psychology and its uses in folklore', in *Journal of American Folklore,* 82, 122–31.

DRURY, Susan, 1994, 'Funeral plants and flowers in England', *Folklore,* 105, 101–3.

DUNDES, Alan (ed), 1965, *The Study of Folklore,* Prentice-Hall.

DUNDES, Alan, 1980, *Interpreting Folklore,* Indiana UP.

DUNDES, Alan, 1987, *Passing Through Customs: Essays by a Freudian Folklorist,* University of Wisconsin Press.

DYER, T.F. Thistleton, 1889, *The Folklore of Plants,* reprinted 1994 Llanerch.

ELLIS, Bill, 'Flying saucers from Hell', *Magonia,* 40, 12-16.

EPSTEIN, James, 1994, *Radical expression: Political language, ritual, and symbol in England, 1790-1850,* Oxford UP.

ESTÉ, Clarissa Pinkola, 1992, *Women Who Run with the Wolves: Contacting the power of the wild woman,* Rider.

EVANS, George Ewart and David Thomson, 1972, *The Leaping Hare,* Faber.

EVANS, Hilary and Dennis STACY (eds), 1997, *UFOs 1947-1997,* James Brown.

EVERETT, Holly, 2000, 'Roadside crosses and memorial complexes in Texas', *Folklore* 111, 91-118.

FABIAN, Johannes, 1983, *Time and the Other: How anthropology makes its object* Columbia UP.

FRIEDMAN, Albert B., 1983, in James Porter (ed), *The Ballad Image*, Los Angeles.

FULLER, Steve, 1991, 'Is history and philosophy of science withering on the vine?' *Philosophy of the Social Sciences* 21(2):149-174.

FULLER, Steve, 1992, 'Being there with Thomas Kuhn: A parable for postmodern times', *History and Theory* 31:241-275.

FULLER, Steve, 1997, *Science*, Open University Press.

GARDNER, Brant, 1997, 'The Impact of the Spanish upon the Record of Native Oral Tradition Among the Nahua'. Retrieved 4 Jan 1999 from www.highfiber.com/~nahualli/Quetzalcoatl/crucible.htm

GAZIN-SCHWARTZ, Amy and Cornelius HOLTORF (editors), 1999, *Archaeology and Folklore,* Routledge.

GAZIN-SCHWARTZ, Amy and Cornelius HOLTORF, 2000, *'On archaeology and folklore',* 3rd Stone, 37, 13-17.

GELL, Alfred, 1992, *The Anthropology of Time,* Berg.

GEORGES , Robert A. and Michael Owen JONES, 1995, *Folkloristics: An introduction,* Indiana UP.

GLASSIE, Henry, 1985, *Irish Folk-Tales,* Penguin.

GLASSIE, Henry, 1988, 'Postmodernism', in *Folklore Forum* 21:2, 221-48.

GRAVES, Robert, 1948, *The White Goddess,* Faber and Faber.

GREEN, Martin, 1993, *Curious Customs,* Impact.

GREEN, Miranda, 1992, *Animals in Celtic Life and Myth,* Routledge.

GRINSELL, Leslie V., 1976, *Folklore of Prehistoric Sites in Britain,* David and Charles.

GOMME, Alice B., 1894, *The Traditional Games of England,* Scotland and Ireland, Vol.1.

GOMME, Alice B., 1898, *The Traditional Games of England, Scotland and Ireland,* Vol.2.

GONZALEZ, Alejandro, 1997, email to Folklore Discussion Group, 27 September.

GORDON, Bruce, 2000, 'Malevolent ghosts and ministering angels: Apparitions and pastoral care in the Swiss Reformation', in B. Gordon and P. Marshall (eds), *The Place of the Dead,* Cambridge UP.

GOSDEN, Christopher, 1994, *Social Being and Time,* Blackwell.

GOSS, Michael, 1991, 'The lessons of folklore' in *Magonia* 38 (Jan), 10-14.

GOSS, Michael, 1996, 'The hypno-heist', *Magonia,* 57, 10-14.

GRAEBER, Matthew J., 1995, 'Godships', *Magonia,* 52, 3-8.

GUREVICH, Aron, 1988, *Medieval Popular Culture: Problems of belief and perception,* Cambridge UP.

HAND, Wayland D. (ed), 1971, *American Folk Legend: A symposium,* University of California Press.

HARKER, Dave, 1985, *Fakesong: The manufacture of British 'folksong' 1700 to the present day,* Open University.

HARPUR, Patrick, 1994, *Daimonic Reality: A field guide to the Otherworld,* Viking.

HARPUR, Patrick, 2002, 'Body and soul', *Fortean Times,* 155 (Feb 2002), 30-34.

HARRIS, Tim, 1989, 'The problem of "popular political culture" in seventeenth-century London', *History of European Ideas,* 10, 43-58.

HARTE, Jeremy, 1997a, 'Cavaliers and phantoms', *3rd Stone,* 26, 6-10.

HARTE, Jeremy, 1997b, 'Hollow hills', *At the Edge,* 5, 22–9.

HARTE, Jeremy, 1997c, 'Pussy cat, pussy cat, where have you been?', *At the Edge,* 6, 30–7; online at www.indigogroup.co.uk/edge/Pussycat.htm

HARTE, Jeremy, 1998a, 'Medieval fairies: Now you see them, now you don't', *At the Edge* ,10, 2–3; online at www.indigogroup.co.uk/edge/fairies1.htm

HARTE, Jeremy, 1998b, 'Sex, drugs and circle dancing', *At the Edge,* 10, 14–15; online at www.indigogroup.co.uk/edge/fairies3.htm

HARTE, Jeremy, 1998c, 'Folk memory', *3rd Stone,* 31, 5–9.

HARTE, Jeremy, 1998d, *Alternative Approaches to Folklore 1969–1996,* Heart of Albion Press. Originally published on disc; online at www.indigogroup.co.uk/albion/aatf.htm

HARTE, Jeremy, 1999, *Research in Geomancy 1990–1994* (2nd edn), Heart of Albion Press (1st edn 1997). Originally published on disc; online at www.indigogroup.co.uk/albion/rig.htm

HARTE, Jeremy, in press, *Explore Fairies,* Heart of Albion.

HENDERSON, Lizanne and Edward COWAN, 2001, *Scottish Fairy Belief,* Tuckwell.

HESS, David J., 1997, *Science Studies: An advanced introduction,* New York UP.

HEYWOOD, Simon, 1998, *The New Storytelling: A history of the storytelling movement in England and Wales,* Daylight.

HILL, Christopher, 1975, *The World Turned Upside Down: Radical ideas during the English revolution* (2nd edn), Penguin (1st edn 1972).

HOBSBAWM, Eric and Terence RANGER (eds), 1983, *The Invention of Tradition,* Cambridge UP.

HOLE, Christina, 1976, *A Dictionary of British Folk Customs,* Hutchinson.

HOPKINS, Budd, et al, 1992, *Unusual Personal Experiences: An analysis of data from three national surveys conducted by the Roper Organisation,* Bigelow.

HOWE, Alex, 2000, 'Kidney devils', *Fortean Times,* 138, 34–9.

HUFFORD, David J., 1982, *The Terror that comes in the Night: An experience-centered study of supernatural assault traditions,* University of Pennsylvania Press.

HUFFORD, David J., 1995a, 'Beings without bodies: An experience-centered theory of the belief of spirits', in B. Walker (ed), *Out of the Ordinary: Folklore and the supernatural,* Utah State UP.

HUFFORD, David J., 1995b, 'The scholarly voice and the personal voice: reflexivity in belief studies', *Western Folklore,* 54, 57–76.

HUFFORD, Mary, 1995, 'Context', *Journal of American Folklore,* 108(430), 528–49.

HUTTON, Ronald, 1991, *The Pagan Religions of the Ancient British Isles: Their nature and legacy,* Basil Blackwell.

HUTTON, Ronald, 1994a, *The Rise and Fall of Merry England,* Oxford UP.

HUTTON, Ronald, 1994b, 'Morris and Marian', *Talking Stick,* 16, 13–15.

HUTTON, Ronald, 1995, 'The English Reformation and the evidence of folklore', *Past and Present,* 148: 89–116.

HUTTON, Ronald, 1996, *The Stations of the Sun,* Oxford UP.

HUTTON, Ronald, 1999, *The Triumph of the Moon: A history of modern pagan witchcraft,* Oxford UP.

INGRAM, Martin, 1984, 'Ridings, rough music and the "reform of popular culture" in early modern England', *Past and Present,* 105.

INGRAM, Martin, 1987, *Church Courts, Sex and Marriage in England 1570–1640,* Cambridge UP.

JAMES, Simon, 1993, *Exploring the World of the Celts,* Thames and Hudson.

JAMES, Simon, 1998, 'Celts, politics and motivation in archaeology', in *Antiquity* 72, 200–9.

JAMES, Simon, 1999, *The Atlantic Celts,* British Museum Press.

JOLLY, Karen, 1996, *Popular Religion in Late Saxon England,* University of North Carolina Press.

JONES, Gareth Stedman, 1983, *Languages of Class: Studies in English working-class history 1832–1982,* Cambridge UP.

JONES, Leslie Ellen, 1998, *Druid, Shaman, Priest: Metaphors of Celtic Paganism,* Hisarlik.

JONES, Leslie Ellen, 2000, 'Stone circles and round tables: Representing early Celts in film and television', in Amy Hale and Philip Payton (eds), *New Directions in Celtic Studies,* University of Exeter Press.

JONES, Leslie Ellen, 2001, 'Everybody must get stoned ...: Megaliths and movies', in *3rd Stone* 40, 6-14. (Completists should also see *3rd Stone* 41 p5 and p59 for obscure movies-with-megaliths missed from Jones' survey.)

JORDAN, Katy, 2000, *The Haunted Landscape: Folklore, ghosts and legends of Wiltshire,* Ex Libris Press.

JOYCE, Patrick, 1991, *Visions of the People: Industrial England and the question of class 1848-1914,* Cambridge UP.

JUDGE, Roy, 1979, *The Jack-in-the-Green,* D.S. Brewer (revised edn c.1998).

KARPELES, Maud, 1987, *An Introduction to English Folk Song,* Oxford UP.

KEARNEY, Richard, 2002, *On Stories,* Routledge.

KEEL, John A., 1970, *UFOs: Operation Trojan Horse,* Putnam.

KING, Lucien, 2002, *Game on: The history and culture of videogames,* Laurence King.

KNOEPFLMACHER, U.C., 1998, *Ventures into Childland: Victorians, fairy tales and femininity,* University of Chicago Press.

KOTTMEYER, Martin, 2002, 'Headhunt', *Magonia,* 77, 3-17.

KROHN, Kaarle, 1926, *Die Folkloristische Arbeitsmethode,* translated and published as *Folklore Methodology: Formulated by Julius Krohn and expanded by Nordic researchers,* American Folklore Society, 1971.

KUHN, Thomas, 1970, *The Structure of Scientific Revolutions* (2nd edn), University of Chicago Press (1st edn publ. 1962)

KUPER, Adam, 1988, *The Invention of Primitive Society: Transformations of an illusion,* Routledge.

LA FONTAINE, Jean, 1998, *Speak of the Devil: Tales of Satanic abuse in contemporary England,* Cambridge UP.

LAKOFF, George, 1987, *Women, Fire and Dangerous Things: What categories reveal about the mind,* University of Chicago Press.

LAKOFF, George and Mark JOHNSON, 1980, *The Metaphors We Live By,* University of Chicago Press.

LAKOFF, George and Mark JOHNSON, 1999, *Philosophy in the Flesh: The embodied mind and its challenge to Western thought,* Basic Books.

LAWSON, Hilary, 2001, *Closure: A story of everything,* Routledge.

LAYTON, Robert, 1989, 'Introduction: Who needs the past?' in R. Layton (ed), *Who Needs the Past?: Indigenous values and archaeology,* Routledge.

LAYTON, Robert, 1996, Discussion on archaeology and folklore session, TAG 96 Conference, Liverpool (unpublished notes).

LAZELL, David, 1993, 'Modern Fairy Tales', *Fortean Times,* 71, 39–41.

LAZELL, David, 2001, *The Fairy Gift and Other Ways to Find Lost Laughter,* published by author.

LE GUIN, Ursula K., 1987, *Buffalo Gals and other Animal Presences,* Penguin.

LEIGH, Dick, 1998, *Fairytales and Therapy,* Daylight Press for The Society for Storytelling.

LESTER, Geoff, 1972, *Castleton Garland,* CECTAL (reprinted 1977).

LEWIS, Philip, 1996, *Seeing Through the Mother Goose Tales: Visual turns in the writings of Charles Perrault,* Stanford UP.

LINCOLN, Bruce, 1991, *Death, War and Sacrifice: Studies in ideology and practice,* University of Chicago Press.

LINCOLN, Bruce, 1999, *Theorizing Myth: Narrative, ideology and scholarship,* University of Chicago Press.

LINDAHL, Carl, 1996a, 'Series editor's preface', in Gillian Bennett and Paul Smith, *Contemporary Legend: A reader,* Garland.

LINDAHL, Carl, 1996b, 'Psychic ambiguity at the legend core', in Gillian Bennett and Paul Smith, *Contemporary Legend: A reader,* Garland.

LOTTES, Günther, 1984, Popular culture and the early modern state in 16th century Germany', in Steven L. Kaplan (ed), *Understanding Popular Culture: Europe from the Middle Ages to the Nineteenth century,* Mounton.

LOWE, Barbara, 1957, 'Early records of the morris in England', *Journal of the English Folk Dance and Song Society,* 8:2, 61–82.

MABEY, Richard, 1998, *Flora Britannica: The concise edition,* Chatto and Windus

MACKINNON, Neal, 1993, *The British Folk Scene: Musical performance and social identity,* Open University.

MCGRANE, Bernard, 1989, *Beyond Anthropology: Society and the other,* Columbia UP.

MCKENNA, Terence, 1992, *Food of the Gods,* Rider.

MAGIN, Ulrich, 2001, 'Waves without wind and a floating island: historical accounts of the Loch Ness Monster', *Fortean Studies 7,* 95–115.

MARCUSE, Herbert, 1956, *Eros and Civilisation: A philosophical inquiry into Freud,* RKP.

MARKOS, Louis A., 2001, 'Myth matters', *Christianity Today,* 23 April, 32–9.

MARTIN, Peter, 1993, 'Series editor's preface' in Georgina Boyes, *The Imagined Village: Culture, ideology and the English folk revival,* Manchester UP.

MARWICK, Arthur, 1970, *The Nature of History,* Macmillan.

MAZA, Sarah, 1996, 'Stories in history: cultural narratives in recent works in European history' *American Historical Review* No.101 p1493–515.

MEDWAY, Gareth J., 2001, *Lure of the Sinister: The Unnatural History of Satanism,* New York UP.

MEGAW, Ruth and Vincent MEGAW, 1996, 'Ancient Celts and modern ethnicity', in *Antiquity,* 70, 175–81.

MEGAW, Ruth and Vincent MEGAW, 1998, 'The mechanism of (Celtic) dreams?', in *Antiquity*, 72, 432–5.

MELLON, Nancy, 1992, *Storytelling and the Art of Imagination*, Element (reissued under the title *The Art of Storytelling* in 1998).

MESKELL, Lynn, 1998, 'Introduction: Archaeology matters', in L. Meskell (ed), *Archaeology Under Fire: Nationalism, politics and heritage in the Eastern Mediterranean and Middle East*, Routledge.

MICHELL, John, 1968, *The View Over Atlantis*, Thames and Hudson.

MIRACLE, Andrew W., 1992, 'Play', in Richard Bauman (ed), *Folklore, Cultural Performances and Popular Entertainments*, OUP.

MONGER, George, 1997, 'Modern wayside shrines', *Folklore*, 108, 113–14.

MORGAN, Prys, 1983, 'From a death to a view: The hunt for the Welsh past in the Romantic period' in Eric Hobsbawm and Terence Ranger (eds), 1983, *The Invention of Tradition*, Cambridge UP.

MORISON, John and Peter DAISLEY, 2000, *Hallaton Hare Pie Scambling and Bottle Kicking: Facts and Folklore of an Ancient Tradition*, Hallaton Museum.

MUNZ, P., 1973, *When the Golden Bough Breaks*, RKP.

NELSON, Gertrud Mueller, 1999, *Here All Dwell Free: Stories to heal the wounded feminine*, Paulist Press.

OATES, Caroline and Juliette WOOD, 1998, *A Coven of Scholars: Margaret Murray and her working methods*, FLS Books.

OBLEKEVICH, James, 1976, *Religion and Rural Society: South Lindsey 1825–1875*, Clarendon.

O'CONNOR, Joseph and John SEYMOUR, 1990, *Introducing Neuro-Linguistic Programming: The new psychology of personal excellence*, Crucible.

ONG, Walter J., 1982, *Orality and Literacy*, Methuen; 2nd edn Routledge, 2002.

OPIE, Peter and Iona OPIE, 1969, *Children's Games in Street and Playground*, Clarendon.

ORING, Elliott (ed), 1986, *Folk Groups and Folklore Genres: An introduction*, Utah State UP.

ORING, Eliott, 1992, *Jokes and their Relations*, University Press of Kentucky.

PENNICK, Nigel, 1998, *Crossing the Borderlines: Guising, masking and ritual animal disguises in the European Tradition*, Capall Bann.

PENNICK, Nigel, 2002, *Masterworks: Arts and crafts of building traditions in northern Europe*, Heart of Albion.

PENRY, John, c.1773, *Three Treatises Concerning Wales*.

PHILLIPS, Julia, 1998, 'Encounters with the little people', *The Cauldron*, 87, 21–2.

PHYTHIAN-ADAMS, Charles, 1975, *Local History and Folklore: A new framework,* Bedford Square Press.

PORTER, John, 1995, *Anglo-Saxon Riddles,* Anglo-Saxon Books.

PRATCHETT, Terry, 2000, 'Imaginary worlds, real stories', *Folklore,* 111, 159–68.

PROPP, Vladimir, 1968, *The Morphology of the Folk Tale,* University of Texas Press.

QUINN, Phil, 1997a, 'A toast to the recently-departed fairy faith in the Bristol region', *3rd Stone,* 26, 21–3.

QUINN, Phil, 1997b, 'The Devil's Eye: Earth lights in landscape and folklore', *3rd Stone,* 28, 20–2.

QUINN, Phil, 1999, *Holy wells of Bath and Bristol Region,* Logaston.

RATTUE, James, 1995, *The Living Stream: Holy wells in historical context,* Boydell.

RENWICK, Roger, 1980, *English Folk Poetry: Structure and meaning,* Batsford.

RIMMER, John, 1997, 'An organised distortion of memory', *Magonia,* 60, 1.

RIMMER, John, 1998, review of La Fontaine (1998) in *Magonia,* 64, 17.

RITU, D.J., 1999, 'England/UK Bhangra/Asian beat', in S. Broughton et al, *World Music: Volume 1 Africa, Europe and the Middle East,* Rough Guides.

ROGERSON, Peter, 1987, 'And the dogs began to howl', *Magonia,* 27, 6–8.

ROGERSON, Peter, 1988, 'Off limits: Ufology and the deconstruction of reality', *Magonia,* 30, 6–8.

ROGERSON, Peter, 1990, 'On a summer's day... ', *Magonia,* 37, 1–4.

ROGERSON, Peter, 1991, 'Somewhere a child is crying', *Magonia,* 38, 3–4.

ROGERSON, Peter, 1993a, 'Fairyland's hunters: part 1', *Magonia,* 46, 3–7.

ROGERSON, Peter, 1993b, 'Fairyland's hunters: part 2', *Magonia,,* 47, 4–8.

ROGERSON, Peter, 1994, 'Sex, science and salvation', *Magonia,* 49, 13–17.

ROTTMEYER, Martin, 1988, 'Abduction: the boundary deficit hypothesis', *Magonia,* 32, 3–7.

ROWBOTTOM, Anne, 1998, '"The real royalists": folk performance and civil religion at royal visits', *Folklore,*109, 77–88.

SAHLINS, Marshall, 1981, *Historical Metaphors and Mythical Realities.*

SAHLINS, Marshall, 1985, *Islands of History,* Chicago UP.

SAID, Edward W., 1978, *Orientalism,* RKP.

SANDELL, Roger, 1991, 'From evidence of abuse to abuse of evidence', *Magonia*, 38 (Jan) 5–9.

SCHAFER, Elizabeth D., 2000, *Exploring Harry Potter*, Ebury.

SCHNABEL, Jim, 1993, *Round in Circles: Physicists, poltergeists, pranksters and the secret history of the cropwatchers*, Hamish Hamilton.

SCRIBNER, Bob, 1989, 'Is a history of popular culture possible?', *History of European Ideas*, 10.

SEGAL, Robert A., 1998, *Jung on Mythology*, Routledge.

SEIFERT, Lewis C., 1996, *Fairy Tales, Sexuality and Gender in France 1690-1715: Nostalgic utopias*, Cambridge UP.

SHERMAN, Sharon, R., 1997, 'Perils of the princess: Gender and genre in video games', in *Western Folklore*, 56, 243–58.

SHIELDS, Rob, 1991, *Places on the Margin: Alternative geographies of modernity*, Routledge.

SIEVEKING, Paul, 2001, 'Millennium moggy survey', *Fortean Times*, 146, 16–17.

SIMPSON, Jacqueline, 1997, '"The rules of folklore" in the ghost stories of M.R. James' in *Folklore* , 108, 9–18.

SIMPSON, Jacqueline and Steve ROUD, 2000, *A Dictionary of English Folklore*, Oxford UP.

SIVIER, David, 2000, 'The limners of faerie', *Magonia*, 71, 3–7.

SIVIER, David, 2001, 'An alien vice: Human sexuality and the pornography of abduction', *Magonia* , 72 , 1–14.

SMITH, Georgina, 1978, 'Literary sources and folklore studies in the nineteenth century: a re-assessment of armchair scholarship', *Lore and Language*, 2, 9, 26–42.

SMITH, Georgina, 1981, 'Social bases of tradition: the limitations and implications of the search for origins', in A.E. Green and J.D.A. Widdowson (eds), *Language Culture and Tradition*, CECTAL.

SMITH, Jonathan Z., 1978, *Map is not Territory*, Brill, reprinted University of Chicago Press 1993.

SMITH, Paul, 1989, 'Contemporary legend: a legendary genre?' in G. Bennett and P. Smith (eds), *The Questing Beast: Perspectives on contemporary legend IV*, Sheffield Academic Press 1989; reprinted in G. Bennett and P. Smith, *Contemporary Legend: A reader*, Garland, 1996.

SMITH, Robert James, 1999, 'Roadside memorials - some Australian examples', *Folklore*, 110, 103–5.

SOUTHGATE, Beverley, 1996, *History: What and Why? Ancient, modern and postmodern perspectives*, Routledge.

STEIG, William, 1990, *Shrek!*, Gollancz.

STEVENS, Phillips Jr, 1989, 'Satanism: Where are the folklorists?', *New York Folklore*, 15; reprinted in Gillian Bennett and Paul Smith, 1996, *Contemporary Legend: A reader*, Garland.

STEWART, SUSAN, 1984, *On Longing: Narratives of the miniature, the gigantic, the souvenir, the collection,* Johns Hopkins UP.

STOCKING, George W., 1996, *After Tylor: British social anthropology 1888–1951,* Athlone Press.

STONE, Kay, 1975, 'Things Walt Disney never told us', *Journal of American Folklore,* 88, 42–50.

STONE, Alby, 1994, 'Celtic fallacy forgone', *Mercian Mysteries,* 21, online at www.indigogroup.co.uk/edge/Celtic.htm

STONE, Kay, 1997, 'Social identity in organised storytelling', *Western Folklore,* 56, 233–41.

STRATHERN, Marilyn, 1987, 'Out of context: The persuasive fictions of anthropology', *Current Anthropology,* 28, 3, 251–81.

SZASZ, Thomas, 1978, *The Myth of Psychotherapy. mental healing as religion, rhetoric and repression,* Oxford UP.

TARZIA, Wade, 1996, email to Folklore Discussion List, 11 September.

TARZIA, Wade, 1997, email to Folklore Discussion List, 3 January.

TAYLOR, David, 1998, 'Spaces of transition: New light on the haunted house', *At the Edge,* 10, 22-27; online at www.indigogroup.co.uk/edge/space.htm

THOM, Alexander, 1967, *Megalithic Sites in Britain,* Clarendon.

THOMAS, Julian, 1996, *Time, Culture and Identity: An interpretative archaeology,* Routledge.

THOMAS, Keith, 1971, *Religion and the Decline of Magic,* Weidenfeld and Nicolson.

THOMPSON, Edward P., 1979, *Folklore, anthropology and social history,* Noyce.

THOMPSON, Edward P., 1980, *The making of the English working class,* Gollancz.

TIDDY, Reginald, 1923, *The Mummers' Play,* Oxford UP.

TOELKEN, Barre, 1986, 'Ballads and Folksongs', in E. Oring (ed) *Folk Groups and Folklore Genres: An introduction,* Utah State UP.

TOELKEN, Barre, 1996, *The Dynamics of Folklore* (2nd edn), Utah State UP (1st edn 1979).

TOLAN-SMITH, Christopher, 1997, 'Landscape archaeology' in C. Tolan-Smith (ed) *Landscape Archaeology in Tynedale,* Department of Archaeology, University of Newcastle upon Tyne.

TREVOR-ROPER, Hugh, 1983, 'The invention of tradition: The Highland tradition of Scotland' in Eric Hobsbawm and Terence Ranger (eds), 1983, *The Invention of Tradition,* Cambridge UP.

TRIGGER, Bruce, 1989, *A History of Archaeological Thought,* Cambridge UP.

TRUBSHAW, R.N., 1990, 'Hallaton Bottle Kicking and Hare Pie Scramble', *Northern Earth Mysteries* 41, 17–20.

TRUBSHAW, R.N., 1997, 'Making time', *At the Edge,* 7, 26–30; online at www.indigogroup.co.uk/edge/makingt.htm

TRUBSHAW, R.N., 1998, 'Fairies and their kin' in *At the Edge,* 10,
    1–8; online at www.indigogroup.co.uk/edge/fairies.htm
TRUBSHAW, R.N., 1999, '"Do not call it fixity": Continuity in
    archaeology and folklore', *3rd Stone,* 34, 6–10.
TRUBSHAW, R.N., 2003, *Explore Mythology,* Heart of Albion.
TURNER, Mark, 1996, *The Literary Mind: The origins of thought and
    language,* Oxford UP.
TURNER, Victor, 1967, *The Forest of Symbols: Aspects of Ndembu ritual,*
    Cornell UP.
TURNER, Victor, 1969, *The Ritual Process,* Aldine de Gruyter.
TURNER, Victor, 1974, *Dramas, Fields and Metaphors: Symbolic action
    in human society,* Cornell UP.
TYLOR, E.B., 1865, *Researches into the Early History of Mankind and the
    Development of Civilisation.*

UNDERDOWN, David, 1985, *Revel, Riot and Rebellion: Popular politics
    and culture in England 1603–1660,* Clarendon.

VALLEE, Jacques, 1970, *Passport to Magonia: From folklore to flying
    saucers,* Neville Spearman.
von FRANZ, Marie-Louise, 1970, *An Introduction to the Interpretation of
    Fairy Tales,* Spring Publications.
von FRANZ, Marie-Louise, 1972, *The Feminine in Fairy Tales,* Spring
    Publications.
von FRANZ, Marie-Louise, 1977, *Individuation in Fairy Tales,* Spring
    Publications.

WALTER, Tony, 1996, 'Funeral flowers: a response to Drury', *Folklore,*
    107, 106–7.
WARNER, Marina, 1994, *From the Beast to the Blonde: On fairy tales and
    their tellers,* Chatto and Windus.
WARNER, Marina, 1999, *No Go the Bogeyman: Scaring, lulling and
    making mock,* Chatto & Windus.
WARSHAVER, Gerald E., 1991, 'On Postmodern Folklore', *Western
    Folklore,* 50, 219–29.
WATT. Tessa, 1991, *Cheap Print and Popular Piety,* Cambridge UP.
WATTERS, Ethan and Richard OFSHE, 1994, *Making Monsters: False
    memories, psychotherapy and sexual hysteria,* Charles Scribner.
WEBSTER, Richard, 1995, *Why Freud was Wrong: Sin, science and
    psychoanalysis,* Harper Collins.
WELLS, Peter S., 2001, *Beyond Celts, Germans and Scythians,*
    Duckworth.
WESTWOOD, Jennifer, 1985, *Albion: A guide to legendary Britain,*
    Granada.
WENTZ, W.Y. Evans, 1911, *The Fairy Faith in Celtic Countries,* H.
    Frowde; reprinted Lemma 1973.

WHELAN, Edna, 2001, *The Magic and Mystery of Holy Wells,* Capall Bann.

WIDDOWSON, J.D.A., 1973, 'Introduction', in S.O. Addy, *Folktales and Superstitions,* E.P. Publishing.

WIDDOWSON, J.D.A., 1993, 'Trends in the commercialization of English calendar customs: a preliminary survey' in T. Buckland and J. Woods, *Aspects of British Calendar Customs,* Folklore Society.

WILBY, Emma, 2000, 'The witch's familiar and the fairy in early modern England and Scotland', *Folklore,* 111, 283–305.

WORKMAN, Mark E., 1989, 'Folklore in the wilderness: Folklore and postmodernism', in *Midwestern Folklore,* 15, 5–14.

ZIPES, Jack, 1979, *Breaking the Magic Spell: Radical theories of folk and fairy tales,* Heinemann.

ZIPES, Jack, 1983, *Fairy Tales and the Art of Subversion,* Heinemann.

ZIPES, Jack, 1997, *Happily Ever After: Fairy tales, children and the culture industry,* Routledge.

ZIPES, Jack, 1999, *When Dreams Came True: Classical fairy tales and their tradition,* Routledge.

ZIPES, Jack, 2000, *Sticks and Stones: The troublesome success of children's literature from Slovenly Peter to Harry Potter,* Routledge.

INDEX

Boorman, John 87
Bord Janet 120, 123, 113–14
Bord Janet and Colin 102, 107, 110
boundaries 36
Bourne, Henry 38
bowdlerisation 12-13
Bowman, Marion 110, 137
Boyes, Georgina 6, 11, 127, 130,
        142, 148, 151–3
Bradtke, Elaine 143
Bragg, Billy 155
Brand, John 38
Breatnach, Deasun 117
Brémond, Claude 20
brewing, home 164
Briggs, Katherine 28, 15, 119
Brighton 136
broadsides 53, 58, 150
Bronson, Bertrand 150
Brookesmith, Peter 125
Brown, Callum 112
Brown, Theo 42
Brunvald, Harold 80, 84
Bryant, Arthur 19
Buckland, Theresa 104, 127–8, 166
Burgess, Anthony 81
Burke, Peter 31–2
Burning Man festival 86
Bushaway, Bob 13, 128–9
Byatt, A.S. 89

Caciola, Nancy 112
Callahan, Kevin 122
Campbell, Joseph 28, 87, 94
Campion-Vincent, Véronique 79
Canepa, Nancy 20, 21, 29, 89
Cape Breton 144
Caribbean carnivals 137–8
Caribbean music 157
Caribbean tales 95
Carpenter, Siri 98
Carr, E.H. 32
Carroll, Lewis 61
Carson, Ciaran 69
Carter, Angela 64, 89
Carthy, Eliza 155

Carthy, Martin 153–5
Cass, Eddie 146
Castleton Garland Ceremony 1,
        129–30, 140
causality 9
chain letters 75
Chamber, Edmund 141
Chandler, Jennifer 137, 142
charity collection schemes,
        spurious 76
Charles II, King 128
Chartier, Roger 30, 32
Chaucer, Geoffrey 65, 117
Child, Francis James 149–51
children's games – *see* games
Chinese New Year 137
Christmas 141, 143, 164
Clarke, Arthur C. p87
Clarke, David 41, 121
Clash 154
Clodd, Edward 11
closure 33, 67–8
Cocchiara, Giuseppe 51
cock fighting 13
cognitive linguistics 33–4, 168
Coker, Crofton 66
Collins, Andy 121
Collis, John 49–50
Colwell, Eileen 94–4
Commonwealth 6
comparative folklore – *see* folklore,
        comparative
computer games 90–1
contamination 81–2
context 29, 74, 167
continuity 2, 43–7
cooking 164
Cooper, Geoff 33
Coppola, Francis Ford 90
Corbett, Ronnie 69
Corfe Castle 12
'corn dollies' – *see* straw craft
Cornwall 1, 130, 134–5, 154
country dancing 143
Cowan, Edward 119
'cowboys and indians' 88, 90